THE HISTORY OF

KENT
COUNTY
CRICKET CLUB

THE CHRISTOPHER HELM
COUNTY CRICKET HISTORIES

Series Editors:
Peter Arnold and Peter Wynne-Thomas

HAMPSHIRE
Peter Wynne-Thomas, with a personal view by
John Arlott

MIDDLESEX
David Lemmon, with a personal view by
Denis Compton

THE HISTORY OF

KENT
COUNTY
CRICKET CLUB

Dudley Moore

With a personal view by
DEREK UNDERWOOD

CHRISTOPHER HELM
London

© 1988 Dudley Moore and Derek Underwood
Christopher Helm (Publishers) Ltd, Imperial House,
21–25 North Street, Bromley, Kent BR1 1SD

ISBN 0-7470-2209-1

A CIP catalogue record for this book is available from the
British Library

Typeset by Cotswold Typesetting Ltd, Gloucester
Printed and bound in Great Britain by Biddles Ltd, Guildford,
Surrey

CONTENTS

A PERSONAL VIEW
by Derek Underwood

WHEN I WAS ASKED to write an introduction to this book, I was aware that the 25 years in which I have been involved with Kent represent a relatively short period in the overall history of the Club. But they have been, I think, years which have seen more changes to the structure and atmosphere of the game than any previous period of the same length. It has been an exciting time, and a successful and glorious one for Kent, and I feel lucky to have played a part in it.

Reflecting on the many great players that have graced the grounds of Kent and elsewhere, I also feel proud to have met and played alongside so many of them. I do have a confession to make, however. Until I joined the staff in April 1962 at the tender age of 16, I had never seen Kent play and, in fact, had closer connections with Surrey. As a schoolboy, I used to receive coaching at Croydon from Tony Lock and Ken Barrington, and often went to The Oval to follow the fortunes of what was then a particularly strong Surrey side. All that was to change when I was 'spotted' and invited to change my loyalties to Kent. Little did I know at the time that I was to become a member of the most successful side in the County's history and go on to play for my country.

By anyone's standards, the last 25 years have been extremely memorable—not only for me but the County. Not only did we win our first Championship for more than 50 years, but we helped pioneer the one-day game and dominated the major competitions through the 1970s. We witnessed the advent of one-day cricket, sponsorship for the game, vastly improved financial incentives for Test players through Kerry Packer's World Series, floodlit cricket, the World Cup competition and much more. We also saw the appeal of the game widen, particularly through the coverage on television—now, of course, in colour.

Whatever the views held about such changes—and, of course, they are many and conflicting—it is fair to say that the lot of the cricketer generally has improved, although not, I am sad to say, in terms of job security. Cricket has been slower to respond to the rapidly changing world around it than many other activities in sport. But it has felt its way cautiously to a position from which it can and should take full advantage.

We in Kent have been most fortunate in having a coaching system that is the envy of the rest of the country. Organized through the Association of Kent Cricket Clubs, this 'school' has been responsible for producing a large percentage of the Kent-born County players. Long may this continue. Certainly many of my contemporaries and I owe much to those early days when we were learning and developing our skills.

My first introduction to Kent came when I was 13. I recall going to Canterbury where I first met that great Kent and England cricketer Les Ames, who by then was managing the side. Having watched me in the nets, Les declared that I showed reasonable potential as a batsman—then added that he thought I could bowl a bit as well! It is ironic, looking back now some 30 years later, that I was to make my name as a bowler and scored only one century. And little did I realise that one day I would be on an England tour with Les as my manager again.

I have always appreciated how lucky I was to have been given an opportunity so early in my career. Having played my first season in the second eleven, I was pitched in to first-class cricket following an unfortunate car accident to David Halfyard. He was a tremendous county player and used to bowl more than 1,000 overs a season. That, for a 17-year-old, was some act to follow. But what it did mean was that I got in plenty of bowling that year and was able to establish myself in the side.

Of course, like anyone else of that age, I had my own heroes. I shall never forget the first time I walked into the dressing room at Canterbury and came face to face with Colin Cowdrey—my schoolboy idol. There was—and still is—a great aura about him, a special quality given to only a few in any walk of life.

My baptism into top level cricket was no gentle affair, for 1963 marked the start of the first one-day competition—the Gillette Cup. Incidentally I think it is important to

Derek Underwood, the greatest left-arm spin bolwer of his era.

remind people that the initial recommendations for this type of cricket were put forward by a former Kent player—David Clark.

Matches are often memorable for the wrong, as well as the right, reasons. I certainly had cause to remember our first cup game—against our old rivals Sussex at Tunbridge Wells. I was only saved from getting the 'ton' up by being taken off after 11 of my 12 allotted overs had cost 88 runs. My blushes were partly spared when that very talented opener Peter Richardson hit a century, although the game still went Sussex's way.

Those early days are full of memories, such as the old pavilion at Canterbury, where during pre-season training the senior players would change in one dressing room while the juniors changed in the other. By today's standards, the conditions there were pretty primitive. Casting an eye round the County Ground today, with the tremendous improvements in facilities, it is difficult to imagine what it was like when I first started playing. There was the original wooden pavilion and adjoining stand, the concrete Frank Woolley Stand and, opposite, the old tin stand, which has since been renamed the Les Ames Stand and given a complete facelift to include the impressive scoreboard and executive boxes.

Kent had the nucleus of a very good side in the mid-1960s and it still surprises me that we won only one competition during that period—the Gillette Cup in 1967, where we beat Somerset in the final. Leading us, of course, was Colin Cowdrey. Peter Richardson was, for me, one of the most exciting of batsmen to watch, and we had strength in the bowling too. There was David Sayer, who toured with the MCC; Alan Brown, who was on the fringe of international selection; and Alan Dixon, one of the best all-rounder off-spinners of the day. Added to that balance of experience you had some solid professionals, such as Stuart Leary. Emerging players included the stylish Mike Denness and his dogged, workmanlike opening partner Brian Luckhurst, whose skills were to blossom some years later. And, of course, there was Alan Knott, Norman Graham and others.

All the while there were important people quietly preparing the side that was to dominate the game during the 1970s. First and foremost there was our manager, Les Ames, ably assisted by Colin Page, who was then still playing and took responsibility for the second eleven. When I started playing, Claude Lewis was the coach and ran the net practices. Under their expert guidance and encouragement a team was being built that would capture all the honours in the County game.

At this time the game saw the introduction of overseas players who were to have an enormous impact, particularly in one-day cricket. There is no doubt in my mind that our own John Shepherd was a player ahead of his time. With all-rounders playing an ever-increasing role in the modern game, his tremendous talent and dedication would be a vital boost to today's side. Then there were the impish skills of Asif Iqbal and the potential brilliance of Bernard Julien.

This was the time of great change in cricket—and in the approach players had to take to the game. Most of us had been weaned on three-day matches, where the game was played in a traditional fashion, without the pressures of over rates and bonus points.

Looking back, it strikes me that the emphasis was almost totally on developing cricketing skills, whereas today it seems to be more on training and fitness. This has naturally brought some rewards, such as the tremendous improvement in the standard of fielding. It is strange to think that in the olden days you used to be considered rather foolish if you dived for a ball and got a green stain on your trousers. Now, if you come off the field without a stain, people would think you had not been pulling your weight.

One of our greatest assets during Kent's 'glory years' was our fielding, exceptional by the standards of the time. We had marvellous fielders of the calibre of Alan Ealham, Mike Denness, Brian Luckhurst and Stuart Leary, and no other County could match us. Their brilliance inspired the rest of the team, some of whom, it must be said—and Norman Graham will not mind if I couple his name with mine—were not famed for our agility.

In fact, if I had to choose the aspect of cricket that has most changed in recent years, then it has to be the quality of the fielding. It is interesting to note that no team has really been outstandingly successful in the 1980s because the standards have improved all round. The difference in slip catching, chasing and throwing in over the top of the stumps between now and when I started in the game is enormous.

Kent's secret for success lay partly in our all-round strength. Of course we were fortunate to have players of the ability of John Shepherd, Asif Iqbal, Bob Woolmer, Bernard Julien and Graham Johnson. There was so much depth in both the batting and bowling that we always felt we were that much ahead of the opposition. This naturally gave us the confidence to win—and there's a world of difference between knowing you are going to win and just hoping you will. Mind you, it was not always that easy and there were times when things never seemed to go right for us. But in the worst times we always managed to find the ability to pick ourselves off the ground somehow. The best example of this must be the 1970 season. By the beginning of July we were bottom of the table, yet incredibly we finished the season winning the Championship. We had learnt how to win, although of course an element of good fortune helped us on our way. You always need this to win consistently.

With all the coaching of young players, it is remarkable that during my career Kent have never produced an international fast bowler, with the exception of Graham Dilley. On his day Kevin Jarvis was pretty quick and Richard Ellison has been known to generate a fair bit of pace, although his speciality is in swinging the ball about. With complete covering of wickets during the 1980s—until the 1987 season, that is—greater emphasis was put on fast bowling. This went hand-in-hand with the devastating success of the West Indies during that period. In turn there resulted a dearth of top spinners in the game and a lack of opportunity for them to mature. A spinner must now be able to bat, especially in one-day cricket, to justify his place in the side, although in certain conditions, all too rarely, he can prove a match winner.

The greatest changes to the game have, in many ways, come from off the field. One thinks particularly of television, sponsorship and the general marketing approach that has made cricket much more like a business than a sport. While we have always had Test Match coverage on television, it really has been the one-day game that has captured the imagination of the viewing public. This in turn has boosted sponsorship in cricket, providing a vital source of income for all county clubs. When I first started playing, revenue for the counties came basically from the money collected at the turnstiles.

Today, with all competitions sponsored, the money-earning potential is far greater. This, of course, puts additional pressure on both club and players to win matches and tournaments.

Sponsorship has developed in several directions. Apart from the now common sight of advertising boards lining the boundary, companies are encouraged to use the entertaining facilities during the cricket weeks and festivals. There is no doubt that without such sources of additional revenue, cricket would not be in the position it is today.

Financial incentives of this size can have an adverse effect. One often feels as a player that winning is of paramount importance, since success can ensure greater security for the club and the individual. This necessarily puts pressure on the players. It is now essential for the county to be successful to get the revenue they need, and if existing cricketers cannot provide this success, then others are found who might have better prospects. There is, of course, no guarantee that they will do any better.

From Kent's point of view, the irony is that having won nothing for more than 50 years, we enjoyed unbelievable success during the 1970s. It is obvious, however, that nobody can go on winning year after year, and the last few seasons have obviously proved somewhat of an anti-climax. But I have no doubt that our turn will come again.

Reflecting on that marvellous period in the Club's history, there are several people who I believe were instrumental in moulding not only my career, but the success of the team as a whole. I must single out my first captain Colin Cowdrey. I was very fortunate to have had someone like him to nurse me along in those early days. His ability to provide encouragement when things were not going particularly well was quite uncanny. Perhaps I had bowled 25 overs in an innings without taking a wicket. Then Colin would put me on again for the tail-enders and I would come off at the end with one or maybe two wickets to my credit. That, I can tell you, was a great boost to my morale after an otherwise unsuccessful day out in the field.

Mr 'Kent Cricket' himself—Les Ames—also made a great impact on my career. His reputation not only as a player but also as a manager is reflected in his spectacular achievements. I owe much, as well, to my coaches at that time—Claude Lewis and Colin Page. In my opinion Claude was the most knowledgeable and experienced man in Kent, having been involved with the game for more than 50 years, while Colin was doing a marvellous job bringing up the younger players. The roles of these players and officials in the success of Kent emerge in the pages of the history which follows.

Of course I could not write these personal observations and leave out a special mention of Alan Knott. We have been colleagues and friends for a long time. In fact our playing associations go back to quite a few years before we started our partnership in first-class cricket. You could say we grew up together since we represented Kent Schools before we joined the County.

Knotty and I got on very well and, I suppose, our 'double act' was one of the most successful ever in the game. Altogether we played 441 first-class matches, including 72 Tests. That alone is probably a world record! In that time we shared 197 victims, of which 134 were caught and 63 stumped.

There is no doubt that Knotty was a tremendous player and his genius behind the

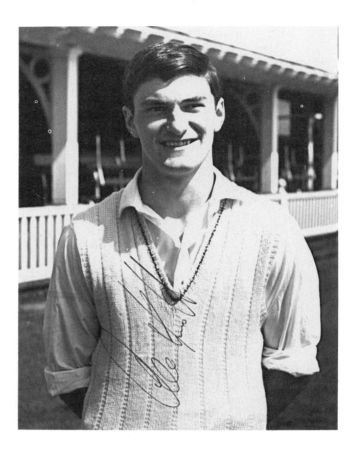

The young Alan Knott in 1965, the year he won his County cap.

stumps really showed on wet, sticky wickets. But, of course, it wasn't just his keeping; he was a great getter of runs, too. I would say he was probably the most unorthodox player of spin bowling in the game—and the most feared.

And what of Kent today? Although the results have been generally disappointing in the last few years, we should not forget the special problems involved in replacing a successful team. Naturally a winning team affords fewer opportunities for newcomers. This makes it harder when the experienced players eventually go and the younger ones must be brought into the side. Of course from time to time this transition period is unavoidable and sometimes seems protracted. What has made it so much harder in recent times is the increased standard of first-class cricket generally. This has widened the gap between the first and second elevens and it is now rare for a young player to come into the senior side and take it by storm.

In the last few years Kent have been able to call on the considerable bowling talents of people like Graham Dilley, Richard Ellison and Terry Alderman and I feel it is in the bowling area that we need to encourage the stars of the future.

We have had to throw some of our young bowlers in at the deep end, but this has given them valuable experience, as it did with me. Certainly Alan Igglesden is potentially a very exciting prospect and Chris Penn and Danny Kelleher also have a chance to prove their worth. Personally, from my new position outside the boundary rope, I shall be taking great interest in the development of Richard Davis, who as a spin bowler will be under tremendous pressure to keep his place—but he must be given his chance.

From a batting point of view, Kent certainly have players of considerable potential, and have rarely lacked them. They have the ability to score their fair share of runs, provided the attitude and mental approach to the game is right. At times some appear to lack confidence in their own ability, but should with more application and experience overcome this. Certainly Kent have the nucleus of a good side, and several players should be able to look forward to rewarding careers in the years ahead. Steve Marsh came into the side at a very difficult time, following in the footsteps of one of the world's great players—Alan Knott. His was certainly not the easiest gap to fill, but he has done an amazingly good job both as a wicket-keeper and a batsman.

Mark Benson is a batsman of high calibre who has been rather unlucky not to have been given more opportunity on an international level. Simon Hinks is another exciting player, who I feel has qualities similar to David Gower. He has that all-important ability to turn a game round completely and should be doing this more regularly in the future. With the experience of Chris Tavaré and Chris Cowdrey, and the return of his brother Graham after his unfortunate injury against Michael Holding, there is certainly depth in the batting line-up from which to build.

The future for the County does, I believe, lie in a much greater emphasis on developing the skills and talents of the young players. Recently I feel there has been too much effort concentrated on training and fitness and not enough attention paid to encouraging the basic cricket skills. It is skill, not calisthenics, which wins matches.

Looking back over 25 years with Kent, I know the successes have been built on skilful players—and what successes. To select particular highlights I find virtually impossible—there were so many. You can look at our first Gillette Cup triumph in 1967 or the first Championship title for more than 50 years in 1970. What days!

I remember that first Lord's Final—in the 1967 Gillette Cup against Somerset—as an especially exciting occasion. It was the first major cricketing experience for all of us in the team and I find it hard to explain quite the feeling as we went out in front of a packed house. The atmosphere was tremendous.

Of course in those days we weren't facing the might of Ian Botham, Viv Richards or Joel Garner. But there was Bill Alley, aged 48 but a great competitor, and it was he that we all felt held the key to the result. Kent got away to a good start, with Mike Denness and Brian Luckhurst putting on 78 for the first wicket. Both got half-centuries and so we were all rather disappointed with the final total of 193.

In the field we put pressure on from the start and gradually Somerset got behind the clock. They got to the stage where they had to force the pace if they were going to overhaul our score and that's when I struck. I had been bowling fairly well without any success and then it all happened. I picked out seven, eight and nine and the game was over. I finished with three for 40 that day and recall that the papers on the Sunday morning referred to my 'devastating late spell'.

It was a wonderful feeling—not only to have been there but to have contributed directly to Kent's victory, although of course it was a great team effort. Mike deservedly won the Man of the Match award for a typical forcing innings.

The memories that last the longest are certainly those of playing in the finals at Lord's. There is something very special about those occasions that anybody who has been there has experienced for himself. The thrill of the day—not only for the players but also the supporters—is, I feel, everything. The winning or losing is secondary. There is usually not quite the sense of disappointment when you lose a final, particularly a well-fought one, since one can at least say: 'I was there'. The hardest pill to swallow is going out in the semi-final, where there is never the same atmosphere.

Hastings has been, without doubt, my favourite and most successful ground and it was therefore rather appropriate that it should be here on the Sussex coast, in the relative tranquility of a County Championship match, that I scored my first—and only— century, in 1984. It was quite a weekend, because I put in my best Sunday League performance as well: six for 12.

My innings started on the Saturday evening, when I went in as night watchman at the beginning of Kent's second innings! Yes, the wickets had certainly been tumbling that day. Having survived till the Monday morning, I was batting with Chris Tavaré and we put on 42. My contribution was an incredible 41!

But the partnership that really mattered was with Terry Alderman, who in fact went on to get a half-century himself in a match made even more remarkable because it ended in a tie. Garth Le Roux was bowling and normally I would have stood little chance against him. But, as luck would have it, he was bowling a bit short that day and gradually the runs started to mount up.

I remember getting to 50 reasonably comfortably, which in fact was my third, and then the runs slowed down. But I pushed on and reached the next milestone of 80, beating my previous highest score. And I suppose it was only then that I realised that magical century was on. Strangely enough I personally didn't feel too much pressure. The person I felt sorry for was poor Kevin Jarvis, who was the next man in at Number 11. He had to sit out the agony in the pavilion, praying that Terry didn't get out!

My heart did miss a beat or two when, having reached 96, I was dropped off a very difficult chance. Then I got a single and I was within three runs of doing it. Rising to the occasion, I hit a four off Ian Greig and I had done it. I shall never forget that shot, as I paddled the ball round to square leg. How could I forget it—it was the only shot in my repertoire, anyway!

Even with all the applause round the ground and in the dressing room afterwards, it didn't really sink in. I suppose the full impact only hit me the next morning when I read about it in the papers! After 22 years, it was well worth waiting for.

As one era comes to an end, so another one begins—and I am sure that Kent will again enjoy the success on which I was fed. Now I have retired, I look back with pride and much satisfaction on those great playing days. More than that, I will cherish not only the friendship of the players but also the many good people I have met throughout the world—and particularly in Kent.

INTRODUCTION

'CRICKET NOW—AND TWO WERE SHOT DEAD and one run through with a bayonet . . .' Had there been television or radio, that might have been the beginning of a news item when Kent encountered Essex in one of their first county games. Since then Kent and their followers have made many excursions across, and in more modern times, under, the River Thames but none of the meetings could have evoked more drama, indeed horror, than that in 1776 at Tilbury Fort.

An extract from a letter from Gravesend, dated 29 October to the *London Chronicle*, published two days later, told the incredible story:

> A terrible affair happened this day at Tilbury Fort. A great match at Cricket being to be played between Kent and Essex, the parties assembled on both sides. When they were met, a man appearing among the former who should not have been there, the Essex men refused playing, on which a battle ensued, and the Kentish men being likely to be worsted, one of them ran into the guard-house, and getting a gun from one of the invalids, fired and killed one of the opposite party. On seeing this they all began running to the guard-house, and there being but four soldiers there, they took away the guns and fell to it, doing a great deal of mischief. An old invalid was run through the body with a bayonet, and a sergeant . . . was shot dead. At last the Essex men took to flight, and running over the drawbridge made their escape. The Kentish men then made off in their boats, and search is making after them.

Another recorded meeting between the two rivals on each side of the Thames was at Swanscombe when Essex won by an innings and 44. At least there was no horror story this time, although it was reported: 'This so exasperated the Gentlemen of Kent that they would not so much as drink with their competitors.'

Since that 'war' on the cricket field in 1776, county cricket has pursued a more sedate course. Cricket in Kent started way back in 1705 and when a county side was inaugurated it was soon one of the strongest, if not the strongest in the country. As early as 1739, after a victory over All England, Kent was dubbed 'the unconquerable county'. In those early days competition between sides was inspired by quite substantial wagers on the result or individual performances and Kent enjoyed the services of some outstanding players.

The first attempt to form a county cricket club foundered in 1787 and it was not until 1836 at Town Malling when there was a more successful effort to form a County Club. Those were the days of renowned players like Fuller Pilch and Mr Alfred Mynn, and in 1842 the first Canterbury Cricket Week was staged. It was the period when Kent could display their tremendous ability in the middle and in the years from 1839 to 1849 they won 16 of the 28 matches against England.

In 1858 another attempt was made to form a County Club. This time there was more success, when the sixth Earl of Darnley presided at a meeting at the Mitre Hotel, Maidstone and became the club's first President.

Twelve years later, at a meeting at the Bull Hotel, Rochester, the County Club

*Lord Harris, Kent captain from 1875 to 1889, and one of the game's
outstanding administrators.*

amalgamated with the Beverley Cricket Club, Canterbury, and Kent County Cricket Club as it is known today was formed. In 1873 the County Championship was inaugurated and points instead of pounds became more the reward for the participating teams, a situation which existed until more recent years when sponsorship has brought pounds very much back into the game.

If success is to be measured by winning trophies, then since 1870 Kent County Cricket Club has been somewhat restricted because there have been only two periods of outstanding achievement. The first was from 1906 to 1913 when the Championship title was won on four memorable occasions, and the other from 1967 to 1978, loosely referred to as the 'Glorious Seventies'. In those 12 years Kent won the Championship twice, shared it on another occasion, took the John Player League title three times, lifted the Benson & Hedges Cup on three occasions and twice won the Gillette Cup, the forerunner of the NatWest Trophy.

Since then, and in between those two triumphant periods, the trophy cupboard has been bare, but the years have produced names legendary in the history of Kent cricket, with entertainment to match.

Lord Harris, Kent's captain for the first 15 years, sowed the seeds for the early success period. Batsmen prospered in the Kent side but the club's history has always been closely associated with the outstanding achievements of wicket-keepers and spin bowlers. F. H. Huish, with 1,253 dismissals in 469 matches and never an England cap to show for his great skills came first, from 1895 to 1914; then J. C. Hubble, followed by L. E. G. Ames, whose 847 victims were accompanied by 28,951 runs for the County, T. G. Evans (554 victims) and finally A. P. E. Knott, who claimed 915 wickets and scored 11,339 runs.

C. Blythe, with slow left-arm spin, made his impact at the turn of the century and had taken 2,210 wickets before the First World War. Thereafter A. P. Freeman emerged to take 3,340 before his first-class career ended in 1936 and D. V. P. Wright carried on the leg-break tradition with 1,709, mostly following the Second World War. More recently it has been left-arm spin dominating the County scene with D. L. Underwood's 2,465 first-class wickets. The most famous name of all in Kent cricket is, of course, F. E. Woolley, who bowled left-arm spin too—taking 1,680 wickets—but he also scored 47,868 runs for the County in his 764 matches, some 158 more than anyone else has ever played or is ever likely to play for the County.

Over the years the County has sent out many of its top cricketers to play for their country with M. C. Cowdrey, who reigned as County Captain for 15 years, as Lord Harris had earlier, winning 114 caps, with A. P. E. Knott (95), T. G. Evans (91) and D. L. Underwood (86) not far behind. In all 46 Kent players have made 815 Test appearances for England, who have also called on five Kent players to skipper the Test side: Cowdrey (27), M. H. Denness (19), A. P. F. Chapman (17), Lord Harris (4) and the Hon Ivo Bligh (4).

It all adds up to a record of which the County can be proud. Throughout the years the Kent side has given pleasure to its supporters all over the County on some of the most beautiful and picturesque grounds in the country.

OLD HEROES

AN ADVERTISEMENT IN *The Postman* on 24 July 1705 referred to the earliest recorded match in Kent. It gave notice of a 'match of cricket' between 11 gentlemen of the west part of the county of Kent against as many of Chatham for 11 guineas a man at Maulden (Malling) to take place on 5 August.

The same journal four years later, on 2 June, reported the earliest recorded match in which the two sides purported to come from different counties—Kent against Surrey for £50. In fact it probably was not a real inter-county match at Dartford Brimpth but one between Dartford and a Surrey town or village.

Games between the Men of Kent and the Men of London were referred to in newspaper reports in 1719 and 1720 and then in 1726 mention was made of a game for 25 guineas between 'the men belonging to Stead Esq., of Maidstone, and the men of London and Surrey'.

Edwin Stead, variously referred to as Edward Stead, Stede and Steede, was the first Kent county player of whom there is any record. An active cricketer himself, living at Harrietsham, he was a very great supporter of cricket in the County during the early part of the 18th century.

When he died in 1735 the *Gentlemen's Magazine,* referring to his death, said he was 'remarkable for several great cricket matches he made with the Prince of Wales and many of the Nobility'.

In 1726 there was a report that a suit of law was to be determined by a cricket match on Dartford Heath between the men of Chingford and Mr Stead's men. There had been a hearing two years earlier before Chief Justice Pratt when apparently the teams had met, with the Chingford men refusing to play out the game when Mr Stead's team had the advantage. The Judge, either not understanding the game or having forgotten it, referred the said cause back to Dartford Heath to be played on where they left off and a rule of the court was made accordingly.

There was no result recorded, but there had been seven years earlier, when the *Weekly Journal* reported that a match between the Londoners and the Kentish men, where there had been a trial at law, was ordered by the court to be played out. The Kentish men, with four men to play and needing 30 to 'come up with' the Londoners, were bowled out after they scored nine and lost the match. It was played for a guinea a man on each side and it was reckoned the law suit would amount to £200.

In 1728 Edwin Stead and his company played the Duke of Richmond and his club for 'a great sum'. The game was not reported but later that summer Edwin Stead of Kent played a match against Sir William Gage of Sussex for 50 guineas, 11-a-side of each county. The match was played in the Earl of Leicester's Park at Penshurst and for the third time that summer the Kent men won. The following year, at the same venue, Kent, headed by Edwin Stead, were beaten by Sussex, Surrey and Hampshire, led by Sir William Gage, in a match for 100 guineas.

Over the next two seasons there were frequent clashes reported between London and Kent and in 1731 Esquire Stead's Cricket Club of Kent travelled to Sudbury Common where they were beaten by the men of Sudbury in a match for 30 guineas-a-side.

In 1731 there were two encounters between Kent and Surrey. The first, in July, was won by the 11 men of Surrey, all named Wood, but the second, in September, did not actually produce a result. It was reported as a 'great cricket match' played on Dulwich Common between the Surrey and the Kentish clubs; His Grace the Duke of Richmond *v* Stead Esq. Several persons of distinction were said to be present, having very considerable bets. When rain intervened it was thought that the match would have ended in favour of Surrey.

Three years later, in 1734, Kent beat Sussex at Sevenoaks in a game in which Lord Middlesex and Lord John Sackville played for Kent and Sir William Gage for Sussex. The tables were turned at Lewes in the following year when Sussex were the winners.

In July of that year, 1735, the Kentish men played for the Earl of Middlesex in a match against a team raised by the Prince of Wales, for whom eight of the London club and three from Middlesex played. The stumps were immediately pitched when the Prince arrived and the £1,000-a-side match was won by Kent, who also won the return a fortnight later.

Kent were successful yet again in 1738 in an encounter between the Prince of Wales' team of Surrey and London against Lord John Sackville, son of the Duke of Dorset, for Kent. The *London Evening Post* of 16 June reported:

> There was a pavilion erected for His Royal Highness, who was accompanied by several persons of distinction. The press was so great on the occasion that a poor woman, by the crowd bearing on her, unfortunately had her leg broke, which being related to His Royal Highness, he was pleased to order her 10 guineas.

Two years later was reported 'the famous match at cricket' played on Bromley Common between Kent and 11 other 'gamesters' selected from All England. The report said:

> It was a very hard match and a fine effort as was ever seen, but was at last won by the gentlemen of the unconquerable county by a very few notches.

When the sides met in a second match it ended abruptly because of a dispute over the dismissal of one of the England batsmen, but Kent would probably have won.

Kent's success continued until on Bromley Common in 1743 their side, chosen by Lord John Sackville played a team from London, Middlesex and Surrey, selected by Lord Mountford, for £500-a-side. On the first innings Lord Mountford's side were ahead by 28 and in their second innings had reached 112 with six still to go in. By then it was eight o'clock and it was agreed to play on the next day. The *London Evening Post* reported that when the game was renewed the following day Lord John Sackville gave up because Lord Mountford's side had gained 'so vast a majority'.

Incidentally, in 1743 there was a forerunner to many of the inter-club games played today, notably at Bank Holiday or pre-season, when 11 married men of Greenwich beat 11 bachelors 'for a great sum'.

On 11 July of that year, in the Artillery Ground, 10,000 spectators saw Three of Kent (Hodswell, J. Cutbush, V. Romney) win by two runs against Three of England (R. Newland, Sawyer, John Bryan) for what was variably reported as 500 pounds or 500 guineas. Betting was five to one in favour of Kent and the six players taking part were reckoned to be the best in the country.

Kent won what the *London Magazine* entitled 'the greatest cricket match ever known' when they beat an All England eleven in the Artillery Ground on 18 June 1744. The Prince of Wales, a frequent spectator at the top games, was present.

Between 1745 and 1748 Kent met England on eight occasions, winning three and losing two, with the other three results unknown. In 1746 Kent and Surrey, who were subsequently engaged in matches against each other, joined forces to play Addington and Bromley in a match at Duppas Hill, Croydon, which attracted nearly 10,000 spectators.

In 1761 the earliest recorded match of 11 against 22 was recorded in the *General Evening Post* when at Woodford Row in Essex, eight from Dartford with three others met 22 from Essex for £50-a-side. Betting apparently did not just cover the result of matches, but extended to the scores made by batsmen. In those days runs were recorded by notches on a stick and in 1772, when Kent beat Hampshire and Sussex, which was the equivalent of the renowned Hambledon club, by an innings and 29 runs at Guildford, great bets were struck on whether the Duke of Dorset would score more than Mr Ellis. The winner was the Duke (John Frederick Sackville) who was regarded as one of the best patrons of the game there had ever been. He played in only ten games for Kent, because he was sent as Ambassador to France in 1783. The famous Vine ground at Sevenoaks belonged to him and he employed several famous cricketers including Bowra, Miller and Minshull. The Duke employed Minshull, regarded as one of the finest batsmen of his time, as a gardener and he played for Kent against Surrey in 1773 as a 'given man'. Believed to be from Middlesex, he also played for England and for Surrey.

A 'given man' was not qualified for the county but his inclusion would increase the strength of a side. He would normally be a well-known player who would enhance the attraction of the match.

The Duke of Dorset was praised for his efforts on behalf of cricket in the *Morning Chronicle* in 1782, when it reported great preparations being made at Knowle for a fête which was to conclude the cricket match at Sevenoaks. It said: 'His Grace is one of the few noblemen who unite the elegancies of modern luxury with the more manly sports of the old English times'.

Another great patron of cricket who played twice for Kent in 1773 was Sir Horatio Mann, who retained the services of several great cricketers and arranged for important matches to be played on his grounds at Bishopsbourne, Canterbury, Linton, near Maidstone, Sissinghurst, and after he moved from Bishopsbourne, at Dandelion Paddock, near Margate. He employed the brothers John and George Ring, as huntsman and whipper-in respectively and James Aylward as his bailiff. Aylward, a hard-hitting left-handed batsman was born in Hampshire and had played with great distinction for Hambledon until Sir Horatio Mann took him to Kent, where he became the first player to score over 1,000 runs for the County.

John Ring, a batsman very strong on the leg side, played for the County for 15 years but died at the age of 42, after his brother George had been bowling to him and the ball suddenly rose and broke his nose. In a single-wicket match at Bishopsbourne between six of Kent and six of Hambledon, Kent still needed 59 to win when Ring went in last but one. While he was walking to the wicket Sir Horatio said: 'Ring, carry your bat through and make up all the runs and I'll give you £10 a year for life.' Ring scored 57 of the runs, and with last man Aylward getting the other two Kent won by one wicket. It was a tense finish, no doubt the equivalent of many of the dramatic conclusions in the limited-overs game today, for Aylward faced 64 balls before he registered his first run and another 30 before he scored his second.

There had been great rivalry between Kent and Hambledon since the first recorded match between the sides at Broadhalfpenny Down in 1768 when John Small, of Petersfield, took the first recorded century off a Kent attack. When the sides met on Windmill Down in 1783 the result was believed to be a tie, although it was discovered after the game that Kent had won. The scorer Pratt, who followed the usual method of cutting a notch on a stick for every run, cutting every tenth notch longer, had by mistake marked in one place the eleventh notch instead of the tenth. He produced his stick after the match but the other scorer would or could not produce his. It seems that around this time scoresheets were taking over from the notch method because some years earlier an advertisement of Pratt revealed that his complete scorecards were ready for sale half an hour after the end of a match. Obviously there was a need for them as evidence in the settling of bets and as a form guide.

In 1787 an unsuccessful attempt was made to form a county cricket club at a meeting at Coxheath, near Maidstone, when among the people who supported that bid was Marsham, a name to be found later in Kent cricket with the Hon and Rev John Marsham, who twice played for the

County in 1873, and Mr C. H. B. Marsham, who captained Kent from 1904 to 1908.

After 1789 the Napoleonic War interfered with cricket in Kent, for apart from 1815 the match between Kent and England did not resume until 1834 when it was played at Lord's.

In 1790 the fourth Earl of Darnley and his brother, General the Hon E. Bligh, played together in the County side for the first time and were regulars in the first-class cricket of the day until 1813. Indeed the Bligh family, whose home was at Cobham Hall, near Gravesend, the seat of the Earls of Darnley, was to be closely associated with Kent cricket for well over a hundred years. The fourth Earl's youngest son, the Hon Sir J. D. Bligh, was President of the Kent club in 1864; the sixth Earl was President of MCC and of the Kent club on four occasions and his two brothers both played for the County. The seventh Earl played for Kent in the years 1871–79 and his younger brother the Hon Ivo Bligh, who

The Hon. Ivo Bligh, who played for Kent as a batsman between 1877 and 1883.

later became the eighth Earl, played for Kent in 1877–83. He also captained England in Australia in four Tests in 1882–83, and was twice President of the Kent County Cricket Club.

One of the great patrons of Kent cricket in the 1830s was Lord Sondes, of Lees Court, who later became President of the Club and whose son Viscount Throwley played for the county.

It was about this time that the style of bowling changed—from under-arm, a move which had been strongly opposed for some years up to 1830. It was introduced, it is reported, by a Sutton Valence man, John Willes. Perhaps at Lord's in 1822, playing for Kent against the Gentlemen of the MCC—the first time the MCC had played Kent without professional assistance—the same Mr Willes had employed his round-arm tactics too early. For *Bell's Life* reported:

> Mr John Willes commenced playing for his county but, being no-balled, he threw down the ball in high dudgeon, left the ground and (it is said) never played again.

Around 1835 Fuller Pilch was induced to settle in Town Malling, receiving £100 a year for making the move from Norfolk, where he had been born and where he had been assisted by his brother in the management of the Norwich Cricket Ground, of which Fuller was the lessee. He had figured in the Gentlemen *v* Players match in 1827 and already he was one of the best cricketers in England. He first played for Kent in 1836 when there was a much more successful inauguration of a County Club, at Town Malling. This was organised by Mr Thomas Selby, a great lover and generous supporter of the game, who had persuaded Pilch to settle in Kent. He backed Pilch and Mr Alfred Mynn in their single-wicket matches and arranged the new club's matches until 1840.

Town Malling at the time had a population of only 1,500 and not all the residents approved of cricket. In 1837 the Vicar, Mr G. F. Bates, proclaimed from the pulpit that attending a match was sinful, even if bets were not placed. His sermon was delivered the day before a Kent *v* Sussex match but *Bell's Life* reported: 'The match was attended on both days by many of the neighbouring clergymen'.

Mr Mynn, born in Goudhurst, and taught the game by Mr John Willes, first played for Kent in 1834 and he was in the side which Mr Selby took to Sheffield to play a team which virtually represented Yorkshire and which was beaten by the visitors by 196 runs. Regarded as one of the finest all-round cricketers the Gentlemen had ever had, Mynn excelled in his stroke play in front of the wicket or on the leg side, and his fast bowling was very destructive. He weighed between 18 and 20 stone and was 6 ft 1 in tall, and when he ran in to deliver the ball it was described by scorer and biographers as 'one of the grandest sights at cricket'.

It was on the Town Malling ground that Mr Mynn won his renowned single-wicket match against James Dearman of Yorkshire in 1838 and he beat him again in the return at Sheffield a week later. Two years earlier Mynn had been badly injured batting at Leicester when he made 125 not out for the South *v* North and there were fears that it might be necessary to amputate his thigh at the hip joint. This mercifully was not the case but he was out of cricket for nearly two years. He and Pilch never met in a single-wicket match, when Mynn's fast bowling may have given him the edge despite the superiority of Pilch as a batsman.

In 1839 Kent met England at Town Malling in a benefit match under the patronage of the MCC for Pilch, who early in his career was successful as a slow round-arm bowler. As a batsman he was commanding, particularly in his forward play, and was reckoned to have won many matches for Kent in his 19 seasons, not only with his batting and fielding but with his management and knowledge of the game. Before moving to Kent he had twice defeated Thomas Marsden of Sheffield, in 1833 for the Championship of England.

Mynn and Pilch, who was reckoned for at least 20 years to be the best batsman in England, dominated much of the cricket at Town Malling. Mynn's bowling was of such pace that his brother Walter used to wear a thick pad over his breast at long stop! When Mynn died, in 1861, 400 people combined to erect his tombstone and to found, in his honour, 'The Mynn Memorial Benevolent Institution for Kentish Cricketers', with £121 16s invested in India five per cent stock. Pilch died some nine years later and over 200 friends marked their admiration by erecting over his grave a memorial consisting of a massive square pedestal and obelisk twelve feet high.

There were contemporaries of Pilch and Mynn in the Kent side who also displayed tremendous form on the cricket field. Mr Nicholas Felix, whose real name was Wanostrocht, was a most interesting Kent cricketing character. A brilliant left-

KENT *v* ALL ENGLAND

Played at Town Malling, 19, 20 August 1839

KENT WON BY 2 RUNS

KENT	FIRST INNINGS		SECOND INNINGS	
Stearman	c Guy	12	b Redgate	15
A. Mynn Esq	b Lillywhite	11	b Redgate	0
Pilch	c Hon Ponsonby	35	b Redgate	0
Clifford	not out	0	lbw	18
R. Mills	c Box	9	b Lillywhite	12
Hillyer	st Box	9	b Lillywhite	0
Wenman	c Box	37	b Lillywhite	8
Dorrinton	b Lillywhite	0	b Redgate	0
W. Mynn Esq	c Cobbet	10	c Lillywhite	1
Adams	b Cobbet	10	b Redgate	6
Whittaker Esq	b Cobbet	1	not out	0
Extras	nb 4, b 3, w 4	11	b 2, w 2	4
Total		145		64

ENGLAND	FIRST INNINGS		SECOND INNINGS	
C. Taylor Esq	c Hillyer	1	b Hillyer	8
Garrett	b A. Mynn	5	c Dorrinton	3
Guy	c Wenman	30	run out	10
Sewell	c Hillyer	4	b A. Mynn	1
Box	c Wenman	3	c Stearman	12
Hon Grimston	c Wenman	46	c Wenman	0
Hon F. Ponsonby	run out	1	run out	2
Cobbet	c Hillyer	10	b A. Mynn	5
Jervis	b Hillyer	9	b A. Mynn	7
Lillywhite	not out	0	b Hillyer	0
Redgate	b A. Mynn	5	not out	20
Extras	b 12, w 4	16	b 12, w 2	14
Total		130		77

Umpires: Messrs Bayley and Good.

Match played for the benefit of Fuller Pilch. This scorecard, as printed on the ground by G. Windsor of Gravesend, contains an error in the England second innings, which as printed totals 82.

handed batsman, during Canterbury Week he would play cricket by day and the violin in the orchestra at the theatre in the evening and he could also dance a *pas de deux*. Twice in 1846 he was beaten by Mr Mynn in single-wicket contests for the Championship of England and in the same year his eleven played Pilch's XI in a benefit match for Felix at Lord's.

Mr Mynn, Mr Felix and Pilch were all in the Kent side which played in 1849 in the County's first game on the Bat and Ball Ground at Gravesend, which had been opened four years earlier by Tom Adams. A fine batsman and a good fielder, Adams played for Kent from 1834 to 1858.

A prize fighter once agreed to box, shoot and play cricket with Adams. The boxing match was first and the winner of two events out of three would take the stakes. The boxer had reckoned that he would give Adams so severe a handling in the glove contest to prevent him being able to take part in either of the other matches. Tom, however, had other ideas. When the prize fighter bore down on him he went down without a blow and was counted out, remarking cheerfully to his baffled opponent: 'There, you've won that.' Adams won the shooting and cricket contests with the greatest ease and drew the stakes.

Kent's wicket-keeper at this time was Edward Wenman, one of seven members of the family who played for the County. Apart from his fine wicket-keeping he was also a successful batsman, a good player off the back foot. It was reckoned to be one of the sights of cricket to see him batting with Pilch, their styles contrasting so well. Supporting Mr Mynn in the pace bowling department was William Hillyer, who was not so quick but was very successful. He was a useful batsman and one of the most brilliant slip fielders, taking many fine catches off Mynn.

There is no doubt that the ten years from 1839 to 1849 were incomparable in the history of Kent cricket. The side won 16 of its 28 matches against England:

> For with five such mighty cricketers, 'twas natural but to
> win
> As Felix, Wenman, Hillyer, Fuller Pilch and Alfred Mynn.

In 1850 Mr Mynn introduced into the Kent side Edgar Willsher, who played until 1875 and was one of the finest cricketers the County had produced. It was his left-arm pace bowling for which he was most famous, but he was also a fine left-handed batsman. He was no-balled six times in succession at The Oval in 1862 for his hand being above his shoulder. The Law was altered two years later, abolishing the restriction on height of hand in delivery. When a benefit match for Willsher at Lord's in 1871 was ruined by the weather, Kent played W. G. Grace's XI at Maidstone two months later and £800 was made for him.

In 1842 the first Canterbury Week had been planned following the success two years earlier of the Beverley Club's match with Shilston. This had become almost a first-class fixture with each side importing leading players. On the first two days in 1840 an entrance fee was charged but crowds were still between 1,500 and 2,000, large in those days. The success of the match obviously inspired the Kent v England match at Canterbury in 1841 on the Beverley club's new ground, just beyond the Cavalry Barracks on the Thanet Road. From the start of the Week in 1842 the features were those that continued throughout the years—large crowds of visitors and a ball in the evenings. The *Kentish Gazette* reported:

> The Beverley ground at eleven o'clock was made the rendezvous of visitors and cits. The ground was very tastefully laid out. The pavilion, in which a first rate cold collation was spread, and the good things of this life supplied at a liberal charge, and of superior quality, under the superintendence of the assiduous host of the Globe Tavern, occupied the farther part of the field, and on each side, in the form of a semi-circle, were marquees, tents, benches, and accommodation of all kinds for the spectators. Several of the tents were tastefully ornamented with bouquets of flowers and evergreens, which contrasted with the verdant lawn, and the varied coloured dresses of the ladies produced a very animated and picturesque scene. There was a considerable number of vehicles upon the ground; and we have infinite satisfaction in auguring from this, the first day's display, that the week will be one of the greatest interest, gaiety, and festivity . . . The remainder of the week, if the weather continues favourable, will draw a greater number of visitors to the city than has been known for many years past.

What joy there must have been for the crowd when two of their favourites, Fuller Pilch (98) and Mr Nicholas Felix (74) dominated the first-innings total of 278, adding 154 for the fourth wicket. England replied with 266, Joseph Guy top-scoring with 80, and then Kent were bowled out in their second innings for 44 by Lillywhite and Dean, with 19-year-old Emilius Bayley carrying his bat for 17 in only his second match for the County. A good deal of money was won and lost on the result and many Kent people, without any known justification, thought their side had sold the match. There was a report that Mr A. Mynn was actually hissed in Maidstone market. On the three following days the Gentlemen of Kent had a convincing victory over the Gentlemen of England by 173 runs. Since then only two world wars have stopped the Week being staged.

In 1847 the Week moved when the St Lawrence ground was opened. The ground went with Winter's Farm, Nackington, from whose tenant it was rented, until it was purchased by the club from Lord Sondes in 1896.

For some years the Week consisted of matches between Kent and England in the first half of the week and the Gentlemen of England and the Gentlemen of Kent in the second. Then the fixtures varied, but since 1882 the Week has always involved Kent meeting another first-class county, the Australians or the MCC & Ground.

It has remained the 'thing to do' to go to Canterbury Week—Les Ames recalled how when he was a boy the family would go into Canterbury from their home at Elham for the Week. Hospitality was on a generous scale in the tents. The tents spread half-way round the ground—the Band of Brothers, the I Zingari, the Old Stagers, the Buffs, the East Kent Yeomanry and the leading Canterbury clubs all had their own. So did the President of the Kent County Cricket Club and the Mayor of the City. There were private tents too. There still are, and although firms and businesses have come into the reckoning for entertaining at cricket and particularly at Canterbury, most of the traditional tents remain.

Woolley had his own very pertinent assessment of Canterbury Week when he wrote in his autobiography:

> At Canterbury, as I am sure at every other famous Week, wherever these are held, there come families who wouldn't miss attending on any account. Kent winning or Kent losing, they come and they go, all the better for having spent the best part of a day in the open air watching the grand old game which has been handed down to us.

The beginning of Canterbury Week had co-incided with the emergence of the Old Stagers, amateur actors, nearly all of them cricketers, who performed on stage during the evenings of the Festival Week at the New Theatre in Orange Street. It was not until their tenth season, in 1851, that they advertised themselves as the Old Stagers and their head-quarters, until it was destroyed during an air raid in the Second World War, was the Fountain Hotel. During their first season several of their members had taken part in the second game of the week—between the Gentlemen of England and the Gentlemen of Kent—including the Hon Frederick Ponsonby who was one of the prime movers in the formation of the Old Stagers. The music at their first performance in 1842 was provided by an amateur band, conducted by Mr Nicholas Felix.

Kent had been playing regular county cricket from 1834, and in 1858 it was decided to try to form a Kent County Club. The sixth Earl of Darnley presided at a meeting held at the Mitre Hotel, Maidstone, when a Club was formed and the Earl became President for the first year. It was resolved that the matches of the Club should not be confined to any particular locality but that Kent, without the assistance of 'given' men, should always be one of the teams taking part. The first year, 1859, was not successful from the playing point of view—only one out of six matches was won, but the record improved. With variable success and in a not very healthy financial position, the Club continued until 1870 when it amalgamated with the Beverley Club at Canterbury. Amalgamation had first been mooted in 1865 when the Kent Club Secretary, Mr W. South Norton, had written to Mr de Chair Baker saying that the unanimous view of his committee was that: 'the cricket of the county might be much improved in the future if an amalgamation with the club at Canterbury could be obtained without interference in the maintenance of the Canterbury Week in its integrity'. Mr de Baker had rejected that approach saying that any amalgamation would be 'injurious to our club'. Five years later, however, further approaches were made to the Beverley club which were to prove successful.

LORD HARRIS: FOUNDING FATHER

Lord Harris was the first President of the newly formed
Kent County Cricket Club, but it was his son, who had such
a tremendous influence on the playing and administrative
side of the County Club for many years, who found the right
way for bringing about the amalgamation with the Beverley
club—and the right man to handle the negotations. That was
Mr Herbert Knatchbull-Hugessen, of Mersham Hatch, who
was his trusted friend and a great lover of the game of cricket.
Members of his family had played for the County and it was
at his instigation that the Kent County Club again made
overtures to the Beverley Club for amalgamation, which was
recommended by their members at a meeting on 22 October
1870.

Those resolutions at the Beverley club meeting were
subsequently confirmed at a meeting of the subscribers to
both clubs at the Bull Hotel, Rochester on 6 December and
the Club, as it is known today, was formed. The resolutions
were:

> 1: that the Kent County Club and the Beverley Kent
> Cricket Club be amalgamated in one club, to be called the
> Kent County Cricket Club; and that the St Lawrence
> Cricket Ground, Canterbury, be the county cricket
> ground.
> 2: that the entire management of the Canterbury Cricket
> Week be retained by Mr W. de Chair Baker.
> 3: that Mr W. de Chair Baker act as the Honorary
> Secretary of the club.
> 4: that a President be chosen alternately from East and
> West Kent and a committee, consisting of ten gentlemen
> from East Kent and ten from West Kent, be formed to
> conduct the business of the club.

Having played a very important part in finding a
successful way to amalgamation, Mr Knatchbull-Hugessen
then persuaded Lord Harris to be the first President of the
new Club and when Harris died in November 1872, he
played an important role in enticing the new Lord Harris to
play for Kent. The new Lord Harris had already been
installed as a member of the Club's preliminary committee

and in 1873 recalled in 'The History of Kent County Cricket' how persuasive a man his friend Mr Knatchbull-Hugessen could be. They met at Faversham station when Lord Harris was travelling to London to see his old school, Eton, play Harrow and, on the preceding day, to play for Lords and Commons in the regular match they had in those days with I Zingari. Mr Knatchbull-Hugessen was travelling only as far as Gravesend to watch Kent's game with Lancashire and, on seeing Lord Harris' bag, was delighted, assuming that he also was making for Gravesend. When he discovered that Lord Harris had other plans he contended all the way to Strood that it would be perfectly reasonable to drop his plans to take part in what was a second-class match and play instead for the County. As for the Eton *v* Harrow game the following day, he argued that he could abandon those plans as well. Lord Harris was eventually convinced, and at Strood station he left the train, wired to Lord's with profound apologies that he would not be playing in the Lords and Commons game and returned to the train for Gravesend to make an unexpected arrival at the Bat and Ball ground. As Lord Harris put it, 'Someone kindly stood out', and he made 26 and 6 on his debut for the County—a winning one.

That was the turning point for Lord Harris and the beginning of his very influential involvement with the Club. In the winter of 1874 he accepted an invitation to act as Honorary Secretary for the conduct and management of the county matches for the following summer. His first task was to try and improve the cash flow and he wrote in March 1875 to the county papers appealing for financial support for the club. The response was generous. Subscriptions for 1874–75 amounted to £338 and in the following year the total was even better: £520. The next step was to derive more revenue from Canterbury Week. The entrance fee there was sixpence (2½p) and for 1875 that was doubled to a shilling (5p) on the Monday and Tuesday and in 1876 standardised at one shilling for the whole week. The effect was encouraging for in 1874 the gate had produced £243, whereas the following year it increased to £306 and in 1876 it had risen to £437. In 1875 the club had 338 subscribers but by 1905 that figure had steadily increased to 2,805, whose subscriptions totalled £2,141.

The new Kent County Cricket Club, formed in 1870, could not have been more fortunate in having Lord Harris making such an early impact on its fortunes. Both off and on the field Lord Harris was the proverbial 'tower of strength'. His efforts on behalf of the club were of vital importance—as administrator and as captain of the county eleven for 15 years from 1875. In fact his playing career for the side spanned 36 years. Captain of England in four Tests, he also had a distinguished political career which restricted his appearances for the County on whose behalf he performed so nobly. Scrupulously fair in his approach to the game, he was admired for his contribution to it on all sides. To him it was more than a game—'a school of the greatest social importance', he claimed—and it was surely appropriate that he made an appearance for the County he loved was in 1906, the year they first won the County Championship.

In Lord Harris' first year of captaincy in 1875 the County played all its home matches at Catford Bridge, made available by the Private Banks Cricket Club. Financially the experiment was not a success but the club derived some lasting benefit from the venture—the start of a very useful association with G. G. Hearne, who was qualified to play for Kent because his father George had just completed two years at Catford Bridge as groundsman. Lord Harris made a bargain with George Hearne that if he selected him for the County he should stay with Kent. G.G. and, subsequently, his brothers Frank and Alec, who might all have played for Middlesex because they had the necessary birth qualification for that County, were to keep their side of the bargain in a most loyal manner. Certainly the acquisition of G. G. Hearne compensated Lord Harris for the loss of wicket-keeper H. Wood. Lord Harris had expected to be able to secure the services of Mr E. F. S. Tylecote, which did not materialise at that stage, and although George Hearne argued that Wood should stay, the captain did not think that his hands would stand up to the fast bowling of Mr William Foord-Kelcey, who had one occasion sent a bail flying 48 yards when he bowled a batsman. Wood had a trial with Surrey and proved the Kent captain wrong by giving them fine service for many years.

Only two matches were won—and six lost—but the captain, admitting that it might seem a poor start, was quick to point out that really it had been a most useful one, because the spirit of enthusiasm in county cricket had been aroused. He paid tribute to the Gentlemen who had supported him—men like Mr Frank Penn, Mr F. A. Mackinnon, Mr C. A. Absolom and Mr Foord-Kelcey. He later wrote:

They used to say of the old Kent XI that they were like a lot of brothers, and I am sure better friendship was never formed among cricketers than that which existed among that little band, who helped to build up from practically nothing the present county club and county eleven.

One of Lord Harris's regrets in that first season of captaincy was that he was without the assistance of his old friend Mr Charles Thornton, whose business commitments meant that he had to live in London, and it was more convenient for him to play for Middlesex. A magnificent cricketer, Mr Thornton had established a reputation as a tremendous hitter. With a straight drive over the pavilion at Lord's and hits out of The Oval on three sides to his credit, Mr Thornton had a hit measuring 152 yards when playing for the South against the North at Canterbury in 1871. That beat his 132 yards hit the previous year at Canterbury for Kent against the MCC. Not surprisingly he frequently dominated stands to such an extent that he once made 107 out of 133 in 70 minutes with 29 hits, which included eight sixes and 12 fours, and he included nine sixes in his career best 124—for Kent against Sussex at Tunbridge Wells in 1869. At Canterbury, playing for Kent against the MCC in 1869, he made four hits out of the ground in a four-ball over from the unfortunate Mr V. E. Walker. On another occasion at Canterbury, against Surrey in 1871, two runs were completed and a third begun before the ball fell to ground after one of his powerful blows.

There was compensation in 1876 from an improved playing record when the side won four and lost the other six of its county games. The captain's most successful move was to persuade Mr W. Yardley to play regularly. Lord Harris said of him: 'Looking back at all the fine bats I have seen for 40 years I say unhesitantly that I have never seen a better natural or a more brilliant bat than Bill Yardley.' As a bowler Mr Yardley included in his repertoire left-arm lobs and right-arm round-arm, and in more than one match bowled both. At Canterbury he would follow a day's cricket by taking important parts at the theatre and then being the life and soul of the Old Stagers' supper.

In 1876 Kent played their only county game at Faversham on the private ground, known as Mount Field, of Mr Percy Neame. Their opponents were Hampshire, who were not then in the County Championship. In that season too,

W. G. Grace, playing for the MCC against Kent at Canterbury, had in the second innings scored 344, still the highest ever innings recorded against Kent at that venue. He batted 375 minutes, hitting 51 fours, eight threes, 20 twos and 76 singles, giving no chances in scoring his runs out of 546. It was quite a happy hunting ground for the great man—three years earlier in the same fixture he had taken ten for 92, and 15 for 147 in the match, still the best-ever innings and match returns at Canterbury against Kent.

Seven of the 12 county games were won in 1877, one being drawn and the other four lost, with Mr F. Penn heading the batting averages and George Hearne taking 96 wickets at 11 runs each. Frank Penn, a free-hitting batsman, was to tour

George Hearne.

Australia with Lord Harris's side in 1878–79. 1877 was the season when the Hon Ivo Bligh made his debut, following in the footsteps of his family in the previous century. That season, too, Kent played Nottinghamshire for the first time for many years. They lost at Canterbury but won the return, much to the delight of the captain who had received a message from the Nottinghamshire Secretary saying that if Kent did not take up a good team the fixture would be dropped!

Lord Harris had the answer to the rumblings among the other counties about Kent playing matches at the Mote, Maidstone, which had a very steep fall in the ground. He defended the slope, saying that it was the reason he liked the ground because it gave the bowlers more chance. He considered that a much more serious drawback was that the wickets were pitched east and west and with the shadows from trees and the sun occasionally glaring through them, batting in the evening could be difficult.

In one game in 1878, against England at Canterbury, Kent were assisted by Mr W. G. Grace, who scored 50 in the first innings and 58 in the second. While younger Kent players made progress during that season, George Hearne was still the mainstay of the attack with 86 wickets at 10 runs each. By the following season he had found a new partner named James Bray, medium-paced round-arm, but 1879 was a depressing season. The wet weather did not help and the side contained so many changes during the summer that only three players appeared in every match. Only two of the nine county matches were won, and the rest lost.

In 1880 a new slow left-arm bowler James Wootton made his debut. Varying his pace and length, he took 30 wickets and went on to claim 628 victims in his 119 matches in 11 seasons with the County. His career was cut short after he sustained a severe blow on the side while batting at Huddersfield in 1888, and six years later he was allocated a successful benefit match at Catford. The most successful bowler in 1880 was Mr Charles Cunliffe who took 54 wickets at 12 runs each. Although he had taken plenty of wickets when at Rugby School, his early form with the County had been shown with the bat. However he became one of the best slow bowlers the County had produced. He was renowned for his break-back from the pitch which his captain described as 'very puzzling'. Unfortunately tragedy struck—in the following season he played no cricket, having left the County for health reasons. He had consumption and in the last year of his life, looking on at the end of Canterbury Week he said: 'Well I shan't be here next year but I'd like to be buried in the middle there to make a good bumpy pitch for our bowlers.'

Not only had Kent lost their best bowler in 1881 but their leading batsman, Frank Penn, who had made a century against the MCC, never played again for the County because of health reasons. On the credit side they acquired the fine batsman and wicket-keeper Mr E. F. S. Tylecote, six seasons after the captain had first hoped to obtain his services. It was a poor season though, with only four victories in eleven county games, and much of the season was missed by the captain, who was travelling in the East.

Little encouragement was forthcoming in 1882 when the batting was strong but the bowling weak. There was, however, a notable debut by Mr Cecil Wilson, later to become a Bishop, against Yorkshire at Sheffield. He went in second wicket down and carried his bat for eight, the other batsmen who followed him making only two, as the last seven wickets fell for five runs. At Canterbury, Kent met the Australians for the first time, losing by seven wickets, and during the match a presentation was made by the club's President, the sixth Earl of Darnley, to Lord Harris. The handsome testimonial consisted of a pair of silver candelabra which cost 400 guineas, and Lady Harris received a silver inkstand. The candelabra was inscribed: 'Presented to Lord Harris by upwards of seven hundred subscribers as a mark of their high appreciation of the services rendered by him to the cause of county cricket.'

There was only slight improvement in Kent's fortunes in 1883. One of the consolations in a disappointing season was the advent of Mr Stanley Christopherson, who took eight for 41 in 23 overs against Surrey at The Oval. A fast right-arm bowler, he showed the form which earned him an international call against the Australians the following year. Reflecting on the season and the side's loss of form the captain felt that the absences of Mr Penn and Mr Cunliffe were the main factors.

In 1884 Alec Hearne, brother of George, and his cousin Herbert, were among the new players drafted into the side and Alec's bowling and some great fielding were the principal reasons for a memorable win over the Australians. It was the only victory recorded by a county side against the tourists that summer. Alec's inclusion in the side had been

Frank Hearne

severely criticised but was justified by his performance. His captain said: 'His was a novel style of bowling then, he and Allan Steel being the first to break from leg at something over a slow pace since the days of Martingell and Buttress and it puzzled some of the Australians a great deal.' After that victory over the tourists, Lord Harris presented the Gentlemen who had played in the game with a cap, embroidered with the White Horse of Kent by Lady Harris. Thereafter any Gentleman who played in Canterbury Week was awarded the cap and subsequently the professionals were accorded the same right. The idea of a county cap had originated in Lancashire and eventually spread to the other counties. About the same time in Kent the Gentlemen were indebted to Mr Mackinnon for the idea of starting the

Cricketers' House. Gentlemen playing in the Week, instead of taking their own lodgings, got together and hired a house for the week, with Mackinnon volunteering to act as housekeeper.

By this season of 1884 Lord Harris had only one other player who had been in the team when he himself started playing ten years earlier—Mr F. A. Mackinnon. He was an old friend of Lord Harris, who told how he had great difficulty in persuading Mackinnon to play county cricket because he was 'very diffident of his own powers'. The captain's remedy was to hang on to Mr Mackinnon's trap when he drove out of Lord's until 'out of sheer alarm, either for himself or myself, he promised to play.' A new bowler, Chris Collins, fast round-arm, had shown considerable promise at the end of the season but the captain rejected him the following summer because he felt the new bowler's action had 'enough suspicion' about it and Kent had to be above suspicion.

The question of action and suspicion was highlighted during the 1885 season when Kent did not play their return game with Lancashire because of a dispute with the northern county about the legality of delivery of two of their bowlers.

The Kent team of 1884. Back row: J. Wootton, H. Hearne, J. Pentecost, G. G. Hearne. Middle row: A. C. Gibson, C. Wilson, Lord Harris, S. Christopherson, F. Marchant. Front row: L. Wilson, F. Hearne.

Lord Harris made his view very clear before the first match between the two counties at Old Trafford, protesting against both J. Crosland and G. Nash. The Kent captain felt that Crosland, who varied his pace, undoubtedly threw his fast ball, while Nash, a slow left-hander, threw every ball. Lancashire would not promise to exclude either, so after the game Lord Harris said in a letter to the press that he intended to advise his committee not to field a side for the return match which Lancashire would win by default. His committee supported him and *Lillywhite's Cricketers' Annual* said 'Though the action of the committee gave rise to considerable discussion it was generally supported'. Middlesex and Nottinghamshire in the two previous seasons had declined to meet Lancashire for similar reasons and Nash dropped out of Lancashire cricket during the 1885 season. Objection was raised by the Nottinghamshire committee about the qualification of Nottinghamshire-born Crosland for Lancashire on the grounds that he did not live in Lancashire regularly and continuously. The MCC, having heard evidence from, among others, rent and rate collectors, a village policeman and a country squire, ruled that the player was not properly qualified for Lancashire.

Later in the season, against Surrey at The Oval, Lord Harris batted 35 minutes, using only his left hand, because his right hand, in which he had broken a small bone earlier in the innings, was in a sling.

George Hearne and his brother Frank both scored a century in the second innings of the game against Middlesex at Gravesend in 1886 when George topped the batting averages and Wootton took 97 wickets at 16 runs apiece. There was an encouraging start for F. Martin, who had played only one game the previous summer but now took 29 wickets in six matches at nine runs each with his medium-pace left-arm bowling. Lord Harris was now finding that his political duties interfered with his cricket appearances and he was prevented from playing three-day cricket until after Parliament had risen.

Whenever he did play he captained the side which was otherwise led by Mr W. H. Patterson, a fine batsman, particularly on sticky wickets. He had a very strong defence and was blessed with unlimited patience.

Only two matches were won in the 1887 season when 28 players appeared in the side's 17 matches, half of which were missed, unfortunately, by George Hearne, who sustained an

Walter Hearne.

ankle injury. A youngster called Walter Hearne, a cousin of George and his brothers, came into the side and showed considerable promise mainly as a right-arm medium pace bowler. On the first day of Canterbury Week in this season, Mr W. de Chair Baker, who had done so much for the Week, was presented by Earl Sondes with a testimonial in recognition of his long and successful management.

Fortune has always made a habit of changing swiftly and in 1888 Kent, having tolerated such a disappointing attack, suddenly found themselves equipped with some top-class bowlers. Martin (60) and Walter Wright (69) were the leading wicket-takers and Wright was Kent's gain and Nottinghamshire's loss. A good right-handed batsman and a fast-medium left-arm bowler, he had played several times for his native county before settling in Maidstone in 1878, where he was married, and was engaged by the Mote Park CC. In 1880 he had played for the Canadians as a 'given' man in several games during their England tour and he played for

Kent as soon as he had qualified. The batting may have been disappointing in 1888 but the top score against the attack was 234 and that improvement in bowling was the secret of Kent's success in winning half of their 14 Championship matches.

Success was achieved despite the loss of Mr Walter Hedley, who had taken 17 wickets for nine runs apiece in three matches, but his action brought complaints by some who had never raised them in years of playing against him in Royal Engineers' matches. Lord Harris immediately had him watched while playing at The Oval by Lord Lyttelton, Lord Wenlock and a third observer. Their verdict was that they

Alec Hearne.

could not say his action was above suspicion. As Kent had taken a strong line about doubtful actions Lord Harris was obliged, with great regret, to ask Mr Hedley to stand down. He subsequently played for Somerset and Hampshire and twice appeared for the Gentlemen against the Players.

The season of 1889 was the last in which Lord Harris played with any degree of regularity. Kent won seven of their 13 County matches and beat the MCC at Lord's in a summer when Martin (87) and Wright (81) spearheaded the attack to good effect. It was the combination of Martin and Wright which gave the captain a tremendous end to his last season by routing Nottinghamshire in their second innings at Beckenham and setting up a Kent victory. So Nottinghamshire had to be content with joint first place in the table with Surrey and Lancashire instead of taking the title outright, which would have been their reward had they beaten Kent. Lord Harris, who had been appointed Governor of Bombay, entertained the side to dinner after the match when he said his 'cricket book was closed' and that the umpire had called 'last over, gentlemen'. He did not suspect it then but he was to play again, albeit briefly, for the County. That season also saw another bad blow for the County because Frank Hearne, who could be a fine batsman and was always a brilliant ground fielder and the safest of catchers, left to take up an engagement in Cape Town on health grounds. After that final game Hearne was presented with nearly £150 by Mr F. A. Mackinnon, the president of the Club.

Lord Harris' contribution to Kent cricket had been immense. *Scores and Biographies* said: 'No cricketer, perhaps, ever did more for a county, if his Lordship's merits and performances as a batsman are considered in conjunction with his ability as a general manager of the Kent eleven.' He worked hard in the interests of cricket, which he recognised was more than a game. In a speech he asserted: 'Cricket has done more to consolidate the Empire than any other influence, and it is certainly the means of consolidating agreeable friendships and originating pleasant reunions.' In another speech he proclaimed: 'Cricket is not only a game but a school of the greatest social importance.'

So in 1890 the Kent side was under joint captaincy. Mr F. Marchant, a brilliant hitter in front of the wicket, especially on the leg side, led the team in the first part of the season with Mr W. H. Patterson, who had frequently deputised for Lord Harris, taking over when allowed by his

Frank Marchant, fine attacking batsman, joint captain from 1890 to 1893 and outright captain from 1894 to 1897.

holidays. If the new captains approached the start of their reign with apprehension it could be understood, but any doubts they might have had were dispelled by a successful season in which nine matches were won, six drawn and only four lost. The Australians were beaten again with two Kent newcomers in fine form—L. A. Hamilton carrying his bat to score 117 out of a total of 205 and Mr Albert Daffen finishing off the Australians by taking four wickets for five runs—the only wickets he took in the three games in which he played that season.

There were mixed fortunes in 1890 for bowlers Martin and Wright. The former bettered his 87 wickets of the previous year by taking 116, and distinguished himself for England against the Australians at The Oval with a match return of 12 for 102. Wright was not so fortunate. Against Surrey at The Oval, in trying to make a return catch, he sustained a compound fracture of the left thumb. He was taken to St Thomas's Hospital in great agony and was detained for five weeks during which his thumb was saved by careful treatment after amputation had been feared.

It was the season which saw the end of county cricket at Town Malling, where Sussex were beaten by an innings despite the efforts of C. Aubrey Smith, later to become as well known in Hollywood as on the cricket field, who took five for 39. The venue had been used by Kent in 1878 and 1879 after an interval of 37 years, but now the accommodation and the lack of spectators were the principal reasons for the withdrawal–symptoms which were still troubling other venues well into the 20th century with the same unfortunate decisions being made.

There was another unique bowling performance in 1891 when Mr W. F. Best, playing against Somerset, performed the hat-trick with his slow right-arm bowling, but he did not play in any other matches during the season. This wet season was ruined for Kent by their faulty fielding. Bad luck did not help either, for during the whole of August, Patterson failed to win the toss once. But for these problems the record of seven wins out of 18 matches could have been better.

That verdict on 1891 would have been welcomed the following season, which was one of the worst in the club's history. Only two matches were won and the season ended with Kent joint bottom with Gloucestershire. The batting was sound enough—it was the bowling that caused the downfall of the side. Martin was feeling the effects of the long tour with England in South Africa and his partner Wright may not have fully recovered from that bad injury at the end of the 1890 season. With Town Malling now off the fixture list, Tonbridge had fixtures with two first-class counties— the start of a cricket week for the Angel ground. The playing consolation of this dismal summer was the bowling of Walter Hearne, who took 93 wickets at a cost of 18 runs each. His short run and easy action at medium pace was accompanied by deceptive flight and the ability to break the ball quickly off the pitch. Unfortunately, he was restricted by injury and ill-health in 1893 when Kent were pleased to move right back up the table to fourth position.

In 1894 Marchant captained Kent throughout the season, with Patterson happily playing on under his leadership. Marchant's association with Kent had started in 1883, when during an interval in the Eton *v* Harrow match he was asked by Lord Harris if he was qualified for Kent. He played in the County side that season and then fairly regularly after the Varsity match during the year he was at Cambridge. One of his biggest problems when he took over the joint captaincy was in fielding the best possible side and he found himself preferring to leave the odd place open rather than having to ask a player to stand down. The policy rebounded on him at York when he found himself with only eight players for the game against Yorkshire and a full side not likely to materialise until four o'clock in the afternoon. He won the toss, decided to bat, hoping to be able to stay in residence at the crease until relief arrived but saw his depleted team all out for 46 by lunch time. Marchant's first full season as captain coincided with the return for a complete season of Walter Hearne, who rewarded him with 116 wickets at 13.29 each, a really superb performance.

Unfortunately for the new captain, for Kent and for Hearne himself, Hearne was injured before the 1895 season began and never played a match. Another telling blow was when wicket-keeper Huish dislocated his shoulder while batting, and for the rest of the season seven different wicket-keepers shared the duties! It was not until later in the season that Mr W. M Bradley came into the side and took over 30 wickets to give the attack a much needed boost.

For cricket fans at Gravesend the highlight of a poor season was the match against Gloucestershire, in which W. G. Grace, then 47, was on the field for the whole match. Twice hit over the pavilion by a Kent newcomer, Percy Northcote, of Beckenham, Grace retorted by going in first and was last out for 257. He then scored an unbeaten 73 when his side made 106 to win.

The Kent team of 1895.
Back row: W. Bradley, G. J. Mordaunt, J. R. Mason, H. C. Stewart, J. Crowe. Middle row: N. Wright, M. C. Kemp, F. Marchant, H. Patterson, F. Martin. Front row: J. W. Easby, A. Hearne.

THE ARRIVAL OF COLIN BLYTHE

ONE OF THE MOST IMPORTANT EVENTS in the history of the Club occurred in 1896 and it was nothing to do with the game itself—it was the purchase of the St Lawrence ground at Canterbury. Originally it had been rented at £40 a year from the tenant of Winter's Farm, Nackington, until 1890 and in the following year the rent was increased to £50 for the next four years. In 1895 the club paid Lord Sondes' agent £75 12s 8d rent and from October until 9 May 1896, when the purchase was completed, the rent was £56 9s 7d. At the November meeting of the general committee in 1895 Lord Sondes' agent had written to say that the executors of the late Earl Sondes wanted to sell the St Lawrence field at Canterbury (about 13 acres) and in the first instance were prepared to offer it to the Club. Lord Harris, who felt the purchase was the wisest possible precaution for the future of the game in the County, was on the committee which was set up to deal with the price negotiations. By February 1896, the asking price was reported as £5,500, while the surveyor had valued it at £4,000. Eventually Lord Sondes informed the County that if the Club was prepared to offer £4,500 the sale could be completed. The money to purchase the unencumbered freehold of the ground was raised by subscriptions (£1,790 5s 7d), the sale on Consols, and the transfer of funds from the General Fund of the club to give a total of £4,614 12s 7d, the extra £114 12s 7d being surveyor's fees, legal expenses and advertisements.

In those days, as now, there were discussions about the practice of the county side playing at different venues. Lord Harris had quite definite views. He wrote: 'I hope that we shall not depart from this wholesome practice.' But he stressed:

> Still Canterbury is our home and the pavilion is becoming the treasure house of our memories, for there are to be seen the likenesses of very many who have fought for the old county at the great game during nearly 200 years—the game which, whether its birthplace was there or not, has always had, and will always have, the most hospitable welcome in the county of Kent.

How well those words would sound nearly 100 years later, for much has been done to make the new pavilion even more of a treasure house, particularly by the efforts of the joint curators of the club, E. W. Swanton and Chris Taylor. Lord Harris would have been proud of them.

In 1895 Mr Bradley had become the first bowler new to the side to take over 30 wickets in the season during Mr Marchant's captaincy. A very fast right-arm bowler, he repeated the feat in 1896 and, to the delight of the captain, two other amateurs also topped the 30 mark—Mr J. R. Mason and Mr E. B. Shine. The side moved up in the table from 14th to ninth but the big disappointment was that Walter Hearne played only three matches before he damaged his knee while batting, and Wright played in only twelve of the 20 matches because he had contracted to play Lancashire League cricket. Huish returned to the side, setting a Kent record with 46 dismissals, which he was soon bettering in subsequent years and Lord Harris re-appeared in two matches, scoring a brilliant 119 against Somerset. Marchant's eight-year spell as captain did not have a happy ending for in 1897 Kent were third from bottom in the table and indeed below all the other counties they had played. In that season S. H. Day became the first player in the club's history to score a century on his debut—101 not out in the second innings of the match against Gloucestershire at Cheltenham, having only left school earlier that season. Marchant, reflecting on his reign as captain, was grateful that his three leading bowlers had endured ten years so well—Martin, Wright and Alec Hearne—for it was mainly on that trio that he had to rely.

The fourth most successful bowler he employed was Walter Hearne, who had only once completed a full season without injury. The other problem Kent had endured over the years was behind the stumps. Until Huish played his first full season in 1896, claiming 46 victims, there had been no reliable wicket-keeper and the average number of dismissals in a season before Huish arrived on the scene was 25.

In 1898 Kent had a Manager for the first time in Mr Tom Pawley and a new captain, Mr J. R. Mason. Pawley had played for Kent on four occasions but was better known for his service to the County at the nursery at Tonbridge.

That appointment of a Manager represented an important change in policy for the running of the club. Membership was increasing, more matches were being played and so the

John Mason, who was appointed captain of Kent in 1898. His best season was 1901, when he performed the 'double'.

staff was doubled from one to two! The work was split between a Secretary and a Manager, with the Secretary keeping the accounts, arranging the fixture list with the other counties and dealing with the MCC. The Manager was responsible for arrangements with the local clubs on whose grounds the County played, the details for all home and away games, and under the jurisdiction of the Canterbury Week sub-committee, dealing with the County Ground throughout the year and especially the organisation of Canterbury Week. Obviously part of his role was to ensure that the captain had less to worry about and was able to concentrate on the side and the match.

The club, as the 19th century neared its end, had a committee of 24, representing East and West Kent. They met about four times a year and from their number were selected the officers of the Club—the captain, the Treasurer, the General Manager and the Secretary, and the Trustees of the different committees. These were the managing committee, which met regularly during the year but was strictly limited in its spending powers, the finance sub-committee, the Canterbury sub-committee, which was responsible for the County Ground and examined the Manager's arrangements for Canterbury Week before adoption, and the young players sub-committee which looked for promising young players, arranged their trials, and if approved, their time at the Tonbridge nursery under Captain McCanlis.

John Mason, who in 1901 was to take 100 wickets and score 1,000 runs in all matches, was educated at Abbey School, Beckenham, and at Winchester. He was regarded as one of the County's best all-round Gentlemen players, certainly the best since Alfred Mynn. A strong forward player, with the off-drive and cuts his main strokes, he bowled right-arm fast-medium and fielded well in the slips. He had headed the bowling averages and returned a batting average of 34 in the previous season, and in his first year as captain the side showed considerable improvement, although only managing to win six of their 21 matches.

There were still problems in the bowling department but relief was on the way, for in 1899 a new bowler, the slow left-arm Colin Blythe, made his first appearance for the County. He had been seen a year earlier in the nets at the Rectory Field, Blackheath, by Capt McCanlis, who was impressed with his gentle easy run-up, the beautiful full swing and the flight. In his debut match against Yorkshire at Tonbridge he bowled Mr F. Mitchell with his first delivery in first-class cricket. He finished with five wickets on a plumb wicket. A great new Kent bowler had emerged, the first in Kent County Cricket Club's long line of distinguished spin bowlers.

He never looked back after that auspicious start, taking 100 wickets the following year, 1900, his first full summer in the game. It was a feat he was to perform with great regularity until his final season in 1914, and during his career he played 19 times for England. Wet or dry, the wickets never seemed to make too much difference to his success story, which played such a prominent part in Kent's halcyon days in the Championship.

The Australians were beaten again in 1899 when the bonus marks for Kent were that Mr Burnup had a complete season and scored consistently while Mr Bradley became one of the top fast bowlers in the country, which was an opportune development because Wright had dropped out of the side. Walter Bradley, who was to take 536 wickets for Kent in his nine seasons with the County, depended on his pace for his success and his victims were mainly caught in the slips or behind the wicket—if not clean bowled. His vital asset was that his pace could be sustained for long spells. In 1899 he twice performed the hat-trick, against Essex at Leyton and against Yorkshire at Tonbridge, and he performed the feat for a third time the following season, against Somerset at Blackheath.

Huish, who had his best-ever total of 77 dismissals, took many superb catches off Bradley's bowling. The wicket-keeper's performance that season was recognised by the presentation of a handsome gold pendant, showing the rampant horse surmounted by a pair of wicket-keeping gloves.

Blythe had played in only four matches, taking just 14 wickets, but he began the 1900 season in brilliant form, capturing 114 wickets for 18.47 runs each as Kent soared up to third position in the table, winning eight of their matches and being beaten in only four. Wickets were good and totals were high but Blythe, who used his head and never lost heart, enjoyed a remarkable first full season. His captain said: 'Even at this early period in his career he looked like being the best of the many good left-handed slow bowlers produced by Kent. There was another bowling achievement of note in that 1900 season when Alec Hearne performed the hat-trick against Gloucestershire at Clifton, but took no more wickets in the innings. In the previous season Hearne had written another entry in the record book with the bat—featuring in the County's highest ever stand for the third wicket of 321 with John Mason at Nottingham. There was distinction for Cuthbert Burnup, because he scored 200, the first double-century recorded for the County, and later in the season at Canterbury had the unusual experience of making his 49 over part of each of the three days of the match against Surrey because of interruptions by the weather.

Kent's first match with the South Africans was played in 1901—at Beckenham—and was marked by a century opening stand in each innings for the County by Mr Burnup and Humphreys. Kent won by seven wickets and in the

Colin Blythe, first of Kent's great spin bowlers and, with Wilfred Rhodes, the outstanding slow left-arm bowler of the 'Golden Age'.

tourists' second innings, Blythe, who just failed to reach 100 wickets in the summer, having been unwell during the previous winter, and Mr Bradley each took three wickets in four balls.

It was also the first season in which Kent played a Championship match on the Nevill ground at Tunbridge Wells, when Lancashire were the visitors. The following year the Cricket Week there was inaugurated and over the years the most traditional fixture has become the local derby meeting between Kent and Sussex. The ground, surrounded by rhododendron bushes, is situated on the border of the two counties with a small part of it actually in Sussex. Tom Webster, the famous cartoonist, commented in the *Daily Mail* in 1920: 'A small corner of the Tunbridge Wells ground is in Sussex. Kent fielders will not stand on it in case they qualify for the other county.'

There were two demonstrations in 1901 of the powers of former captain Frank Marchant as a hard-hitting batsman. Against Yorkshire at Sheffield he hit 111 out of 150 in 95 minutes and on a rain-affected wicket at Lord's he punished the Middlesex bowling for 100 out of 141 in 75 minutes. In two successive matches Kent had three batsmen making a century. Against Somerset at Taunton it was Mr Mason (145), Mr Burnup (134) and A. Hearne (103); against Hampshire at Tonbridge the happy trio were Mr Burnup (144), Mr. S. H. Day (118) and Mr P. C. Baker (108). In the game against Surrey at The Oval there was a very curious sequence. The first over bowled by Mr Dillon saw a single scored off each ball with the fielder in every instance being Mr Burnup. In fact each of the first eight balls and nine of the first ten bowled by Mr Dillon were singles, and the first seven hits were fielded by Mr Burnup!

Blythe may have missed the century of wickets by just seven in 1901 but there was no such problem in 1902 when he captured 127 wickets, 111 of them in inter-county matches. With John Mason, he took the bowling honours in a dramatic collapse of Surrey at Canterbury. Having reached 55 for one, Surrey were bowled out for 59 with Blythe taking five wickets for three runs, while Mr Mason at one stage had four wickets for one run.

Cuthbert Burnup, who in 1902 had topped the 2,000 runs mark in all matches and completed 1,000 for the fourth successive season, looked such a good batsman, particularly on wet wickets, that he was considered unlucky not to gain a place in the England side. There was some compensation because he became the Kent captain in 1903, when Blythe thrived on the wickets of a wet summer to take 137 at 13 runs each. He bowled well even on good wickets. The Kent attack contained a new fast bowler, Fielder, who replaced Mr Bradley. Off a long run with a high delivery action Fielder was at times very fast. *Wisden Cricketers' Almanack* reported: 'Taking a good run, Fielder brings the ball well over and is particularly awkward on a wicket with any life in it, his best ball being one which swings away with the arm.' Born at Plaxtol, he had played only a couple of matches, one in each of the preceding seasons, but his performances in 1903 when he took 61 wickets for the County at 18 runs each earned him immediate recognition, for he was selected for the winter tour of the MCC side to Australia. There was a tour for Kent at the end of the season too, for the County made history by being the first to be invited to play in America, when they won all four matches they played in Philadelphia.

Cuthbert Burnup had only one year as captain, and was succeeded in 1904 by Mr C. H. B. Marsham, second cousin to the Earl of Romney, who had been the Club's President in 1880. The new captain's uncle, Mr George Marsham, had played for Kent in 1876 and 1877 and had been the Club's President in 1886. For Kent in general, and the new skipper in particular, the 1904 season could hardly have started more disappointingly. The side lost three of the first four matches, including the opening game against the MCC when Marsham had his middle stump broken when he was bowled. Things had to improve and they did with the batting of

C. H. B. Marsham, who played for Kent from 1900 to 1922 and captained the side from 1904 to 1908.

*The Mote Ground,
Maidstone, in 1905.*

Humphreys and Seymour contributing much towards the County's rise to third place again.

Seymour, whose brother John had played for Sussex, was born in that county, at Brightling, and had been offered a place on the Kent staff after scoring 66 not out for the Kent Club & Ground against Gravesend. Twice in the summer of 1904 he wrote his name into the Kent record books. Against Worcestershire, at Maidstone, he became the first Kent player to score a century in each innings—108 and 136 not out. In the second innings he had scored only 70 when the last man Fielder arrived at the crease. Fielder scored 37 in a stand of 103 in 35 minutes. Against the South Africans at Canterbury, Seymour, at slip, took six catches in an innings—a feat which has been equalled by only one Kent player since—ironically by South African, Stuart Leary, in 1958.

Blythe again spearheaded the attack, taking 121 wickets for 19 apiece, and in the game against Sussex at Tunbridge Wells he bowled his first 12 overs for just one run. Blythe, going in last, showed his usefulness as a batsman against Somerset at Taunton when he made 70 out of 98 added. It was a game in which John Mason displayed his magnificent all-round ability. He made one and 100 and had a match

return of ten for 131, having in the first game between the counties at Beckenham scored 126 and enjoyed a bowling figures in the match of ten for 180.

In that season of 1904 Kent completed only one of their two games with Yorkshire—the match at Harrogate being declared NOT a first-class fixture after the pitch had been rolled, watered, and doctored by persons unknown between the end of play on the first day and the start of the second day's play. In fact play took place on the second day, but only so that the crowd should not be deprived of some entertainment; but there was no play on the third day.

There was an important development in 1905 when the ground at Tonbridge was secured by the local club and used as a nursery so that young talent from within the County could be developed rather than the County having to rely, if necessary, on the introduction of players from other counties. It certainly achieved its purpose in helping to discover young professional players who were to have an important part to play in the Club's subsequent successes. That season of 1905 though saw Kent slip three places down to sixth position. Although the side won the same number of matches, ten, they lost seven as compared with four the previous season. The batting was no problem—although S. H. Day, Mason and Humphreys all showed a drop in their average, Dillon, Blaker and Seymour all increased theirs, and A. P. Day, a newcomer, scored 1,149 runs for an average of 32 in his first season in first-class cricket. It was the bowling that caused concern, for inadequate support was given to Blythe, who captured another 130 wickets at 19 runs apiece. During the season, Kent failed to win a game in any of the Cricket Weeks and the captain embarked on an extraordinary long run when he failed to win the toss in the last six matches of the season, and indeed went 17 matches plus another two for MCC teams before he won the toss again on 2 July the following year.

The last match of the season provided Kent with their first-ever experience of a tie—against Surrey at the Oval. Eight were needed for Surrey to win when No 11, N. A. Knox, arrived at the crease. The scores were level when Smith (W. C.) skied the ball to Murrell at cover point. Kent had certainly kept their cool in this tense situation, as Murrell

Fred Huish, first in a line of distinguished Kent wicket-keepers that has included Ames, Evans and Knott.

rubbed his hands on his trousers before catching the ball. Before it was in his hands Blythe is reported to have said: 'This is the first tied match I have ever played in.'

The season was notable for the continued brilliance behind the stumps of Huish, who set up a new record, yet again, by claiming 78 victims (54 caught and 24 stumped)—one more than he had in 1899. It was an appropriate year in which to be so successful, for the game against Lancashire at Canterbury was allocated as his benefit match. Even in those days, it was no fun being the deputy wicket-keeper for Kent. The player who had that unfortunate role was Murrell, rated a very clever wicket-keeper by Mr Mason when captain, but although his chances behind the stumps were severely restricted, he did get the odd game as a batsman. Without a win in their last four games of the 1905 season there was little to suggest that 12 months later the club and its supporters would be celebrating the greatest possible success in County Cricket: winning the Championship.

FOUR CHAMPIONSHIPS IN EIGHT YEARS

FOUR TIMES WINNERS of the Championship in eight years—that was the major success story unfolding for Kent as they won their first title in 1906 and embarked on the most successful period in the club's history. Certainly that kind of success in the Championship has never been equalled, although in the 1970s they were to win it twice and share it once in nine seasons. Success in winning the Championship in 1906 coincided with the introduction to the County side of a brilliant young player, Frank Woolley, who in that first season played in 16 matches, scoring 779 runs for an average of 31.16 and taking 42 wickets at 21.11 apiece. Born at Tonbridge on 27 May 1877, Woolley batted and bowled left-handed. His bowling, deceptive in flight and pace, was likened to that of Blythe, while with the bat he soon won renown for his off-drive. Woolley's name has become a legend in Kent cricket. His ability to entertain and to take apart opposing attacks stamped him as one of the game's greatest all-rounders. He was to play 64 Tests for England in a career which did not end until 1938, and played 764 matches for Kent—a record which surely will never be exceeded. In every season he played, apart from his debut summer of 1906, he scored over 1,000 runs and in six seasons he completed the double of 1,000 runs and 100 wickets for his County, achieving the feat in all, eight times. No wonder that when he chose to retire at the end of the 1938 season, then aged 51, he was accorded a tremendous ovation wherever he played.

The 1906 season had started where 1905 had left off, in disappointing fashion. The first county game against Yorkshire at Catford was lost, as had been the opening match of the season when the MCC won by 69 runs. The match against Essex at Leyton was drawn before victory was tasted for the first time with a win by an innings and 117 runs over Sussex at Brighton. At Manchester the side was back on the losing trail, beaten by ten wickets by Lancashire in a match which saw the debut of Woolley because Blythe, whose haul of wickets for the season was 111, had sustained a hand injury in the previous match.

For Woolley that first appearance, gained at the expense of his injured boyhood hero, was one that he would remember

for its conspicuous lack of success—for himself and the side.
He twice dropped J. T. Tyldesley, who scored 295 not out in
a total of 531, he took one for 103 with the ball and was out
for a duck. He marked his second innings by scoring 64, but
Kent lost heavily. Thereafter Kent did not lose again during
their wonderful summer. Woolley had a spell where
everything went right, whether he was batting or bowling;
wicket-keeper Huish made his best score for the County, 93,
and fast bowler Fielder, going in at No 11, stayed with
Woolley while 19 were scored for a one-wicket victory over
Surrey at The Oval.

Fielder's outstanding performance with the ball in 1906,

*Arthur Fielder, an
outstanding fast bowler in the
years before the First World
War. Ironically his most
memorable feat was to score a
century at No. 11 and share
in a last-wicket partnership of
235 with Woolley, a record in
county cricket.*

indeed of his career, was not for Kent but for The Players—he took all ten wickets in the match against The Gentlemen at Lord's. Overall, too, it was his finest season, because he claimed 172 wickets for Kent alone.

The Tonbridge Week marked the first appearance of the season of Mr K. L. Hutchings, who, in the second game of the Week against Middlesex, hit 125 and 97 not out to set him on the road to a great summer in which he scored 1,454 runs for an average of 60.58. Hutchings, only 23, was referred to in *Wisden* as: 'the sensation of the season, the English Trumper.' Kent fans have always appreciated top-class fielding and in this department he was brilliant, specialising at cover, and renowned as one of the best throwers in the history of the game.

The return game with Yorkshire at Sheffield was drawn—a match in which Lord Hawke was bowled by Fielder but was invited by the Kent skipper to continue his innings because the bails had been blown off before the ball hit the stumps. His Lordship rejected the offer. Kent's first-ever match with Leicestershire resulted in a win by eight

The Angel Ground, Tonbridge, in 1906. Kent played here until the Second World War.

wickets—and then in the next game against Worcestershire
the Kent captain's luck changed and he finally won the toss
again, bringing to an end the flow of coins with which people
were supplying him in the hope of restoring his fortunes.
Certainly his side appreciated his success with the toss, none
more so than Alec Hearne, now 41 and in his 23rd season
with the County, who scored 154 in a mammoth total of 576.
The next match was another first for Kent—when the West
Indians opposed them for the first time. The match was at
Catford and Lord Harris returned to play for the County,
who won by an innings and 14 runs. That match marked the
return of Blythe, who had missed seven Championship
matches. By bowling long spells in both innings, and earning
a match return of ten for 134, he proved all was well again.

Both matches of Tunbridge Wells Week were won—
against Essex and Gloucestershire. Leicestershire were easily
beaten by ten wickets at Maidstone, and then came an
amazing 164-run victory at Blackheath in the great battle
with Surrey. Blythe won the game for Kent with some
brilliant bowling on an easy batting wicket. Kent had been

bowled out for 136, although they scored 327 in their second innings. Surrey were favourites to win but collapsed and were dismissed for 80. Canterbury Week was a real success story. Both matches were won, the weather was almost perfect, and there were record attendances on four of the days. It was the sort of form that the crowds loved and was worthy of Champions-elect. Progressing at the rate of around 100 runs an hour they amassed totals of 568 and 479 to beat both Sussex and Lancashire by an innings.

Easy victories followed at Cheltenham and Taunton before the side returned to Canterbury for another convincing win over Worcestershire, which took them to the top of the table. It was on to Lord's for a seven-wicket victory, set up by Blythe's bowling, and then to Bournemouth for the final match of the season against Hampshire. A draw would have gained Kent the title—and there was little doubt that would be achieved when Kent, having dismissed Hampshire for 163, amassed 610, with Burnup scoring 179. In their second innings Hampshire made 410; but Kent had won their first title in style. It was a great end of the summer for Burnup personally. He had topped the national batting list, scoring 1,207 runs for an average of 67.

As Champions Kent played England at The Oval where they lost by 251 runs, but had the satisfaction of playing before 40,000 people over the four days. After expenses had been deducted there was £825 left to share between the Cricketers' Fund and the London Playing Fields Society, the joint beneficiaries of the match.

Kent, in their first Championship success, had lost only two games, drawn four and won 16 with a percentage of 77.77, with Yorkshire, in second place, registering 70.00. The success was greeted rapturously throughout the County. The captain, C. H. B. Marsham, received over 500 telegrams, letters and picture postcards offering congratulations. It was Marsham's third season at the helm. A sound batsman, he could score freely when set, as he had proved in the game against Sussex at Canterbury. He made 119 and with Huish (30) added 74 for the eighth wicket in 30 minutes and with Blythe (53) 111 for the ninth in 35 minutes.

Such a memorable year was difficult to follow. It did not seem too difficult, though, when the County, having beaten MCC in their opening match, won their first three County matches in succession and by the end of Tonbridge Week were still going well with seven wins out of eleven County

games. But then came a slump in fortunes. They lost to the South Africans at Catford, were beaten in their next two county matches, rallied with three successive victories, but then managed only one win in their last eight games.

There were problems. Hutchings was struck such a bad blow on the hand against the tourists that he missed the next seven games before reappearing to score a century in each innings at Worcester. In addition Burnup, who had scored 1,207 runs the previous year, played in only three matches in 1907. It was also questionable whether the decision to dispense with the services of Alec Hearne had been correct. The committee's policy was to try out young, promising players which they felt would be of more benefit to the County in the near future, but in 1906 Hearne, with Cuthbert Burnup, had been a steadying influence when required in the batting department.

Seymour, with 1,547 runs, took the batting honours in a wet summer which saw the Champions slide to eighth place in the table. The pace of Fielder, the best fast bowler in the County, and the spin of Blythe, who took his 1,000th wicket during the season, dominated the attack. Blythe had one

The Championship-winning Kent side of 1906. Standing: F. Humphries, F. E. Woolley, F. Huish, J. Seymour, W. Hearne. Seated: A. Fielder, R. N. R. Blaker, C. H. B. Marsham, J. R. Mason, K. L. Hutchings. On ground: J. C. Hubble, W. Fairservice.

unbelievable day at Northampton when he took 17 wickets for 48 runs. In the first innings, when he took all ten for 30, he had seven wickets for one run in the first 36 balls he bowled. There was also a 'first' for Woolley, who reached 1,000 runs for the season, though few would have dared to predict that he would repeat that feat 26 times, indeed in every season until 1938, when he retired.

Once a side wins something it is always likely to be under pressure for a repeat performance, and Kent came very close to producing one in 1908 when they finished runners-up, winning 18 of their games and losing just three, one of those defeats by a staggering margin—an innings and 318 runs at the hands of Surrey at The Oval. Some compensation was earned by the defeat of Surrey at Blackheath, and a dramatic win over Middlesex at Lord's in the final game of the season, when Woolley took the last six wickets for eight runs in 27 balls. Blythe again dominated the bowling figures, taking 174 wickets, his total steadily increasing every year, despite the handicap for a time of having water on the knee. Fielder, owing to injury, could play only infrequently in the second half of the summer and had to be content with 86 wickets compared with his 159 the previous season. W. J. Fairservice, who had taken 70 wickets the previous season, again proved a most useful member of the attack, with 86 victims.

The batting was brilliant and most entertaining, and Hardinge, who established himself in the side, made 1,341 runs, including a century in each innings of the game against Essex at Leyton. Woolley raised his aggregate to 1,244 runs, and also took 71 wickets. With Hutchings he figured in a fourth-wicket stand of 296 against Northants at Gravesend, which was to stand as a Club record for 18 years. Hutchings enjoyed the reputation of being a brilliant driver of the ball; 'The hardest driver I ever saw, bar nobody', was Woolley's verdict. He added: 'I never see a "silly" point positioned on a hard wicket without wishing Mr Hutchings was at the wicket, or in next.'

Against Somerset at Bath Humphreys and A. P. Day scored 248 for the seventh wicket, still a Club record, and the last 201 of those runs were scored in 75 minutes. After a successful season with the bat, in which he failed by only 37 runs to reach his 1,000, Marsham resigned as captain and was succeeded by Mr E. W. Dillon. Educated at Abbey School, Beckingham, Rugby and Oxford, he was a left-handed batsman who had been playing for the County since

K. L. Hutchings, who played for Kent between 1902 and 1912, was renowned for his fierce driving and his agile fielding.

1900. An international rugby player, he embarked on a reign as Kent's captain which was to prove the most rewarding in the club's history. Not only did they win the title under him in 1909 and 1910, his first two seasons, they did it again in his final summer of captaincy in 1913.

What a record the side enjoyed in 1909—losing only two of their 30 matches, and winning 18, ten of them by an innings. The new captain performed his duties skilfully, and when he was not in the side for business reasons for most of August, Mr Mason deputised.

During the season Kent introduced a 37-year-old bowler, Mr D. W. Carr, who had played only in club matches in the south of England, but suddenly came upon the Kent scene because he had developed the 'googly'. Encouraged by the success of Mr Bosanquet, with whom he had played, Mr

SOMERSET *v* KENT

Played on the County Ground, Taunton, 13–15 August 1908

KENT WON BY AN INNINGS AND 114 RUNS

SOMERSET	FIRST INNINGS		SECOND INNINGS	
Mr P. R. Johnson	lbw Seymour	31	st Huish b Blythe	126
Braund	b Fielder	6	c Huish b Seymour	53
Lewis	c Blythe b Fielder	42	c Hardinge b Seymour	3
Mr B L Bisgood	b Seymour	0	c Huish b Blythe	4
Whittle	c Huish b Fielder	10	c Hutchings b Blythe	0
Robson	c and b Seymour	49	c Seymour b Blythe	8
Mr V. T. Hill	b Blythe	14	c Huish b Seymour	0
Mr M. M. Munden	c Huish b Fielder	0	c Seymour b Blythe	0
Mr E. J. Leat	st Huish b Blythe	11	b Seymour	1
Mr W. T. Greswell	c A. P. Day b Blythe	6	c Huish b Blythe	41
Mr A. E. Newton	not out	3	not out	50
Extras	b 6, nb 7, w 1	14	b 8, lb 2, nb 3, w 2	15
Total		186		301

BOWLING	O	M	R	W	O	M	R	W
Fielder	22	10	55	4	16	5	71	0
Blythe	20	2	73	3	37.3	6	115	6
Woolley	3	2	1	0	10	4	16	0
Seymour	10	2	43	3	21	4	62	4
A. P. Day					3	0	9	0
Humphreys					2	0	13	0

KENT	FIRST INNINGS	
Mr C. H. B. Marsham	c Braund b Robson	37
H. T. W. Hardinge	c Newton b Lewis	0
J. Seymour	b Braund	129
Mr S. H. Day	c Newton b Lewis	4
F. E. Woolley	c Braund b Robson	105
Mr K. L. Hutchings	b Robson	35
Mr A. P. Day	c Hill b Braund	118
E. Humphreys	c Leat b Robson	149
F. H. Huish	not out	7
C. Blythe	} did not bat	
A. Fielder		
Extras	b 10, lb 2, nb 5	17
Total	for 8 wkts declared	601

BOWLING	**O**	**M**	**R**	**W**
W. T. Greswell	31	4	157	0
Lewis	30	2	122	2
Braund	22	1	99	2
Robson	26.3	1	151	4
V. T. Hill	5	0	55	0

The only occasion in a County Championship match when Kent had four batsmen scoring a century. The stand between Humphreys and Mr A. P. Day of 248 for the seventh wicket took just 100 minutes. The feat of four centuries in an innings was repeated in 1982 against Oxford University at The Parks by the first four in the batting order: R. A. Woolmer (126), N. R. Taylor (127), C. J. Tavaré (125) and M. R. Benson (120).

Carr, during the winter of 1905–06, succeeded in developing the googly, only to discover he had lost his ability to bowl the leg-break. During the summers of 1907 and 1908, Mr Carr, who was born at Cranbrook, and educated at Sutton Valence and Oxford, recaptured the ability to produce both the leg-break and the googly. Brought into the Kent side in 1909, his 61 wickets in 11 matches for 165 runs had a great effect on the potential of the team to win games. His success for Kent did not go unnoticed—within a fortnight of making his County debut he played for England against Australia.

Blythe's total rose again, to 185, the highest number of wickets ever taken in a season by a Kent bowler. His skill and popularity were recognised when his benefit game against Hampshire at Canterbury realised £1,516. At Leicester, Blythe captured 14 wickets for 56 runs in a day and at Bristol, in Gloucestershire's first innings, he had a spell of six wickets for six runs. He was human, of course, and at Canterbury, Lancashire batsman Mr K. G. Macleod punished him for 41 runs in three overs, including a six and eight fours.

There was another record partnership during the season, for the tenth wicket, and this has stood the test of time. Fielder, who took 95 wickets in the summer, went in No 11 against Worcestershire at Stourbridge, and scored an unbeaten 112, helping Woolley (185) to add 235 runs in 150 minutes, a record in all first-class cricket by an English pair to this day—beaten only by a last wicket stand of 307 in Melbourne (1928–29), and 249 for India at The Oval in 1946. During the season Woolley had made the first of his 84 appearances for England.

Kent's only two defeats of the season were during Tonbridge Cricket Week—by Worcestershire and then Lancashire. Their retort to these reverses was to thrash the Gloucestershire attack at Catford in the next match for 593 in $4\frac{1}{2}$ hours with Humphreys (208) and Seymour (86), engaging in a stand of 224 in 100 minutes for the second wicket. When Hutchings (100) joined Humphreys, the pace was accelerated, with 102 being added for the third wicket in 35 minutes—Hutchings, who hit 20 fours, reaching 50 in 30 minutes and 100 just 20 minutes later.

John Mason, who headed the batting averages (65.25), was indebted for one of his three centuries to Blythe, who going in at No 11 at The Oval when Mason was on 45, resisted resolutely to score 29, while his partner reached an unbeaten 152. Supporters were delighted at this second Championship success and on 23 October the team were entertained to a banquet at Canterbury, when the Mayor read a telegram from the Archbishop of Canterbury: 'Please convey to your eminent guests an expression of very proud recognition of the county's prowess.' Tradition had demanded for over 700 years that on important occasions in the city, there should be a blast on the ancient burghmote horn, and that duly followed. All over the world, Men of Kent and Kentish Men celebrated. In Canada, William Wenman, a member of the County team of 1862–64, congratulated the side on their success when he spoke at a public function. Hopes for the future of Kent cricket were suitably expressed by Mr E. B. Christian: 'If the county's motto "Invicta" be one no team can hope always to bear unchallenged as regards results, it can be borne—and long may Kent bear it!—unchallengable as regards devotion to the game and loyalty to its best traditions.'

Of course, if you can stay on top, so much the better, and that is exactly what Kent did in 1910 when a new system of deciding the Championship positions was introduced—the percentage of wins to matches played. It made absolutely no difference to Kent's runaway title success. Their percentage was 76.00 with their nearest rivals Surrey (57.14) and Middlesex (50.00) well in arrears and by the second week of August, with four games still to play, Kent's success was assured. The opening match of the season against MCC was cancelled because of the death of King Edward VII, and the match against Lancashire at Manchester was restricted to two days because of the King's funeral at Windsor and did not count in the Championship. Of the 25 county games, 19 were won, many of them by overwhelming margins. The first, against Middlesex at Lord's, set the pattern—victory by an innings and 198 runs. And what a debut for Percival Morfee, who bowled 'Plum' Warner twice in a day for a duck, with the third ball in the first innings and first in the second. A very fast right-arm bowler, he played in only nine matches for the County in three seasons but after the First World War figured prominently in the Lancashire and Central Lancashire League.

Skilfully led by Edward Dillon, the side's all-round performance was of the highest possible standard. The batting was brilliant. Driving with greater power than ever Hutchings scored 1,461 runs, averaging 42.97. Humphreys (1,618) and Seymour (1,546) averaged 36.78 and 36.80 respectively. Yet Seymour was left out of the side for the

Edward Dillon, Kent's captain from 1910 to 1913. He also played three-quarter for Blackheath and England.

game against Middlesex at Canterbury but played because Fielder was unwell—and scored 193, his highest innings of the season! There was another annihilation of the Gloucestershire attack—this time at Cheltenham, when Kent scored 607 for six in five hours with Humphreys (162), Mason (121 not out) and Seymour (90) leading the run-spree. Young players who got their chance included Mr F. H. Knott, a former captain of Tonbridge School, who, in his third game for the County, scored 114 against Worcestershire at Dover.

Woolley completed the 'double' (1,050 runs and 132 wickets), taking over at the top of the bowling averages. He and Blythe (163 wickets) bowled unchanged throughout the match against Yorkshire at Maidstone, dismissing them for 120 and 78. Blythe twice performed the hat-trick, and on the first occasion against Surrey at Blackheath he had five wickets for no runs in ten balls, including four in five balls. His second hat-trick success was against Derbyshire at Gravesend.

Fielder was prevented by illness from playing in more than 18 games but he captured 77 wickets and Douglas Carr, who played only from the end of July, picked up 63 wickets at 14.20 each. All the bowlers benefited from the superb form behind the stumps of Huish, whose 73 victims consisted of 43 catches and 30 stumpings—a proportion unlikely to be encountered today!

It would have been a hat-trick of title wins in 1911 but for a change in the system to decide the placings. Under those previously adopted Kent would have landed the Championship, instead their percentage of 73.84 saw them pipped on the post by Warwickshire (74.00). Five points were awarded for a win outright, three for the side leading on the first innings and two for the team behind on the first innings, with no points awarded when a first-innings result was not obtained.

During the season, in the game against All India at Catford, Lord Harris, then 60, made positively his last appearance for the County side, batting for an hour for his 36 and taking one for 34, so ending a career in the team which spanned from 1870 to 1911. Hubble made his first century for the County but it was as a batsman that he played when he was in the side, his wicket-keeping being not required, for Huish had his most brilliant season ever behind the stumps. He claimed ten dismissals in the match against Surrey at The Oval, one caught and nine stumped (a record then for stumpings in a first-class match) and the ten victims, equalled by Hubble 12 years later, has remained a County record. Huish finished the season with 100 wickets (62 caught and 38 stumped) a feat never before achieved in a season in first-class cricket, but one which he himself was to repeat two years later.

It was quite a year for thrilling individual performances and Woolley again illustrated his all-round ability. He made 42 out of 78 in 28 minutes against Surrey, hitting six fours and a two off eight balls from Hitch and breaking his bat in going for another big hit off the next delivery. Then, in the return against Surrey, he had an analysis of seven for nine—the wickets being taken in 24 balls for five runs.

Lacking the assistance regularly of their amateur players Kent's professionals were not found wanting in the run-scoring department. Seymour (1,737) and Humphreys

James Seymour, who scored over 26,000 runs for Kent between 1902 and 1926.

(1,773) led the way, with Woolley close behind on 1,676 and Hardinge (1,146) showing improved form as he passed a thousand in a season for the second time.

Fielder, appreciating the fast pitches in his benefit season— the second match of Canterbury Week yielded him a return of £1,174 10s 3d—took 119 wickets while Blythe, despite the conditions, captured 138. The best support came from Woolley (72) and Carr (55), the latter continuing to puzzle batsmen on any wicket.

Shrugging off as best as possible the handicap of injury, unavailability and Test calls in 1912, Kent did extremely well to slip no further than third place in the table. An eye injury and then business commitments restricted the captain to only ten matches. Other amateurs' appearances were curtailed for varying reasons and Woolley, the great all-round strength of the side, missed five matches because he was required for England in the Triangular Tournament. Yet he still completed the 'double' (1,373 runs and 107 wickets) and he, Blythe (178) and Donald Carr (56) produced the goods on the slow wickets. Blythe and Woolley delighted the Kent fans by bowling out Nottinghamshire twice at Canterbury, operating unchanged. Blythe had 15 for 45 at Leicestershire, who were dismissed for 25 in one innings with Blythe claiming seven for nine, and he and Carr bowled throughout the match at Dover when Gloucestershire were dismissed for 67 and 95. Apart from Woolley only Hardinge and Humphreys passed the thousand-run mark.

During the season Capt William McCanlis resigned as coach to the young players after a career with the County which had started as a player in 1862. During his coaching at the nursery at Tonbridge he could reflect with pride on some of the young players who had passed through his hands: Blythe, Seymour, Humphreys, Hardinge, Hubble and Woolley. He was succeeded by Mr G. J. V. Weighall, who had played in 130 matches for Kent between 1891 and 1903. In its tribute to Captain McCanlis the committee's report read:

> What the club owes to him for his life long services to the county as cricketer, counsellor and friend it is impossible to estimate but so far as his coaching is concerned he has the extreme satisfaction of having lived to see and enjoy the most satisfactory results.

Certainly, the results which Captain McCanlis and

everyone else in Kent savoured were eminently satisfactory as the Championship title returned to the County in 1913 for the fourth time in eight seasons. With 20 of their 28 games won they had an eleven-point lead over the runners-up, Yorkshire, and so well did the team perform in every department of the game, with perhaps a slight reservation that the fielding was not quite of its usual high standard, the County did not use any new players. Any worries about the balance of the attack were dispelled by Fielder returning to his best form, showing his appreciation of the hard wickets by claiming 115 victims. Blythe, with 163 wickets for an average of just under 16, again shouldered the burden of the attack, despite the hard wickets; and he and Woolley (who took 83 wickets) brought about the humiliation of Warwickshire at Tonbridge, in the first meeting between the two counties for 14 years. How Warwickshire must have regretted renewing acquaintance with Kent as they were bowled out in their second innings for 16, still the lowest score ever recorded against Kent. Blythe and Woolley each returned five for eight as the innings was over in 43 minutes and 62 balls. Kent, who had been bowled out for 132 in their first innings, 130 behind, were given an unexpected chance of victory. They survived early shocks, losing two wickets for 16 runs, but Woolley steered them to a six-wicket win with an unbeaten 76.

Although Hutchings did not appear throughout the summer, the batting was still at its brilliant best, with Hardinge scoring 2,018 runs and Seymour failing by 20 to reach the 2,000 mark. Hardinge, whose debut in 1902 had been at the age of 16, wrote his name into the Club's record books by scoring four successive centuries, and the consistency of Humphreys (1,056) was rewarded with a £1,336 benefit match at Canterbury. Although sidelined in the late stages of the summer by a thumb injury, Woolley still registered 1,737 runs, showing all-round form of the highest quality.

In the match against Northamptonshire at Northampton there was the unusual sight of two Kent players in direct opposition to their brothers. At one stage C. N. Woolley and John Seymour were batting against their respective brothers Frank and James.

A very important part of the success of any top side is the performance of the wicket-keeper and Huish, then 42 and first a member of the side in 1895, recorded his own brand of

KENT *v* WARWICKSHIRE

Played at Tonbridge, 18–21 June 1913

KENT WON BY SIX WICKETS

WARWICKSHIRE	FIRST INNINGS		SECOND INNINGS	
Charlesworth	c Hatfield b Woolley	47	c Seymour b Blythe	1
Parsons	b Day	0	st Huish b Woolley	5
Mr F. R. Foster	b Fielder	13	c Hubble b Blythe	2
W. G. Quaife	c Seymour b Blythe	31	b Blythe	0
C. S. Baker	c Dillon b Humphreys	59	c Humphreys b Woolley	4
Jeeves	b Woolley	30	c Blythe b Woolley	0
Mr G. Curle	b Woolley	1	st Huish b Blythe	0
Mr W. C. Hands	lbw b Blythe	21	b Woolley	0
Santall	c Dillon b Woolley	31	c Huish b Woolley	3
L. Bates	lbw b Woolley	4	not out	0
Brown	not out	0	st Huish b Blythe	1
Extras	b 14, lb 9, nb 2	25		0
Total		262		16

1st inns: 1-2. 2-33, 3-83, 4-118, 5-178, 6-190, 7-192, 8-255, 9-259, 10-262
2nd inns: 1-5, 2-6, 3-6, 4-12, 5-12, 6-12, 7-12, 8-12, 9-15, 10-16

BOWLING	O	M	R	W	O	M	R	W
Fielder	21	4	56	1				
A. P. Day	18	4	61	1				
Blythe	22	4	50	2	5.2	1	8	5
Woolley	16.5	4	44	5	5	1	8	5
Humphreys	10	2	26	1				

KENT	FIRST INNINGS		SECOND INNINGS	
E. Humphreys	c Baker b Jeeves	11	lbw b Santall	1
H. T. W. Hardinge	c Jeeves b Foster	15	b Foster	27
James Seymour	c Hands b Jeeves	24	c Jeeves b Foster	9
F. E. Woolley	c Hands b Jeeves	8	not out	76
J. C. Hubble	c Bates b Foster	24	b Charlesworth	10
Mr E. W. Dillon	c Baker b Foster	15	not out	18
Mr A. P. Day	b Foster	0		
Mr C. E. Hadfield	b Foster	10		
F. H. Huish	not out	7		
C. Blythe	c Quaife b Jeeves	6		
A. Fielder	b Foster	0		
Extras	lb 8, w 4	12	b 5, lb 1	6
Total		132	for 4 wkts	147

1st inns: 1-23, 2-27, 3-40, 4-66, 5-104, 6-104, 7-113, 8-116, 9-129, 10-132
2nd inns: 1-1, 2-16, 3-73, 4-93

BOWLING	O	M	R	W		O	M	R	W
F. R. Foster	29	8	62	6		10	1	44	2
W. C. Hands	8	2	14	0		3.4	0	27	0
Jeeves	12	5	27	4		7	0	20	0
Santall	10	5	17	0		11	0	27	1
Charlesworth						6	0	23	1

Umpires: Moss and Atfield.

Warwickshire's 16 is still the lowest score against Kent. The innings was completed in 62 balls, and lasted 43 minutes. Incidentally, the Warwickshire batsman Jeeves gave his name to P. G. Wodehouse's famous butler!

century, claiming the highest ever number of dismissals in a season by a wicket-keeper—102 (32 stumped and 70 caught). He was the first in a long line of brilliant wicket-keepers who were to grace the Kent scene in the years ahead and he must have wondered just what he had to do to obtain some sort of representative recognition, for he appeared in only one Gentlemen *v* Players match. So the 1913 season had brought more distinction on the captain Edward Dillon, who although he had played in more games than usual that summer, was forced to resign from the post because of his business commitments. People always talk about going out

Kent, County Champions 1913. Back row: W. Hearne, C. Blythe, E. Humphreys, J. Seymour, J. C. Hubble, W. Fairservice. Seated: F. E. Woolley, C. E. Hatfield, E. W. Dillon, W. A. Powell, F. H. Huish. On ground: H. T. W. Hardinge, D. W. Jennings.

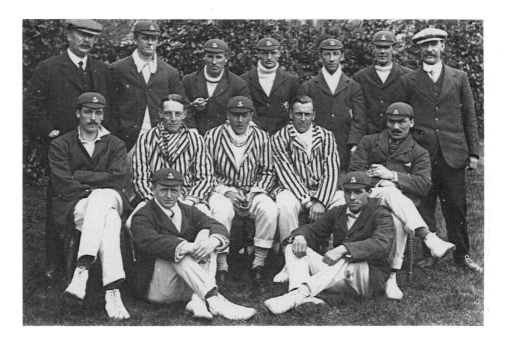

on a high note and certainly Dillon did. Kent were on the proverbial crest of the wave, with four Championship titles in eight years and the stage was set for more success. But at the end of that great season the First World War was only a year away and Kent's next title success was to be far in the future.

Frank Woolley, all-rounder supreme. His career record of 58,959 runs, 2,066 wickets and 1,018 catches is unlikely to be surpassed.

FREEMAN AND WOOLLEY SUPREME

THE 1914 SEASON was of the utmost importance in the history of Kent cricket—not because its closing stages were interrupted by the outbreak of the First World War, but because the year marked the final appearance of one great spin bowler, Colin Blythe, and the debut of a new one who was to become equally great—A. P. 'Tich' Freeman.

Freeman had joined the staff at Tonbridge in 1912, an event reported in anonymous fashion by the young players' committee chairman, Captain McCanlis, whose report read: '. . . two other young men have been engaged for 1912'. By perusing the batting and bowling averages of those young players the name 'Freeman' could be found. He had finished second in the averages, having taken 21 wickets in second eleven matches at eight runs apiece. In the next report of the young players' committee it was acknowledged: '. . . Freeman promising well as a googly bowler.'

Freeman, a right-arm leg spinner and googly bowler, took over for Kent where Blythe left off. Astonishingly his first-class career did not start until he was 25—yet he returned career bowling figures which Kent will never see bettered. First with Woolley and then virtually single-handed he shouldered the main burden of attack for Kent, often being called upon to open the bowling. Just 5ft 2in tall, Freeman had been born at Lewisham but had first played for Essex Club and Ground—his older brother and cousin both played for that county—before he joined Kent. He was to play only twelve times for England and their loss was the County's gain as during his career he wrote numerous new entries in the record book, finishing with 3,340 wickets in his 506 games for Kent.

The 1914 season for Kent in county cricket had started under a new captain, Dillon's successor being Mr L. H. W. Troughton, a cousin of M. A. Troughton, who had played for Kent in 1864–73. Born at Seaford and educated at Dulwich, the new skipper had filled a similar role with the County's second eleven. Unfortunately his first season in charge of the senior side was a disappointing one, although the side managed third place in the table, winning 16 of their 28 Championship games. It was a dry summer and Woolley headed the run-getters, scoring 2,102, recorded six centuries and still finding time and the energy to take 119 wickets, enjoying his most successful season. It was the last in which he and Blythe were to be in harness. Blythe had announced his retirement, and he ended a distinguished career in the best possible style by taking 170 wickets at 15.19 runs apiece, a tremendous performance in such dry conditions. On any sort of pitch he was feared, and when the pitch offered him any assistance he was irresistible—just the kind of label which was to be attached to another slow left-arm bowler some 50 years in the future.

Meanwhile Freeman, whose wicket-taking had gathered strength the previous season, when he headed the second eleven averages, was waiting in the wings. Freeman was a week past his 26th birthday when he made his first-class debut against Oxford University at The Parks. It was a very ordinary beginning. He took one for 88 in 18.2 overs, his wicket a stumping, the first of 484 taken off him in his career. He went back to the second eleven and England was soon at war—the declaration was made on 3 August. Kent continued their fixtures and because The Oval had been requisitioned by the Army, Kent's fixture there—Jack Hobbs' benefit match—was transferred to Lord's, where Freeman was recalled to the side for his Championship debut in place of Fairservice. Kent were beaten in two days; Freeman took none for 42 in 11 overs, and the man he was to replace, Blythe, bowed out of county cricket by taking nine for 97. Surrey wanted only 47 to win and got them for the loss of Hayward, bowled by Freeman with a cleverly flighted leg-break, his first Championship victim. He stayed in the side for the game against Warwickshire at Birmingham, where he took five wickets in an innings, the first of 386 occasions on which he was to perform the feat in the next 22 years, his final return being seven for 25. He played in the rest of the Championship matches, and when the season ended he had claimed 29 wickets with his leg-spin and googlies at 27.55 runs each.

No-one knew then that the war would last for four years, nor whether Freeman, having given that glimpse of his obvious potential, would find such a gap in his cricket career harmful. His answer was to come back with bowling displays that have never been equalled and statistics which will probably never be reached again in the history of cricket, let alone Kent.

Donald Carr, who had taken over 50 wickets in each of his restricted seasons for Kent between 1909 and 1913, had played only once in 1914, so with his departure from the first-class scene and Blythe's retirement much was to depend on the little spinner when play was resumed.

Meanwhile Kent had defended its decision not to follow the lead of other counties and stop at least some of their fixtures which remained after war had broken out. The annual report subsequently declared:

> The committee have been subjected to some criticism over their decision to complete the programme of the season: in doing so the committee were solely guided by the desire to comply with the wishes of Government not to add to the number of unemployed by cancelling their arrangements and as far as it lay in their powers to hold to normal conditions. Some of their critics were perhaps forgetful of the fact that during the greater part of August there was no recruiting allowed for the Territorial Army and that the maximum age was 30, which disqualified a large proportion of the Kent County players.

Financially Canterbury Week in 1914 was a disaster and the Old Stagers' performances and the two balls during the week were cancelled. Because Dover had become an armed camp the two games at The Crabble were switched to Canterbury, and just to round off the traumatic end to the season the final two games against Middlesex at Lord's and Hampshire at Bournemouth resulted in overwhelming defeats.

For four years there was no first-class cricket, but such was the support in the County that 1,382 members sustained their financial contributions during the war years, although the income in 1915 of £2,275 had fallen to £320 by 1918. For those members of the professional staff who volunteered for service the club made up the difference between Army pay and allowances and their ground pay. The ground at Canterbury was not entirely idle because the club lent it free of charge for matches and for practice to soldiers stationed locally.

Needless to say the war took toll of Kent cricketers who embarked on active service but no loss made more impact than that of Colin Blythe, who was killed at Ypres on 8 November 1917 at the age of 38. He had volunteered for active service on the outbreak of war and was enrolled in the Kent Fortress Engineers. He was quickly promoted to Sergeant and in 1917 was transferred to the King's Own Yorkshire Light Infantry with whom he was serving when he was killed in action.

The memorial at Canterbury, on the St Lawrence ground, unveiled by Lord George Hamilton during a match there in August 1919 between the Band of Brothers and the Kent Club & Ground, bears the following inscription: 'He was unsurpassed among the famous bowlers of the period and beloved by his fellow cricketers.' An inscribed mural tablet was also placed in the parish church at Tonbridge by Blythe's widow and his many friends in the County. To him and his eleven comrades of the Kent teams who fell in the service of their country, including Ken Hutchings, that gifted batsman, the obelisk was raised by the Kent County Cricket Club. Every year, during Canterbury Week, members of the County Club's supporters' club gather to lay a wreath on the memorial on the St Lawrence ground.

When first class cricket resumed after the war the 1919 season was one in which Kent were rebuilding and experimenting under the renewed captaincy of Lieutenant-Colonel Troughton. Membership was only just over half the pre-war figure and inevitably subscriptions and entrance fees had increased. Championship matches were restricted to two days, with longer playing hours, and the table positions were resolved by the percentage gained of actual wins to matches begun. Kent played 14 matches, losing only one, and had they won their final match against Middlesex at Lord's they would have taken the title. But Middlesex, twelve runs ahead with nine wickets down in their second innings, narrowly avoided defeat. So Kent, with a percentage of 42.85, had to be content to finish runners-up to Yorkshire who returned 46.15. Still it was a final position which was probably much better than expected, considering that the County had lost its greatest bowler, Blythe.

Woolley, with 848 runs and 96 wickets for the County—he completed the 'double' in all matches—served notice that he was the best all-rounder in the country and performed the hat-trick for the first and only time, when Surrey were the victims at Blackheath. Freeman took 60 wickets to establish himself in the side and Hubble, a competent wicket-keeper-batsman, filled the gap left behind the stumps by the retirement of Huish. The weakness in the Kent attack was in the pace bowling department but there were no problems in dealing with the Sussex batsmen at Tonbridge. After rain had washed out play on the first day the match was completed on the second, with Kent winning by an innings and 123 runs. They had scored 261 for six declared and Sussex were bowled out for 60 and 78, with Woolley taking 12 wickets in the match and Fairservice nine.

The lack of a fast bowler was again felt in 1920 but fortunately there were plenty of slow wickets to be found. The County had to settle for fifth place, with Woolley having a really memorable summer. He topped the County's batting averages (1,548 runs at 39.69), hitting four centuries, and the bowling list (164 wickets at 13.43) in a season which was marked by the return of three-day Championship cricket. Freeman and Fairservice both took over 100 wickets, with Freeman recording the first of the two hat-tricks of his career—against Middlesex at Canterbury. Of the new players tried, Mr G. J. Bryan immediately wrote his name into the County's record book with a century in the second innings of his debut match. Ashdown had no such fortune in his first game for the County, but his was a name which was

Harold Hardinge, prolific opening batsman in the years spanning the First World War. He played one Test, in 1921, and was capped for England at soccer in 1910.

to play an important role in the County's fortunes for years to come. He had, in fact, made his first-class debut in 1914 for Mr G. J. V. Weigall's, XI against Oxford University at the age of $15\frac{1}{2}$, the youngest player ever to appear in a first-class game in England.

The Kent attack was now becoming very much dependent on the abilities of Freeman and Woolley, and in 1921 they did not let their supporters or the side down, taking 163 and 129 wickets respectively. It was just as well that they could sustain such consistent form because a fast bowler was still to be found—over the years that cry was to echo very firmly in Kent cricket circles. Freeman used the googly to good effect in that summer, although his employment of that delivery was to diminish as the years progressed. Certainly he was twice too good for his brother Jack, dismissing him when Kent played Essex at Leyton and again when the two teams met at Tunbridge Wells.

The batting department, however, was tremendously strong, with Hardinge scoring 2,126 runs and in the match against Surrey at The Oval distinguishing himself by scoring a double-century in the first innings and an unbeaten century in the second. So Kent were able to finish fourth in the table, and when their leading amateurs played there were some fine batting performances, notably by the brothers John and Godfrey Bryan, with A. J. Evans, a former Oxford blue, who made a Test appearance for England that season, scoring a century on his County debut at Northampton. The brothers Bryan were both left-handers as was a third brother Ronald who played less often for the County. Woolley, of course, completed the 'double' yet again—he achieved the feat on eight occasions during his career—scoring 1,638 runs and emphasising once more how fortunate the County were to have such a superb all-round player—a fact the County itself was always very quick to acknowledge.

They had another chance to do so in 1922 when Kent cricket followed its now regular pattern. Woolley performed the 'double' again in his benefit season—his game against Hampshire at Canterbury yielding £2,550. He and Freeman dominated the attack, and he, Hardinge and Seymour were the most successful batsmen. It all added up to enough for Kent to stay fourth in the table. Freeman (194) and Woolley (142) shouldered the bowling burden, with the former's accuracy even more pronounced. *Wisden's* verdict on Freeman was:

He was at the top of his form, keeping a remarkable length to his leg breaks and every now and then bowling genuine and well disguised googlies. Seldom, or never, did he fail to take advantage of a treacherous wicket.

While he and Woolley took 336 wickets between them, their colleagues managed just 145. Of those 75 fell to the fast medium right-arm bowling of George Collins, who had first played for the County in 1911 but only established himself in the side after the war. His father Christopher and uncle George had both played for the County and in 1922 the latest member of the family to appear for Kent distinguished himself at Dover by taking all ten Nottinghamshire wickets in their second innings for 65 runs, finishing with a match return of 16 for 83. A left-handed batsman, who could adapt to the needs of the side, he also scored 108 against Lancashire at Manchester that season, when he demonstrated his all-round ability in the match by taking six for 89.

There was prolific scoring by the more recognised batsmen in 1922 when Hardinge set a new record for the County with an unbeaten 249 at Leicester. He scored 80 out of 88 in a stand with Ashdown who made only four—there were also four byes—and while Ashdown took 55 minutes to obtain his last run Hardinge made 78. In years to come Ashdown was himself to find a patient partner as he in turn completed a memorable innings. Hardinge was on the field throughout the match at Leicester, scoring 13 not out in the second innings, and he repeated that feat of endurance against Northamptonshire at Tunbridge Wells.

The burden on Woolley to sustain such dominating all-round form must have been at times intolerable, and in 1923 the effect of the strain showed somewhat. Kent dropped down a place to fifth and weak batting and Woolley's loss of spin, and therefore of effective bowling, were blamed as the main factors. Yet he still took 89 wickets! Freeman shouldered the extra work and responsibility well, taking 157 wickets in a season which proved eventful for him as a batsman. Against Lancashire at Gravesend he hit a ball from R. Tyldesley over the pavilion; at Leicester a ball from Geary hit the little fellow's off stump, going for four byes, but the bail, although removed from its groove, did not fall. Then in the final match of the season at Lord's, while running between wickets he was hit on the head by a long throw-in from the boundary.

Hubble, now the main wicket-keeper, had the satisfaction of equalling a Kent wicket-keeping record set up by Huish in 1911 by claiming six victims in an innings (five caught and one stumped), a feat to be equalled subsequently by five other Kent wicket-keepers but never exceeded. In that same match, against Gloucestershire at Cheltenham, Hubble claimed ten victims in all, equalling Huish's feat in 1911 and that record has never been achieved by any other Kent wicket-keeper.

As a batsman Woolley marched on with reputation enhanced as he scored 1,805 runs, with his 270 against Middlesex at Canterbury beating the previous best for Kent set only the year before by Hardinge, who had compensation when his benefit match at Canterbury realised £1,649, including a collection on the Bank Holiday Monday of £195. He again had a match when he was on the field throughout—at Tunbridge Wells against Gloucestershire, while Kent's third leading run-getter Seymour, now 43, scored two centuries in the game against Essex at Leyton, 19 years after he had first achieved the feat.

There was an unusual feature too in J. L. Bryan's season. During his innings of 236 out of 345 against Hampshire at Canterbury one of his brilliant drives sent the ball into the pavilion, where it became so firmly embedded in the glass of the old Canterbury picture that a new ball had to be obtained. The season, which ended with a short five-match tour of Scotland, had its tragic note when Tom Pawley died suddenly on 3 August. The founder of Tonbridge Week, he had been associated officially with the club since 1898 when he became Manager, and his efforts in making the different Kent Festivals so financially successful had been much appreciated. He was succeeded by Lieut-Colonel Troughton, the captain, whose post was accepted by Captain W. S. Cornwallis. G. J. V. Weighall took over as coach at Tonbridge for 1924 in succession to Alec Hearne and also became captain of the second eleven.

Captain Cornwallis' first year as captain in 1924—he had to stand down in the closing stages of the season because of injury—was marked by the debut, in just one match, of a player who was to have an important impact in Kent cricket—Mr A. P. F. Chapman. Born in Reading, he had enjoyed a brilliant cricketing career at Uppingham school and at Cambridge University, and had been playing Minor Counties cricket with great success for Berkshire before he moved to Kent to qualify by residence when he went into the

*Percy Chapman, whose
illustrious career began in
1924. A typical amateur,
dashing in his stroke-play and
brilliant as a close field, he
actually captained England
before leading his county.*

brewery business with a firm at Hythe. He was, however,
allowed to make his debut for the County against Oxford
University in The Parks, scoring three and 28 (top score) as
the University won by six wickets. For the rest of the season
he was unable to play for the County but he played twice for
England against South Africa before he was thrown from his
motorcycle in a freak accident, his raincoat being caught in
the back wheel of the machine. He escaped with a badly
bruised face but was severely shaken. However, he finished
the season with 74 in a stand of 124 in 50 minutes with
Woolley for the Rest of England against the Champions
Yorkshire, before setting off as a member of the MCC party
to tour Australia.

Meanwhile his new County had finished fifth in the

Championship table with another newcomer, C. S. Marriott, who had played for Lancashire, making his presence felt in the attack. His slow-medium leg-break and top-spin was immaculate, and provided good support for Freeman, who dominated the attack. It was the beginning of the deadliest leg-break combination in county cricket. Freeman in that year made the first of only twelve appearances for his country. Woolley performed better with bat (1,604) than ball (68) a pattern which became very much the order of the season from now on. There was another batting performance in the record category when against Essex at Gravesend, A. C. Wright and A. L. Hilder added 157 for the eighth wicket. Hilder became the fourth player in the County's history to score a century in his debut match.

Woolley, Hardinge and Freeman were outstanding again in 1925 when 'Father' Marriott and J. L. Bryan made their presence felt with ball and bat respectively from the beginning of August. There was even a century by Freeman, but John not 'Tich', playing for Essex against Kent at Gravesend, and the following season on the same ground this brotherly touch was repeated when Claude Woolley scored 111 for Northants. The sad note of the season was the death of Captain McCanlis, whose great ability as a coach had been appreciated by everyone who had been through his nursery.

Business commitments had restricted Chapman to just four first-class matches for the County but the situation improved marginally in 1926 when he played nine Championship matches, scoring an unbeaten 159 in the first at Southampton, and winning a bet with a former director of the brewery where he worked, who had offered him two bottles of port for each 50 and bet him fifty cigars that he wouldn't score a century. The director received the following telegram: 'Six Cockburn 1896: 2 large Coronas, Percy.' During his innings Chapman was partnered by Hardinge in the County's record fourth wicket stand of 297.

Not surprisingly, Woolley and Hardinge dominated the batting overall during the season, Freeman the bowling, and Kent rose to third place in a summer which saw the debut of Ames, who played two matches but did not keep wicket in either, although he took four catches in the match, three of them in the outfield.

The County played for the first time on the Royal Navy and Royal Marines ground at Chatham, attracting a crowd of over 8,000 on the first day. The following season two matches were allocated but they were the last to be played at the venue.

The season saw the retirement of Seymour, who had brought his total of runs for the County to 27,064 since he first played for Kent in 1902. His most important success that year, however, was off the field, in litigation which was to be of considerable significance to all professional cricketers. He had received a demand for income tax on the gate money which was included in his benefit receipts. When he appealed to the Income Tax Commissioners they found in his favour. The case was then taken by the Crown to the High Court, which upheld the decision of the Commissioners. Still it was not over, for the case went to the Court of Appeal, where the Crown was successful. Then came Seymour's successful appeal to the House of Lords.

Kent began the 1927 season under the captaincy of A. J. Evans, who succeeded W. S. Cornwallis, and with its nursery moved from Tonbridge to Canterbury, where the St Lawrence ground belonged to the club, the soil was much drier and there were better facilities for practice pre-season. The new concrete stand, which had cost £5,918 and could accommodate 1,700 people was completed in time for Canterbury Week.

Chapman played in only eleven matches but scored 985 runs, average 70.35, and featured in another record County stand, of 284 for the sixth wicket with G. B. Legge against

The 1927 Kent side. Standing: J. C. Hubble, W. H. Ashdown, G. C. Collins, A. C. Wright, C. J. Capes, L. E. G. Ames, A. P. Freeman, A. Hearne (scorer). Seated: H. T. W. Hardinge, A. P. F. Chapman, A. J. Evans, G. B. Legge, F. E. Woolley.

Lancashire at Maidstone. Ames established himself as a fine wicket-keeper-batsman, reaching 1,000 runs in virtually a full season. The batting could not be faulted, but the bowling, spearheaded by Freeman with support from Woolley, lacked depth.

It was a good first season for the new captain, but he handed over to G. B. Legge for 1928, when Kent were runners-up in the Championship, their title hopes sunk in three successive defeats towards the end of July. Freeman had a spectacular season, taking 304 wickets, of which 246 were for Kent, 216 of them in the Championship. He had reached his 200th wicket on 27 July and his 300th on 15 September. *Wisden* reported:

> Kent owed most to Freeman who, putting a rare amount of spin on the ball and flighting it cleverly, bowled with such skill that he went from one triumph to another.

His 300th wicket had been achieved with the help of the wicket-keeper who had stumped so many batsmen off his bowling—Ames—and the victim was Lancashire's Richard Tyldesley. The ball with which this feat was achieved—one never likely to be equalled again in the history of the game—rests in a glass show case in the Stuart Chiesman pavilion at Canterbury.

Meanwhile Ames was claiming victims behind the stumps in equally staggering style—114 for Kent, 121 in all (69 caught and 52 stumped). It was his first full season behind the wicket, taking over from Hubble with whom he later went into the sports goods business in Gillingham, where the shop still stands, loosely speaking a six-hit distance from the old RE Officers ground. The new keeper was to serve Kent in two capacities: first as a wicket-keeper-batsman of England class—he played in 47 Tests—and then as an administrator, where his talents also saw him attain international status. Runs flowed from his bat in a vastly entertaining and aggressive style while behind the stumps he claimed victims with almost monotonous regularity—twice performing the wicket-keeper's double of 1,000 runs and 100 victims in a season. Back trouble finally ended his playing career just when it was hoped he might have become Kent's first professional captain. He did return, however, in 1957 as Secretary and subsequently Secretary-Manager to embark on a successful administrative career which was to end with his retirement in 1974 when Kent won the Gillette Cup.

The opening batting combination in 1927 of Hardinge and Ashdown featured 13 times in century stands as they and Woolley all exceeded 2,000 runs. Chapman, who was selected to captain the MCC in Australia, did not have such a successful summer for Kent, whose batsmen were criticised for their failure in several matches, notably against Lancashire and the West Indies.

In 1929 the side slipped to eighth in the table with their usual good form in August badly lacking, only one match being won after 22 July. It did not stop Ames having an even better summer behind the stumps, claiming now 127 victims in all games, 70 caught and 45 stumped being his record in County matches. It was also the season in which he won the first of his 47 caps for England. During the season Weighall retired as coach and former player E. Humphreys took over.

It was Freeman's benefit year. How appropriate that he should, in that season which brought him 214 wickets for the County, take all ten wickets in an innings for the first time. It was ten for 131 in 42 overs against Lancashire at Maidstone and feats like this helped to inspire over 20,000 people to attend his benefit match against Gloucestershire at Canterbury over the August Bank Holiday. His net return was £2,381 6s 1d, which was to remain a Kent record until after the Second World War.

There was an improvement in position in 1930, back to fifth, and at the end of the season G. B. Legge retired from the captaincy, being succeeded by Percy Chapman, with Bryan Valentine as vice-captain. It was ironic that Chapman had played for England before making his Championship debut for Kent and that now he was leading his County when his career as England's captain was over. Nor in that 1931 season could he reproduce his best batting form, scoring only 432 runs at 14.89; but in *Wisden* Norman Preston wrote:

> He exercised an invigorating influence. No doubt the dead pitches were detrimental to his free left-handed style and if he often disappointed with the bat his presence in the field—quite apart from his own brilliant work—made him invaluable to the side.

Kent were a formidable team to lead when at full strength, and in that season had provided four players for the Gentlemen *v* Players match, including both wicket-keepers, Ames and W. H. V. Levett. The summer saw the County's

'Tich' Freeman, whose astonishing tally of 3,340 wickets for the County will surely never be surpassed. From 1928 he took 2,090 wickets in eight seasons—an average of 261 per season!

record fifth-wicket stand of 277 by Woolley and Ames against New Zealand at Canterbury.

By the end of that season the amazing Freeman had taken 226 wickets and in the process smashed four records. He had exceeded Blythe's total of 2,231 wickets for Kent; set up a new record of 1,122 wickets in four seasons, taken over 200 wickets for four successive summers, and become the first bowler to take all ten wickets in an innings three times—in successive campaigns. He and 'Father' Marriott were back in harness again, displaying their contrasting styles of the short and the tall spinner, with Marriott being one of the quicker leg-break bowlers.

Before the start of the 1932 season Kent cricket sustained the loss of its greatest figure with the death of Lord Harris. A fine player and an England and Kent captain, he had also been

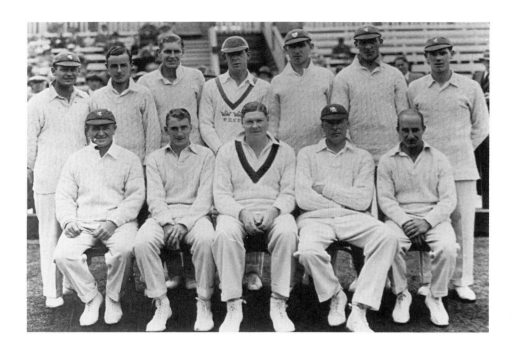

The Kent team, 1931.
Standing: W. H. Ashdown,
H. J. Hubble, C. Fairservice,
W. O'B. Lindsay, A. E.
Watt, A. C. Wright, L. J.
Todd. Seated: H. T. W.
Hardinge, B. H. Valentine,
A. P. F. Chapman,
F. E. Woolley, A. P.
Freeman.

a great administrator and no-one had done more to enhance the game in every possible way. A County memorial fund realised £1,000, with which a portrait for the pavilion at Canterbury was purchased and a tablet was built in the wall of Queen Bertha's Way in the Cathedral Precincts. The balance of £722 was donated to the benevolent fund for Kent cricketers. The side maintained third place in the table in 1932, thanks mainly to that little man Freeman, who took 253 wickets, 209 of them in Championship matches. During the summer two youngsters who were to have an impact on the County scene in future years made their debuts—Arthur Fagg and Doug Wright. Wright was, like Freeman, a leg-spinner, but with a different approach and delivery. With his tiring-looking 'kangaroo' run he had been taught to add the googly to his leg-break by his cricket school coach, Aubrey Faulkner. To follow the act of a spin bowler like 'Tich' Freeman was not easy but Wright achieved it with remarkable success. He won the first of his 34 Test caps in 1938. After the Second World War he was to play a vital role in spearheading the Kent attack and he became Kent's first professional captain in 1954 to round off a most distinguished career. When he retired, like so many of his Kent cricketing forebears, he held a record that will probably never be broken, for during his career he had taken the hat-trick on seven occasions—still a world record.

Kent again had two other Counties above them in 1933 when the County sustained the loss of another former captain with the death of Lieut-Colonel L. H. W. Troughton. He had skippered the second eleven from 1900 to 1913 and the first eleven from 1914 to 1923, subsequently becoming Manager.

After a dubious start to the season, when Woolley was not well, the County found its form. After the Week at Tunbridge Wells it never lost a match, despite the fact that Freeman lacked support in attack. In his 45th year he bowled 12,234 balls, more than anyone had ever achieved in a first-class season, and he failed by only two wickets to reach the 200 mark. Ames, who scored a century in each innings of the match against Northamptonshire at Dover, had a tremendous season, scoring 2,428 runs, while Ashdown and Valentine both exceeded 1,500 runs. It was the final season for Hardinge, who signed off his first-class career with 32,767 runs for Kent, averaging 36.32, and with the distinction of having carried his bat through a completed innings on twelve occasions—at the time more than anyone else apart from

Frank Woolley batting for the Players against the Gentlemen, Folkestone, 1932.

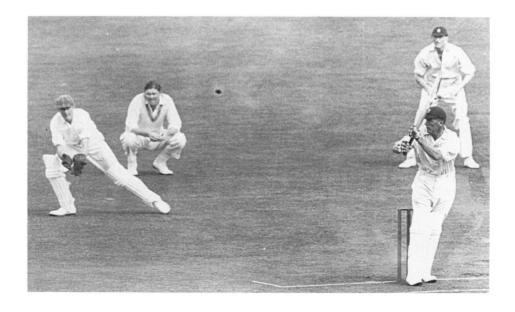

ESSEX *v* KENT

Played on the County Ground, Brentwood, 30, 31 May and 1 June 1934

KENT WON BY AN INNINGS AND 192 RUNS

KENT	**FIRST INNINGS**	
Ashdown	c Ashton b Nichols	332
Fagg	lbw b Smith (R)	31
Woolley	b Ashton, C. T.	172
Ames	not out	202
Watt	c Smith (R) b Ashton, C. T.	11
I. D. K. Fleming	not out	42
Extras	b 8, w 4, nb 1	13
Total	(4 wkts dec)	803

Todd, B. H. Valentine, A. P. F. Chapman, Wright and Freeman did not bat
Fall: 1-70, 2-422, 3-667, 4-707

BOWLING	**O**	**M**	**R**	**W**
Nichols	20	1	93	1
Smith (R)	22	1	115	1
C. T. Ashton	31	2	185	2
Smith (P)	36	2	208	0
O'Connor	16.2	0	83	0
Cutmore	12	0	63	0
Taylor	7	0	36	0
Pope	2	0	7	0

ESSEX	**FIRST INNINGS**		**SECOND INNINGS**	
Cutmore	c Ames b Watt	30	c Fleming b Wright	0
Pope	c Woolley b Valentine	100	c Ames b Wright	11
T. N. Pearce	c Ames b Valentine	79	c Woolley b Freeman	17
O'Connor	not out	105	lbw b Freeman	25
Nichols	c Valentine b Wright	3	lbw b Wright	20
C. T. Ashton	st Ames b Freeman	11	not out	71
Taylor	st Ames b Freeman	1	st Ames b Freeman	1
Eastman	c Chapman b Wright	52	c Woolley b Freeman	4
Smith (P)	c Woolley b Freeman	11	c Ashdown b Freeman	0
Sheffield	c Woolley b Freeman	0	c Watt b Ashdown	31
Smith (R)	b Freeman	0	st Ames b Freeman	1
Extras	b 7, lb 8, nb 1	16	b 14, lb 8	22
Total		408		203

1st inns: 1-75, 2-231, 3-242, 4-259, 5-333, 6-358, 7-360, 8-394, 9-394, 10-408
2nd Inns: 1-35, 2-36, 3-42, 4-86, 5-92, 6-97, 7-105, 8-115, 9-201, 10-203

BOWLING	O	M	R	W		O	M	R	W
Watt	23	4	85	1		9	0	20	0
Ashdown	6	2	22	0		1	1	0	1
Freeman	50.5	15	116	5		34.2	13	60	6
Wright	38	9	117	2		27	12	59	3
Todd	6	0	11	0					
Woolley	7	2	10	0		5	1	26	0
Valentine	9	2	31	2		5	2	16	0

Umpires: W. Hitch and E. A. Street.

Kent's total of 803 for four declared remains the County record. W. H. Ashdown's 332 is the highest individual innings played for the County. His second wicket stand of 352 with Frank Woolley is also a record for any wicket for the County.

W. G. Grace, L. Hall and C. J. B. Woodhead. Recognised as a very fine bat, Hardinge was also a very good slow left-arm bowler, and would have bowled much more but for the presence of Freeman, Woolley, C. S. Marriott and before the war, Blythe. He twice took more than 50 wickets in a season, 66 in 1930 being his best for Kent, and although he bowled left-arm he always threw with his right hand.

Ashdown hit Kent's first-ever treble-century in 1934 when his 332 at Brentwood against Essex was made in a total of 803 for four declared in seven hours. Both Ashdown's score and the innings total have remained records for the County ever since, as has his second wicket stand of 352 with Woolley. Ames made an unbeaten 202 in the same innings and Woolley 172 as Essex replied with 408 and, following on, lost by an innings and 192 runs. That typified the batting for the season with Ames, Woolley and Todd all in good form and Fagg showing promise for the future. The amateur batsmen were in form, too, with B. H. Valentine completing 1,000 runs, and towards the end of the season Woolley won the Lawrence Trophy for the season's fastest century—obtained in 63 minutes against Northamptonshire at Dover.

Winning 12 of their 30 County matches the side dropped down from third to fifth place in the table with Freeman again having to shoulder the main responsibility in attack, sometimes opening the bowling. It was his benefit season, the second of his career, which netted him £1,586, and his response was to take 205 wickets, including the third hat-trick of his career, although he suffered late in the season from a nagging foot injury. There was one match in August, by which time 'Father' Marriott was back in the side, when such support was given by the amateur that he bowled 624 balls in the Northamptonshire match at The Crabble. He bowled 55 maidens, ten of them in succession, and failed by only six balls to equal the record number ever bowled in a County match.

That fifth position would have been welcome in 1935 when the County dropped to tenth, its lowest place in the table since 1897. Once again there was too much reliance on the veterans of the side: Woolley now 48, but still managing to score over 2,000 runs, and Freeman, only two years younger, who again took over 200 wickets. Fagg continued his improvement as a batsman and Todd as a bowler—he was already scoring centuries as a batsman—and the captain, Chapman, hit what was to be his last century in first-class cricket. It was his first for four years, when at Maidstone he thrashed the Somerset bowlers for 107 out of 130 in 85 minutes, restoring memories of his illustrious past as he struck two sixes and 17 fours. For the second successive season

W.H. Ashdown made his first-class debut in 1914, aged 15, for G. J. V. Weigall's team, and is the only player to appear in first-class matches before, between and after the two world wars.

Ashdown made a treble-century, scoring an unbeaten 305 against Derbyshire at Dover, when he owed a debt to the No 11 Claude Lewis for achieving it—as they invariably remembered when in later years they scored together, Lewis for Kent and Ashdown for Leicestershire. Ashdown was on 295 when Lewis went to the wicket and the Kent scorer remembered how he made nine while his partner scored those very vital last five runs.

WAR AND CHANGE

ALL GOOD THINGS have to come to an end—and 1936 was the beginning of a decade which was to see Kent cricket undergo a great measure of change. It was the last season for the captain, Percy Chapman, and for the most successful Kent bowler of all time, 'Tich' Freeman; two years later ended one of the greatest careers cricket has known with the retirement of Frank Woolley; and then a year after that the outbreak of the Second World War ended first-class cricket altogether until 1946.

As far as the captaincy was concerned, there was a hint of what was to come in 1936 when the post was shared by three men—Chapman, Valentine and I. S. Akers-Douglas. Valentine had first played for Kent in 1927 and had been a regular member of the side since 1931 and Akers-Douglas had first represented the County in 1929. All three led the side efficiently but the constant change of leadership must have had its effect on the side, although Kent advanced two places up the table to eighth. Woolley and Freeman could not maintain their usual prolific standard of run-getting and wicket-taking, and Ames was out of the side for most of the season with back trouble, but some of the younger players took the chance to reveal form that was encouraging for the future. Todd, who bowled and batted left-handed, performed the 'double', only the second Kent player to have achieved the feat after Woolley, who did it on six occasions for the county, although Ames, of course, had done the 'double' as a wicket-keeper-batsman twice, in 1928 and 1929. In all matches Todd scored 1,211 runs at an average of 26.91 and took 102 wickets at 20.98 apiece. Wright had his best season with 59 wickets while Watt had his most productive summer to date, taking 88 wickets with his medium pace, and astounding spectators with his big hitting. Three years earlier he had caned the Nottinghamshire attack for five sixes and three fours in an innings of 42 and this summer in the match against Gloucestershire at Gravesend he hit 60 of the 78 he made in the two innings of the match in sixes. The other match of the week on the Bat and Ball ground against Derbyshire was one to remember, as the spin of Freeman and the man who was to take over his role, Wright, spearheaded the ten-wicket victory with respective match figures of nine for 52 and eight for 80.

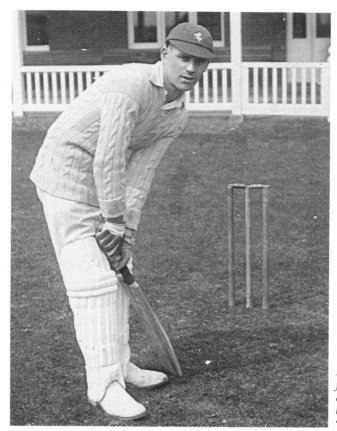

L. J. Todd, Kent stalwart from 1927 to 1950. A sound opening bat and left-arm bowler, he achieved the 'double' in 1936.

At the end of the season Chapman announced that he was resigning the captaincy because of his increasing business commitments. There was a story told that summer at Folkestone that he had sent out a message to Todd who was batting against the Glamorgan attack: 'Tell Todd he's boring me. If he doesn't get a hundred he's dropped for the next match.' Unfortunately Todd could find little support in his quest for the century until Freeman arrived to resist stubbornly in a last-wicket stand which saw Todd's mission achieved. Chapman was reported to have smiled—the occasion was probably worthy of a celebration drink. *Wisden*, reporting on the captain's last season at the helm spoke for all Kent cricket followers: 'Chapman always brought such an inspiring influence to bear on the side, particularly in the field, that, if his intention remains unaltered, his familiar figure will be greatly missed.' In fact he played in one game in 1937 and two in 1938, scoring 36 in his final innings for the County at Worcester.

Ames regarded Chapman as a brilliant player. He said: 'He was a bit of a showman and the crowd loved it. He would lead the team out, for example, and then walk to the middle with himself and Woolley on each side of "Tich" Freeman.' Chapman and Woolley, of course, were the sort of batsmen who attracted the crowds. Ames recalled how when Kent played Lancashire at Old Trafford before the war the attendance would probably be bigger than any other match apart from the Roses duel with Yorkshire. He said: 'Probably 80 per cent of it would be because of Frank and Percy Chapman. They knew that if those two got runs they were going to see some entertainment.'

For Freeman and for Kent the season had begun on the right note. The County won its first four matches and in the first two months of the season Freeman had taken 79 wickets. In the last two months of the season it was a sadly different story. He took only 29 and his colleagues felt they knew the answer—at 47, he was suffering the strain of putting his right arm to such exacting exertion—his muscles just could not tolerate it. His last wicket for Kent was taken at Folkestone against the MCC and the last of his career on the same ground for the Players against the Gentlemen. His final tally of wickets for the County, never likely to be surpassed, was 3,340 and his career record was 3,776. With Wright on the way up as a spin bowler with great potential and with Freeman having taken only 108 wickets that season (how many players would give their right arm to take that many in a season today), the Kent committee suggested that in the following season he should only play on a match-to-match basis, with long rest periods in between. He declined that offer and in the November it was announced that he would not be re-engaged. Was that the complete picture? Some of his colleagues contended that he had been sacked and that there was another element to the story—a letter he had written to a local newspaper criticising the Essex fast bowler Ken Farnes for bowling bouncers at Kent earlier that season. Apparently Essex took umbrage and so did the Kent committee when the matter was reported to them. Whatever the truth of the matter the Kent report for that year said:

In view of the importance of doing everything possible to encourage our young bowlers, the committee has decided, with great regret, to terminate Freeman's contract. As a mark of appreciation of his services the sum of £250 has been paid to him and payment of winter money will be continued until the beginning of next season. He has borne the brunt of the bowling for so long and his record for the County is such a fine one that the committee feel sure this action will be endorsed by members of the Club.

There would certainly have been no dissent to such action. Freeman's outstanding characteristics were his sustained effort and humility. Everyone loved him. He may not have wanted to have been one of the game's characters but he was. All knew that determined hitch of the trousers and the Napoleonic fold of the arms, revealing the satisfaction from doing a job well. Now they were to be no part of the Kent scene again. Ames, who kept wicket to him for so many years, said: 'They were his little mannerisms. If Percy Chapman—and he only did it once or twice—put "Father" Marriott on before "Tich" that's when he would hitch his old trousers up and say "let him get on with it then."' Woolley had written of Freeman in his book the 'King of Games': 'What we should have done without him it is not possible for me to put into words.' Equally it is difficult to put into words the record of the little man over the years. He spent the next two seasons playing for Walsall in the Birmingham and District League before retiring to Maidstone where he appropriately called his house 'Dunbolyn'.

Not only was it a taste of life without Freeman in 1937 but also a completely new management team, for Mr G. de L. Hough was the new Secretary. He had taken over from Mr A. J. Lancaster, who had died the previous year shortly after his retirement, having been in the post for 50 years, succeeding his father Mr J. J. Lancaster. The new captain was R. T. Bryan, a left-handed batsman, for the first part of the season, with Valentine taking over in August. It was not a good season, for the County dropped to 12th in the table. Fagg, who had played in two Tests the previous season, was not available at all in 1937, having been taken ill with rheumatic fever on the winter tour of Australia. Woolley scored 1,632 runs and took 31 wickets for the County, the most he had achieved for eight years, and Ames was happily

Les Ames batting against the
South Africans at
Canterbury, July 1937.

restored to full fitness, scoring 1,997 runs. His wicket-keeping, and that of Levett, were the redeeming features in what was a disappointing season in the fielding department. Todd had developed into the all-rounder of the side, taking 79 wickets and scoring over 1,000 runs while Wright and Watt both exceeded 100 wickets for the first time in their careers.

So Wright had done what was expected of him in the absence of Freeman and John Arlott once wrote of him:

> Each time he bowls his fast leg-break to a length he achieves the difficult plus the impossible. To bowl a length with a fully finger-spun leg-break as distinct from the rolled leg-break is difficult, to bowl a leg-break really fast is impossible for everyone who ever played cricket, except Doug Wright.

In this season at Dover Kent recorded one of their most memorable victories when they scored 219 to beat Gloucestershire, winning by eight wickets with 19 minutes to spare after obtaining the runs in 71 minutes, averaging nine an over. It was clean, controlled batting allied to consistent, scientific hitting, aided by speedy running between the wickets. The victory emphasised Valentine's daring and imaginative approach to captaincy. He decreed that the run-chase was on and Woolley hit 44 out of 68 scored in 25 minutes. Then the spinners Goddard and Sinfield came in for the punishment. When Woolley went, Ashdown joined Ames, who scored 70 out of a 100 in 36 minutes. When Ames was dismissed, Watt took over, hit 39 in 10 minutes and won the game when the ball soared from his bat out of the ground. The Kent fans had been so excited and caught up in the atmosphere that they had ringed the boundary to make sure the ball was returned as quickly as possible.

This was also the season when the County returned to play at the Royal Engineers Officers' Ground at Gillingham, a venue first used in 1862 against Cambridgeshire, although the ground actually played on then was adjacent.

It was the farewell season of Ashdown, who retired to take up duties as coach at Rugby School. He scored 1,437 runs that summer to bring his total for the county to 22,218. A medium paced bowler he took 595 wickets, was an excellent slip field and could keep wicket. During that 1934 run riot at Brentwood, when he had scored 332, he indulged in a stand of 352 with Woolley for the second wicket, still a record stand for any wicket for the County. He made many return trips to Kent grounds when he was scorer with Leicestershire and had the distinction of playing first-class cricket before the First World War and after the Second World War. He played in 1947, at the age of 48, for M. Leyland's XI against The Rest at Harrogate, opening the innings, scoring 42 and 40, and taking five wickets in the match.

In 1938 Kent had a new captain. Like Chapman before him, F. G. H. Chalk was a product of Uppingham School and had played in the Oxford elevens of 1931–34, skippering the side in his final year. He built up a good reputation for handling his bowlers and setting his field, but although the side rose one place to ninth it was a difficult summer for the new captain. Because of injuries and representative calls it was never possible for Chalk to lead the best side. Kent certainly had a fine team at full strength, reflected by the

KENT *v* GLOUCESTERSHIRE

Played at Dover on 18, 19, 20 August 1937

KENT WON BY 8 WICKETS

GLOUCESTERSHIRE FIRST INNINGS

				SECOND INNINGS		
Barnett	b Watt	70		c Valentine b Harding	0
G. W. Parker	b Watt	210		b Wattt	20
B. O. Allen	c Spencer b Watt	21		c Woolley b Todd	9
Hammond	c Ashdown b Woolley	3		c Woolley b Wright	52
Crapp	c Ashdown b Watt	2		b Watt	1
Sinfield	not out	74		b Watt	26
B. H. Lyon	c Pearce b Watt	0		b Watt	21
Neale	lbw, b Watt	0		c Chalk b Todd	3
Stephens	c Ashdown b Woolley	4		run out	15
Goddard	c Ames b Woolley	6		b Harding	9
Watkins	b Harding	25		not out	11
Extras	byes 9, lb 9, w 1	19		byes 7, lb 4, nb 4	15
Total		434			182

BOWLING	O	M	R	W		O	M	R	W
Harding	24.1	2	104	1		14.1	2	43	2
Watt	29	2	129	6		26	7	69	4
Todd	8	0	22	0		18	8	26	2
Wright	25	7	78	0		12	4	29	1
Woolley	24	6	82	3					

KENT FIRST INNINGS

				SECOND INNINGS		
Ashdown	c Hammond b Parker	45		not out	62
Woolley	c and b Sinfield	100		c Barnett b Sinfield	44
F. G. H. Chalk	b Neale	34			
Ames	b Neale	1		c Barnett b Sinfield	70
Todd	b Parker	12			
B. H. Valentine	c Hammond b Parker	30			
T. A. Pearce	b Sinfield	59			
Spencer	b Sinfield	53			
Wright	c Watkins b Goddard	29			
Watt	c Barnett b Sinfield	0		not out	39
Harding	not out	14			
Extras	byes	22		byes 2, lb 2	4
Total		399		2 wkts	219

BOWLING	O	M	R	W		O	M	R	W
Barnett	16	2	45	0		3	0	23	0
Lyon	8	0	39	0					
Sinfield	31	5	83	4		9	0	69	2
Goddard	23.1	2	77	1		8.2	0	98	0
Parker	24	5	78	3		3	0	25	0
Neale	11	0	55	2					

Umpires: Reeves and Chester.

selection of B. H. Valentine, Ames, Wright and Fagg for the MCC South African tour.

Fagg marked his return to first-class cricket after illness by scoring 2,322 runs and becoming the first and only player to score a double-century in each innings of a match. He hit 244 and 202 not out against Essex at Colchester, his individual match aggregate of 446, the highest ever recorded in a first-class game in England. In that match he and his opening partner, P. R. Sunnucks, registered Kent's record first-wicket stand of 283. The main feature, however, of the 1938 season concerned Woolley, not because of his performances, although there were several which thrilled, but because it was his last season for the County. Wherever he played, the farewell ovations were naturally completely deserved, for his had been an extraordinary career. 'It is impossible to speak too highly of his service to Kent cricket', said the annual report. How right—anyone attempting to deal with Woolley's career would soon run out of superlatives. He scored his obligatory 1,000 runs in the season (1,467) with a final century for the County at Tunbridge Wells against Sussex, where he and Bryan Valentine added 220 for the third wicket. At Oakham he had a final fling with the ball, returning a match analysis of 11 for 106 against Leicestershire.

Six years earlier in the foreword to Woolley's book 'The King of Games', a former Kent captain, W. H. Patterson, had written:

> To say that with us in Kent Frank Woolley is popular is altogether too commonplace. In Kent Frank is loved, our cricket revolves around him and has done so for many years. But in spite of the never concealed admiration of our sporting crowds, Frank is utterly unspoiled. He's still the modest, unassuming boy of whom that sound judge of cricketers, the late Captain McCanlis, never had a moment's doubt. For young professionals Frank's life has been a permanent model, loyal to his employers and his captains. Quiet, almost shy, by nature—a gentleman always.

Patterson, like all those who watched and enjoyed Woolley's batting, reckoned that two of his shots alone placed him in the most attractive class of the mighty batsmen: the off-drive and cut. 'Plum' Warner, captain of England and Middlesex, had paid this tribute to Woolley:

That his name will go down to posterity as one of the greatest cricketers the game has ever produced is as certain as tomorrow's sun. It was I who wrote of him as 'the pride of Kent' and I'm proud of it for it is true.

'One of the finest players who have graced the game', was *Wisden*'s final verdict on Woolley, adding: 'Often it was difficult to believe that he became 51 on May 27th.'

He was honoured by the MCC, who chose him to captain the Players at Lord's against the Gentlemen and his last Championship game for Kent was at Dover, where they were beaten by Notts by ten wickets. He opened the innings, scoring seven and 18, dismissed both times by Voce, and bowled only in the first innings, just two overs conceding five runs without getting a wicket. The Kent report on the season said:

> It's impossible to close this report without a special word of farewell to Woolley, one of the greatest cricketers of our time. The committee would like to take this opportunity of expressing their great appreciation of all he's done for Kent and to extend to him their good wishes for the future.

The testimonial fund inaugurated on his behalf raised £1,397 10s 3d.

Woolley had indicated in the preface to his book that he had not welcomed the day when he would start the role of playing permanent looker-on. He wrote: 'I feel now, however, if when that time comes I see half-volleys gently patted back to the bowler that I shall never go to a match again.' Those feelings must have been in his mind many years later when he was welcomed on his visits to Kent grounds in the 1970s. He could not appreciate some of the batting he saw. Taken to a Sunday League by his former colleague Les Ames, the then Kent Manager, it was explained to him that each side had only 40 overs to bat. He looked out at the field and remarked 'Why aren't all the fielders back on the boundary then?'

Woolley's attitude had been that he always believed nobody could bowl. Ames said: 'He always thought he could knock the bowlers all over the place and the only bowler I ever heard him say was a fine bowler was Sid Barnes.' Ames saw at first hand an example of the Woolley philosophy when Kent played Yorkshire at Bradford and encountered for the first time Hedley Verity. Yorkshire had won the toss, put Kent in to bat and quickly dismissed Ashdown and Hardinge. Ames went in next and he recalled how Frank had walked down the wicket and said: 'I don't know who this left-hander is, I haven't seen him before but he's a good bowler. You stay at the other end and I'll try and look after him.' Woolley proceeded to hit Verity all over the place, dominating the Kent innings to such an extent that he scored 188 out of 260.

He loved to open the innings and did so almost throughout that final season when he left behind so many memories, particularly to players like Ames and Fagg, who had been youngsters joining the staff when Woolley was established at County and international level. Ames remembered: 'The first time I ever kept wicket to "Tich" Freeman was in the nets at Tonbridge in 1925 and Frank was batting. He asked if I could pick the "googly" and I said that I didn't know. I'd hardly ever seen it. Frank replied: "I'll tell you every time he bowls one", which I thought was very kind—he didn't know then that I was going to make the grade.' Fagg always contended that Woolley was the player who helped him most as a youngster. He once told the writer: 'Instead of getting down to the different coaching techniques, elbow up and all that sort of thing, his view was that if anyone bowled a length to you then you had to do something about it. His philosophy was that you only got runs if you were on top which meant you had to control the situation.'

Kent and the skipper, F. G. H. Chalk, made a great start to the 1939 season, beating Sussex by an innings at Tonbridge with the captain scoring 198. Todd made 143 and Fagg 91 in a total of 580 for nine declared. Then Harding, Watt and Wright dismissed Sussex for 95 and in the second innings for 364, with Wright taking eight for 84. That created the pattern for the season for what was one of the youngest sides in the country. They won 14 of their games, finishing fifth in the table, and attracted increased interest in the sides' fortunes. Excluding the tourists' match, attendances went up by 7,000 and for the first time the services of a masseur were engaged. His role was to assist in keeping players fit, particularly the bowlers, and to help in maintaining the spirit of the side.

During the 1939 season the Hoppers Tie Club was formed, two of the founder members being Ames and W. H. 'Hopper' Levett. In fact, the title was nothing to do with Levett's

Ames attempts to stump Martin. Kent v Worcestershire at Tunbridge Wells, June 1938.

nickname, but with the pattern of the tie, logos of a beer barrel and hops on a navy background. Ames explained how a Club tie had been inaugurated for members but was not apparently available for players. So the players decided to have their own tie, and the Hoppers Tie Club has flourished ever since. Membership was subsequently extended to non-players who were proposed by a player member and the tie has to be worn on Mondays—with the forfeit, if caught not wearing it, of buying a drink for the challenger.

During the 1939 season wicket-keeper-batsman T. G. Evans, who had been on the staff for two years, made his debut. Educated at Kent College, Canterbury he played in seven matches and immediately showed great promise. Sports fans love a character, particularly if he has outstanding talent and Evans was to become a natural entertainer on a cricket field. His ability, of course, was confirmed by his selection for England in 91 Tests, and at a very early stage in his career it was quite obvious that the great Kent wicket-keeping line would be continued. Whenever he was in the middle the game was alive and he had the same exuberant approach to his batting as to his wicket-keeping. Behind the stumps he was brilliant, displaying wonderful powers of concentration, energy and enthusiasm.

That summer of 1939 was wonderful for batsmen, and the attack performed well too. Ames (1,846) and Fagg (1,812) led the way with Valentine (1,518), Chalk (1,288) and Todd (1,056) all passing the 1,000-run mark. Todd also took 84 wickets, but Wright, with 131, topped the bowling averages. There was good support from the slow left-arm spin of Lewis, whose 56 wickets cost 17.12 each, from Watt (76) and the fast bowler Harding (69). Because of the developing international situation, one county game and the match against the West Indies were cancelled and the last game of the season finished at Dover on 29 August, with the Second World War breaking out on 3 September. That habit of exciting wins at Dover continued as the side scored 382 for five to beat Lancashire with Fagg (138) and P. G. Foster (49) scoring 181 for the first wicket. Then Valentine (68) and Chalk (94) added 94 for the third wicket to set up the win.

Within a week England were at war and the first-class season was over. Nearly all the eleven players who had represented Kent in that last game found themselves taking part in the war: Ames (Squadron Leader, RAF), Chalk (Flight Lieutenant, RAF), J. G. W. Davies (Colonel, Army), T. G. Evans (Sergeant, Army), Foster (Captain, Army),

The Kent side of 1939. Standing: T. W. Spencer, P. R. Sunnucks, D. V. P. Wright, N. W. Harding, A. E. Watt, P. G. Foster, A. E. Fagg, A. Hearne (scorer). Seated: W. H. V. Levett, B. H. Valentine, F. G. H. Chalk, L. E. G. Ames, L. J. Todd.

Harding (Lieutenant, Army), Todd (Sergeant, RAF), Valentine (Major, Army), Wright (Lieutenant, Army).

Back at Canterbury the St Lawrence ground was maintained in playing condition. Troops stationed in the neighbourhood were able to hire it for games and one unit asked for a tent in the first post-war Canterbury Week in order to hold its reunion there. The St Lawrence and Beverley clubs amalgamated and frequently provided opposition to service sides, while at some matches collections for service charities were made. Special matches were arranged on August Bank Holiday when the Mayor of Canterbury provided hospitality during games which helped to keep alive the spirit of Canterbury Week.

For a considerable time the Army was in occupation of most of the buildings, with the surrounds used for parking lorries, guns, ambulances and other vehicles. There was an explosives store in the ladies' lavatory at the Nackington Gate, the City authorities had a control room and air raid shelter under the concrete stand, and the hospital had a coal dump and emergency kitchen in the surround. For some time quarters were supplied for the Salvage Corps and the iron stand was used as a petrol store. Physical training by a girls' school, cross-country practice by Army motorcyclists, Home Guard training, and a Women's Land Army rally were all features of the wartime activities in the St Lawrence grounds.

Some 250 incendiary bombs fell on the property, 138 of them on the playing area, but fortunately the damage was negligible. In fact their ingredients appeared to be good for the grass. The most costly damage was that the blades of the motor mower were badly bent by shell splinter.

Kent County Cricket Club was accorded special mention in the German press according to this following extract from the *Daily Telegraph* of 25 July 1940. Headed 'On the German Frontier', it read:

The German 'Lokah-Anzeiger' over-reaches itself with a front-page account of a revolt by cricketers in England against ploughing up the pitches. The revolt, it seems, is worst in Kent. It is headed by the leader of the club who pleaded that their rights had been handed down from forefathers who played cricket before defeating Spaniards. Non-cricket inhabitants of Kent, says the paper, in a fury of rage decided to reduce the Club by force of arms. As a result, club members, armed to the teeth, patrol the pitch nightly, peering into hedges. Not for parachutists, but for the advanced guard of Sixth Column plutocrats.

During the war the business of the Club was carried on by the Canterbury Committee, which consisted of not more than four members of the committee with power to co-opt not more than two members of the club. It was responsible for the management of the St Lawrence Ground and for recommending to the Managing Committee all arrangements for the Canterbury Cricket Week.

One sad feature of the war for Kent cricket was news of the death in February 1943 of the Club's captain, F. G. H. Chalk, killed while flying a fighter plane.

A BARREN DECADE

FOR THE FIRST TWO SEASONS after the Second World War Kent maintained their immediate pre-war form in the County Championship, finishing sixth and fourth. They were fortunate to be able to welcome Bryan Valentine back to the captaincy to fill the gap so tragically left by the death of F. G. H. Chalk. Valentine was an enthusiastic, aggressive leader with plenty of pre-war experience in the job and he settled immediately into the role. There were, of course, obvious difficulties. A very promising side in 1939 was handicapped by the long absence of first-class cricket. After two years of maintaining their form the side, weakened by the tragic death of fast bowler N. W. Harding in 1947, plummeted to 15th position in the table. For the next 15 years the side only twice figured in the top nine as the County embarked on a rebuilding programme in which giving youth its chance was always a main objective.

In 1946 however, first-class cricket was welcomed back in Kent so warmly that attendances rose to 125,611, compared with the total of 95,891 in 1939. Kent's only Test match trial, on the St Lawrence ground at Canterbury during that season, attracted 13,782 paying customers. Membership showed an immediate increase—up from 886 the previous year to 2,453, encouragingly approaching the 1939 figure of 3,166. The August Bank Holiday crowd contributed £375 to J. Murrin, who was scheduled to retire later that year after 41 years as head groundsman, but who died still in harness on 8 November.

The six years of war had naturally taken its toll on the St Lawrence ground, where considerable money needed to be spent on repairs and renewals. The old wooden gates were beyond repair and were replaced by new iron ones; chestnuts were planted as an avenue up the drive. The cricket started badly but did improve, the side constantly changing with players short on experience of first-class cricket being pressed into first-eleven service. No fewer than 29 players appeared on first-team duty. One of the newcomers to make an instant impression was H. A. Pawson, who nearly scored a century on his debut, and always entertained with his running between the wickets and brilliant fielding.

Pawson, who played soccer as an amateur for Charlton,

Arthur Fagg, whose long career for Kent spanned the Second World War, remains the only first-class player to score a double-century in each innings of a match.

recalled years later in his autobiography *Runs and Catches* how as he had walked down the pavilion steps for his first innings against Hampshire, he heard a voice proclaim loudly: 'It's ridiculous the committee allowing untried youngsters to play in Canterbury Week.' To his delight he eventually found himself on 90 and a century on his debut seemed there for the taking. His own swift running was to prove his downfall. He pulled a ball to midwicket and, realising the fielder was an occasional Hampshire player who had been clumsy in his picking up and weak in his throwing, he called loudly 'easy two' and sprinted for the second without looking. The call must have prompted the fielder into action for the pick-up was clean and the throw right over the stumps, leaving Pawson run out by a yard.

Fagg did not appreciate Pawson's quick singles. In a subsequent match he loudly refused several and eventually went down the wicket to exclaim: 'Look here, Mr Pawson, you've only come into the side since August, I'm tired out playing since May. And if you call me for one more quick single I will make sure you are run out.' Fagg had not returned to the Kent scene in 1946, still being employed at Cheltenham College, but Valentine persuaded him to play in 1947 when Fagg took a job with Sharp's toffee company at Maidstone.

Some of the younger players, because of their time in the services during the war, had received no training in the club's nursery, and this was another reason for inconsistent form, particularly in the batting department, which was spearheaded by Todd. He scored 1,864 runs, with the captain totalling 1,566 and Ames and J. G. W. Davies, another superb fielder, also passing the 1,000 mark. Doug Wright was the top bowler with 113 wickets and he and wicket-keeper Godfrey Evans were selected for the party to tour Australia. Evans, Pawson, J. W. Martin and R. R. Dovey were all awarded their county caps and off-spinner Dovey, from Chislehurst, gave most support to Wright in the attack, taking 89 wickets with his off-breaks.

The immediate post-war boom for first-class cricket and Kent continued in 1947 when the County won 12 of its Championship matches to finish fourth in the table. Total attendance during the season was 182,452, which included 45,470 through the junior turnstiles. They saw a galaxy of entertainment from a formidable first four in the batting order: Fagg (2,025), Todd (2,057), Ames (2,156) and the inspiring and popular captain, Valentine (1,375). Hearn, a left-handed batsman from Tunbridge Wells, had the distinction of scoring a century on his debut: 124 against Warwickshire at Gillingham. Wright, with 142 wickets at 19.01 apiece, was again the leading bowler with Dovey (89) providing most support but the pace of Ridgeway (who had played for Stockport in the Central Lancashire League in 1942) and Harding, who took 56 and 68 wickets respectively, was encouraging. Assistance to the pace bowlers was provided by the amateur J. W. Martin, from Catford, who was awarded his cap the previous summer and in 1947 was selected for England in the Trent Bridge Test against South Africa. He played only occasionally, some half-a-dozen matches in each of the eight seasons he was with the County, on whose cricket committee he subsequently served.

Hearn, Ridgway and Harding were awarded their county caps which made the death of Harding just a few weeks after the end of the season even more tragic. He had first played for the second eleven in 1936, joining the nursery staff a year later, when he made his Championship debut. His 69 first-class wickets in 1939 heralded great promise, but he then was commissioned in the Royal Artillery only to be invalided out of the Army. His health was affected and it was not until the 1947 season that he seemed to be showing his best form.

Bryan Valentine batting against Middlesex at Lord's, 1947. He took over the Kent captaincy after the Second World War.

Kent also lost the services at the end of the season of W. H. V. 'Hopper' Levett, who announced his retirement from the first-class game. In Mr Levett Kent had been blessed with a reserve wicket-keeper of Test Match standard, and the popularity he enjoyed as a player was to be sustained over the years in his long and devoted association with the Club he loved, whether as committee man, President or just a Kent supporter. He had first played for Kent in 1930, being awarded his county cap in the following season. He toured India and Ceylon with MCC in 1933–34 and played in one Test on that tour, against India. Even 40 years after his retirement the man who has Kent cricket so much at heart was an automatic choice for his own brand of 'speech' at the 'Hoppers' Dinner.

It was a disappointing season for Kent in 1948 when they dropped to 15th place in the table. The loss of Harding obviously had a serious effect on the attack, which was weakened even further by the frequent absence of Wright, who had a leg muscle injury. The batting continued to be dominated by Fagg (2,420), Ames, who contributed 1,943 in his benefit year, which totalled £4,336, and Todd (1,415)—the only players to top the 1,000 runs.

The match against Australia at Canterbury that year, with Sir Donald Bradman on his final tour, had special significance in more ways than one. It played a major role in boosting membership from 3,310 to 3,918 and it was estimated that the game was watched by crowds totalling nearly 39,000. The Aussies were unbeaten and Pawson told later how the Kent side had felt they must do better than England, who had been bowled out for 52 in the Test at the Oval. In fact Kent were shot out for 51 with Todd, receiving the first ball of the match from Lindwall, being hit on the toe. The lbw appeal was rejected but Pawson wrote: 'Todd then appeared to hobble down the wicket and argue that he had been plumb lbw. Getting no satisfaction, he made no attempt to play the next ball, which bowled him'. Back in the pavilion he claimed he could take no further part in the match because of injury, but the physiotherapist reported no damage. Added Pawson: 'As Todd still declined to take further part he was suspended for the few remaining games of the season.'

When Kent batted again a Kent supporter had offered £50 for the first batsman to make 50. Pawson and Evans were batting together with Pawson unaware of the reward offered. Evans, on 49, went for a quick single but Pawson was not backing up. Evans had danced down the wicket to the spinner McCool, pushed the ball and kept on running. Pawson sent him back and Evans was run out because the ball had gone straight to the only close fielder, Bradman.

There was a warning in the annual report of that year for future beneficiaries. It read:

> While having every sympathy with professionals who wish to increase their Benefit Funds, the Committee has reluctantly decided to limit the number of local matches played for this purpose. First-class cricket is hard work and county matches must come first. Rest days should not be interfered with.

How times have changed—in the modern game beneficiaries do not have many rest days in which to cram their activities.

For business reasons Bryan Valentine resigned the captaincy at the end of the season, a decision accepted with regret for he had always been a leader who set out to entertain and to sustain a policy which could never be branded 'safety first'. He was the positive skipper and very much the positive batsman, reputedly the best leg-side hitter of his time and boasting an average rate of scoring at around 50 runs an hour. He had made his debut for Kent in 1927, won a Blue at Cambridge in 1929 and became the County's vice-captain in 1931. He represented England in seven Tests, when he toured India in 1933–34 and South Africa in 1938–39. His interest in the County's fortunes never diminished and was always based on an encouraging approach.

In March 1948 the Club made enquiries into the idea of setting up an Association of Kent Cricket Clubs, which was eventually formed. Valentine, who was one of the club representatives on the association, reported considerable keenness and stressed that everything should be done to encourage cricket among the youth of the County. It could be done in a variety of ways: coaching of boys by experienced club cricketers; parent clubs to hold trials of promising boys and to invite them to play; holiday matches for schoolboys; possible decentralisation of coaching by Kent professionals. Clubs could be helped by a panel of visiting experts like groundsmen and advisers on insurance, the purchase of materials, the setting up of cricket schools for helping coaches and umpires, and by the establishment of a fixtures bureau. The Association blossomed. Indoor cricket schools were established in the County, and former players like Claude Lewis and later Colin Page dedicated themselves to finding and developing young talent. Soon the hard work and commitment was to pay off as a steady stream of talented youngsters emerged to give wonderful service to Kent cricket—players like Underwood, Knott, Johnson, Woolmer, Ealham and Tavaré—the production seemed unlimited.

With the retirement from the captaincy of Valentine, the side was led in 1949 by D. G. Clark. Educated at Rugby school, he had played for the County's second eleven and during the war had served in the Army, being taken prisoner at Arnhem. He had made his first-class debut in 1946 but had not played much in the first eleven. Now he had agreed to lead the side for three years and he pursued an objective of trying to build a side that would last for ten or 15 years. His senior professional was Ames, described by the new captain as 'God's gift to any young amateur coming in to captain a county side with very little experience.' Clark and his senior pro had lengthy discussions about the long-term position in the game of the part-time player—amateur or professional. Ames' view was that the amateur might be very valuable from the point of view of the way cricket was played, but he was never likely to contribute to the game to the same degree as a professional. Clark was never really completely persuaded to that point of view but Ames was right—to the extent that cricket did eventually become almost entirely a professional game.

In fact Clark had wanted Ames to be captain when he himself was appointed for the 1949 season. Clark recalled: 'We had a long evening together, when I suggested that it was really nonsense for me to do the job when he was available. His reasoning for not accepting the role was that he felt that if things went wrong an amateur captain was more able to go to the committee and say if you don't do what I think is right in the interests of the team you can find another captain. A professional captain would not be able to take that stand.' In fact Ames had already been approached about leading Kent—Bryan Valentine had told him the previous season, in the dressing room at Southampton, that the County would like him to take over. There was a proviso— that he would have to take amateur status. This Ames declined to do on the grounds that he had started as a professional and was not ready to change when he was approaching the end of his career.

While the new captain had some satisfaction in seeing Kent move up the table by two places, to 13th, Ames registered 2,125 runs, averaging over 47. Fagg and Todd, who featured in an opening stand of 251 against Leicestershire, each passed the 1,000-run mark and a young 16-year-old batsman who had played with such distinction at Tonbridge School, M. C. Cowdrey, made his debut in the second eleven.

With Wright again in such tremendous form—128 wickets at just over 21 apiece—there were times when the opposition really suffered, as Leicestershire and Hampshire found, with Wright taking 15 for 163 and 10 for 84 respectively against them. He had good support in the spin

department from Dovey, with 73 wickets, and Ridgway's pace earned him 97 wickets. Slightly built Ridgway could generate real pace and he was to be rewarded with a place in the Test Trial the following season and on a tour of India with a Commonwealth XI in 1950–51. In the following winter he won five Test caps on the MCC tour of India, Pakistan and Ceylon. In 1949, at Tunbridge Wells, Ridgway had written his name into the County's batting records when he and Brian Edrich, a brother of Bill Edrich, of Middlesex and England, had established a best-ever ninth-wicket stand of 161 against Sussex.

Frank Mann, c Fagg, b Wright, Middlesex v Kent, Lord's, 1947.

In April 1950 the club received the resignation, through ill health, of G. L. De Hough, who had been appointed General Manager in 1933 and subsequently combined the duties of Manager and Secretary. He was succeeded by Nevill Christopherson, a nephew of Stanley Christopherson, the England and Kent cricketer. He himself played for Blackheath and was a member of the Free Foresters and the Band of Brothers, and had been on the Kent committee since the war and was a trustee.

In 1950 Kent enjoyed the first of two seasons when they got out of 'double figures'—finishing ninth in the Championship. Ames and Fagg were the most successful batsmen. Ames started the summer in great style with a century in each innings against Gloucestershire, and in the match against Essex he, Pawson and Hearn all scored centuries in a total of 552.

During a summer in which Wright (141) and Dovey (102) dominated the bowling, Kent experienced their first tied match since 1905, when they needed 171 to win but, with Ames retired hurt, could only reach 170.

The season marked the end of his Kent career for Todd, who decided to retire and become an umpire. Awarded a benefit in 1947, Todd, who was born at Catford, had joined the staff in 1923. He had made his first-class debut in 1927, and was awarded his cap two years later. He had played 426 games for Kent, scoring 19,407 runs at an average of 31.50 and taking 55 wickets at 27.38 apiece. He still remains the last Kent cricketer to perform the 'double' of 1,000 runs and 100 wickets, which he achieved in 1936.

As Todd played his last game for the County, so Cowdrey made his first-class debut—against Derbyshire at Derby, scoring 15 and 26 and taking a wicket. He continued in the side for the last three matches of the season for the skipper had said that it was time to 'break-in' the promising 17-year-old. Cowdrey had been in the Tonbridge School first eleven at 13, and before he played for the Young Amateurs of Kent, he had played twice for the corresponding side in Surrey.

There was no doubt from the very beginning that Cowdrey was destined for the top honours in the game, and it was virtually a certainty that he would soon lead the County. He was to take over in 1957, reigning for 15 years as Kent became a force to be reckoned with again; and he was to play 114 times for his country, which was a record until passed by Gavaskar for India, and he was captain on 27 occasions.

In his second season Cowdrey played regularly while waiting to go up to Oxford, scoring 891 runs and being awarded his cap. For Kent it was a disastrous season for they slid seven places down the table to 16th position. It was the lowest they had ever been and it was a season that marked the end of the playing road for Ames, who, being injured, played in only the opening game. Fagg dominated the batting, scoring over 2,000 runs, with his best support coming from Hearn and Edrich. The burden of the bowling was borne mainly by Wright, Dovey and Ridgway, but no-one reached 100 wickets. There was a bitter pill to swallow during Tunbridge Wells week, when Kent suffered two humiliating defeats, first by Sussex, by an innings, and then by Lancashire. Consolations were few. Dovey had a return of eight for 38, as Glamorgan were shot out for 99 at Swansea, and Fagg scored 221, almost half the Kent total of 462 against Notts at Trent Bridge. Then in the final game of the season, when Kent were 22 for five, Evans entered to hit an amazing 101 out of a total of 158.

Ames' retirement was a dreadful blow. That breakdown in the first match of the summer against Nottinghamshire at Gillingham meant that there was no farewell season, or even farewell game, for one of Kent's all-time greats. He had ricked his back at home about three days before the match and was really not fit to play. He was prevailed upon to do so and it did not assist his cause when Kent had to field first on a bitterly cold day. He recalled: 'I remember fielding at short leg when someone skied a ball. I only had to move about four yards but I don't know how I ever got to it and caught it.' There was no respite for the casualty. When Kent batted he told his captain: 'It's no use putting me in because there's no way I can bat.' But the side lost six wickets quickly and he had to go in. He said: 'I went to play a ball round to leg and just collapsed in a heap. That was my last game.'

His career figures speak for themselves but tribute was paid to him for his magnificent achievements. A special feature article in the County's annual recorded:

> It was not only what Leslie Ames did, but the way in which he did it, which will mark him for all time as one of the finest exponents of the game of cricket. His whole-hearted enthusiasm and extraordinary efficiency were only equalled by his personal modesty. He might have earned his place in any team by his wicket-keeping or his batting alone, but he had not the single-mindedness of the specialist. Always a great-hearted player, his best efforts were at the disposal of his captain as long as the game was in progress.

In recognition of his achievements in the field and his influence on cricket generally the MCC elected him, among the chosen few professionals, to be an Honorary Life Member, and he was made a Life Member of the Kent County Cricket Club.

Kent scorer and former player and coach Claude Lewis played with him over the years and, of his wicket-keeping ability, said:

The 1949 Kent side. Standing: P. Hearn, T. G. Evans, B. Edrich, E. Crush, R. R. Dovey, A. Phebey, F. Ridgway. Seated: A. E. Fagg, L. E. G. Ames, D. G. Clark, L. J. Todd, D. V. P. Wright.

He was a natural. He was also so reliable, did everything very quietly without any show at all . . . As a batsman, he could really make bowlers suffer. He was predominantly a front-foot player and drove with tremendous power. He was one of the finest straight hitters I've ever seen.

When it was finally realised that Ames would never play again, he accepted the post of coach to the first eleven. Unfortunately he had to resign from the job because he was unable to attend all the matches and therefore felt he was not in a position to carry out his duties properly. Ames was more practical about the matter. He said: 'The county had endured a bad season financially and were looking for ways of saving money. I suggested that there was no better way than to start with myself.'

Clark, who has always given his best to Kent cricket in whatever capacity, player or administrator, stepped down as captain as he had said he would after doing the job for three years and W. Murray Wood was appointed to lead the side in 1952. Born at Dartford, he had first played for the County in 1936, when he represented Oxford University.

It was another disappointing season with the only consolation the rise of just one place in the table with the usual pillars of the side doing their best to restore flagging fortunes. The batting department was yet again led by Fagg, with over 1,500 runs, receiving best support from wicket-keeper Evans, who scored 1,000 runs in a season for the first and only time in his career. Wright, after missing out on 100 wickets the previous summer, led the way with 118 wickets in an attack which saw him receive most assistance from Dovey and from Page, then a pace bowler, and who in his first full season took 61 wickets. There were the customary overwhelming defeats, as at Southampton when the side was dismissed for 32 and 91 by Hampshire. Cowdrey was now up at Oxford University and available only when term ended. He then made his presence felt with his maiden century for the County, obtained against India at Canterbury.

The see-saw fortunes of Kent in the lower reaches of the table continued in 1953 when they reverted again to 16th place after the confidence booster of victory in the opening Championship match against Warwickshire. They then went 15 games, 11 of them lost, before they won again, beating Worcestershire. Triumph was short-lived—Middlesex dismissed them for 43 in the next match, as if to put them

126

in their place, and before the end of the season Yorkshire's paceman, Fred Trueman, with ten wickets in the match, plunged them to another defeat. Despite an injury problem Wright was still the spearhead of the attack and, as usual, Fagg, who included an unbeaten 269 against Notts in his aggregate of 1,377 for the season, held the batting together. His best support now came from Arthur Phebey, who scored

Godfrey Evans catches Lindsay Hassett off Alec Bedser in The Oval Test against Australia, 1953, the match in which England regained the Ashes.

1,300 runs. Phebey, from Catford, a correct and sound opening batsman, had played for Kent Schools in 1939 and made his County debut seven years later, being awarded his county cap in 1952. Known for his immaculate appearance, his calm unruffled approach had gained him respect wherever he played during his career.

The difficult time which Murray-Wood was experiencing in leading Kent became no easier in 1953, and during Canterbury Week committee members were canvassed for their views after the whole team had indicated that they would not play for Kent again if Murray-Wood captained another match. So as the second match of the week drew to an end—resulting in defeat by Middlesex by 99 runs—the committee issued a statement saying that Murray-Wood would be relieved of his post. That defeat by Middlesex had been the 13th of the season in 23 Championship matches to date. In Wright's absence, Cowdrey led the side in the next match but Wright took over for the remaining matches of the summer. In the first match in which he skippered Kent, against Somerset at Dover, he had a match return of 12 for 102 and Kent won by eight wickets.

In 1954 Wright officially took over the leadership of the side, becoming the County's first professional captain, and the new role did nothing to restrict his success as a bowler. He led the way with 109 wickets in a season which saw Kent's fortunes improve to the extent that they climbed to 11th place in the table. Dovey, who left the County at the end of the season to take up a school coaching appointment, Ridgway and Page all played a useful part in the attack but there was a change of emphasis in the batting, where Fagg, troubled by injury, just failed to make it to 1,000 runs. That target was achieved though, by four batsmen: Phebey, Hearn, the Australian Pettiford, and the young left-handed Wilson. Again Cowdrey was restricted by his time at Oxford, where, for the University, he had scored a century against Kent. In the second eleven during that summer, there was an interesting debut—by the 15-year-old Brian Luckhurst (as a bowler!).

Kent's cause in 1955, when they slid back two places to 13th in the table, was not helped by Test calls, injury and illness which restricted the appearances of Cowdrey, Evans and Ridgway. Wright's total of 127 wickets was almost a third of those taken by Kent all season, and the next best returns were the 58 by Page, and 42 by J. M. Allan, like

Doug Wright, whose idiosyncratic action was a feature of Kent and England cricket either side of the Second World War. He took a record seven hat-tricks in his career.

Cowdrey now finished at Oxford University. He also scored a century in each innings of the match against Northampton-shire, a feat which Cowdrey had achieved against Essex at Gillingham, where Doug Insole had returned the compliment for the opposition. Phebey, who had a bad spell in the middle of summer, reached 1,000 runs again, and the leading run-getters, all exceeding 1,300, were Fagg, Wilson and Pettiford.

It was almost a carbon copy of 1953 in 1956, when after winning the opening championship match against Glamorgan, Kent endured an even longer time without victory: of 17 games. The result was another taste of 16th position in the table, with Test Match calls and injury mainly responsible. Cowdrey, despite his England commitments, scored 1,000 runs in a season for Kent for the first time. Phebey, with 1,300 runs, was the top run-getter and Wilson also reached 1,000 but Fagg, for only the second time since the war, did not reach that landmark. The most serious of the injury problems was that to Wright. It affected him almost throughout the summer, in which he took only 48 wickets, including a return of eight for 30, when he bowled out Middlesex for 64. Fortunately, Ridgway was back to full fitness, and took 82 wickets, while the advent of a human 'bowling machine' named D. J. Halfyard boosted the attack. Halfyard, born in Middlesex, at Winchmore Hill, had played for Surrey before his move to Kent. What a rewarding switch it was to be for the medium-pace bowler and the County.

This was the last season for the very reliable Fagg, who had given such tremendous service. In 1957 he captained the second eleven but only for a season before he embarked on a countrywide coaching job. That too was for the one year—then the first-class game which he had served so creditably lured him back—as an umpire. He became one of the best in the game, operating over a long period at Test level.

The 1955 Kent side. Standing: A. L. Dixon, R. G. Wilson, J. C. T. Page, P. Hearn, J. S. Pettiford, A. H. Phebey, A. F. Brazier. Seated: A. C. Shirreff, A. E. Fagg, D. V. P. Wright, T. G. Evans, F. Ridgway.

COWDREY AT THE HELM

THE CAPTAINCY REIGN OF COLIN COWDREY, taking over the side at the age of 24, began in 1957 and was immediately heralded as an important advance in the fortunes of Kent cricket. Educated at Tonbridge School and Oxford University he had captained the Public Schools in 1950, the year in which he made his debut for the County side. He had won Blues at Oxford in 1952, 1953 and 1954, skippering the University in that final season. He had toured Australia in 1954–55, scoring a superb maiden Test century at Melbourne, and at home was an automatic selection against South Africa in 1955 and Australia in 1956.

He was on tour in South Africa when he received a cable asking him if he would succeed Wright as Kent's captain. Cowdrey, in *MCC—the Autobiography of a Cricketer*, admitted that his first thoughts were of the men who would be playing under him—Arthur Fagg, Fred Ridgway, Jack

Colin Cowdrey, one of the giants of post-war English cricket, a child prodigy who richly fulfulled his potential.

Pettiford, Wright himself, Evans, an England veteran then approaching 90 Tests—all established cricketers while he was still a schoolboy. He wrote:

> Now I was being invited to lead them. It was a daunting prospect and I challenged Godfrey Evans, who was also on the tour, to ask him how men of his calibre would react to me as captain. Evans' reply typified the man: 'We'll all be behind you master. Give yourself everything you've got and we'll all give you a hand.'

Cowdrey accepted. His qualities as a batsman were undoubted—now Kent wanted him to show he had similar talent as a leader, for since the end of the war the County had been served by four different skippers. Having finished sixth and fourth respectively in 1946 and 1947 the County's highest position thereafter had been ninth and three times they had finished with only one team below them in the Championship table. The new captain opened his season at Lord's by being dismissed for a duck, but Kent went on to win the match by an innings and 59 runs—a start which easily compensated the skipper for his personal failure. Cowdrey, of course, was required throughout the summer for England duty, missing 12 of Kent's games, and he and his side had to wait until mid-July before they achieved their next victory—over Worcestershire at Folkestone. Four more victories followed before the end of the season, which saw Kent rising by just two places to 14th in the Championship table.

It was a start, and there was plenty more to encourage Kent and their supporters in a season when, of course, they had wicket-keeper Evans away on Test duty with Cowdrey. The batting was certainly more consistent. For the first time since the war five batsmen topped 1,000 runs: Phebey, Wilson, Cowdrey, Pretlove and Leary. The openers Phebey (1,576) and Wilson (1,831) had warned opposition attacks of their prowess with a stand of 179 in that opening game at Lord's. They proved to be the most consistent opening batting combination in the country, scoring between them five of Kent's ten centuries, six more than in the previous summer.

To a Kent bowler went the distinction of the best return of the summer. Halfyard took nine for 39 against Glamorgan, and he well deserved his season's tally of 116 wickets, easily the best in the Kent camp. Page, bowling off-spin from mid June, took 69 wickets despite being sidelined by injury for six matches. Topping the bowling averages was G. Smith, who played in ten matches during his holidays, and took 57 wickets at 16.19 apiece.

Ridgway missed six weeks because of a leg injury, which provided a chance for a new young paceman, A. Brown, to play nine matches in the County side and show great promise for the future. Wright, persistently troubled by injury, did not play after mid-July and that was obviously a great handicap to the side. At the end of the season, he announced his retirement, having become one of the select few bowlers to take over 2,000 wickets. His career had lasted 25 years, had been distinguished off and on the field and the County paid him a permanent and deserved tribute by electing him as honorary life member of the club.

Wright, during his distinguished and very successful career, established one record which will almost certainly never be broken—by taking seven hat-tricks, six for Kent and one for the MCC against Border at Eastbourne in the winter of 1938–39. His sequence had started with two in the 1937 season—at Worcester and at Nottingham—then one in 1938 against Gloucestershire at Gillingham then came the South African hat-trick, followed by another against Gloucestershire at Bristol in 1939. There was then a lapse of eight years before he completed the next hat-trick, against Sussex at Hastings in 1947, and the staggering sequence was rounded off in 1949 against Hampshire at Canterbury.

Wright, the most modest and unassuming of men and a very popular figure, had one secret which he kept with his wicket-keeper—the signal for his faster ball. There was no secret for the googly or leg-spinner but he said: 'Whenever I was going to bowl the faster ball I always tossed the ball up and caught it as I turned at the end of my walk back to my mark. As far as I'm aware no-one ever twigged it.'

When he finished playing for Kent, he went to Charterhouse as cricket coach and is still coaching today—for the Kent club and for two schools in Canterbury—King's and St Edmunds. He thoroughly enjoys it and so must his pupils.

Looking back on the 1957 season, the Kent annual report was optimistic, and enthusiastic about the impact of the new captain. His tremendous enthusiasm and example had played an important part in the growing confidence and determination to win among the players. Kent had found a skipper, who, 'by his own prodigious efforts, both on and off the field, can and will raise the team to great heights.' It was a bold prediction, and one which was to be realised, but there was still much hard work to be done before the ultimate success of winning something could be achieved.

There was another important decision taken by the Kent committee in 1957, which was to have a vital influence on the future and the eventual emergence of Kent again as a cricketing power. It was resolved to revert to the former policy of employing a Manager as well as a Secretary, and the post was filled by Ames. It was no great surprise because D. G. Clark, who, since he stopped playing, had been chairman of the Young Players sub-committee, had always referred in his days as captain to 'my exceedingly wise senior professional Les Ames'. Now those qualities which Clark and everyone else in Kent cricket appreciated were being put to another and very important use. Ames was blessed with fairness and experience and was able to enjoy the respect of the players to an enormous degree. Not only that, he also commanded the respect of the committee, the members and the supporters which was, for an administrator, a very vital asset.

With Cowdrey totally involved in his cricket, his dressing-room enthusiasm and exuberance could not fail to keep a side buoyant. So as a pair the manager and the captain had plenty to offer Kent cricket and Clark was not alone when he contended: 'It was that partnership which really put Kent back on its feet without any doubt at all.' Cowdrey agreed. Writing in his autobiography he asserted:

> So began a friendship and partnership that eventually was to bring the success that looked unobtainable in those early days. We knew it was going to be a long haul and agreed, ironically, that it would probably be the 1970s before we would be set to become the champion county of England.

Paid attendances went up in 1957 from 83,731 to 100,950 and by 1958 another very important change had taken place; C. Stuart Chiesman, father of Cowdrey's wife Penny, had been elected Chairman. While his son-in-law revealed his qualities of leadership on the field Mr Chiesman displayed his own particular brand of dynamics in the committee room. A highly successful businessman, he gave not only financial assistance to the Club but showed a flair as an administrator which was to prove equally valuable as the Club's attitude and approach underwent a noticeable change. His tremendous drive and enthusiasm could not fail to be infectious. He had the ability to sweep people up into his almost fierce loyalty for Kent cricket. He was good with people—with all the different types of member and supporter. He would make it his business to tour the perimeter of the ground during a match, talking to everybody and anybody, sometimes being on his circuit for hours.

Up six places—that was the encouraging improvement in 1958 when the captain, missing for 11 games because of Test and representative matches, still passed 1,000 runs for the County, accompanied by Phebey and Wilson. Prodger, who got into the side at the start of the season, played 25 matches, totalling 847 runs. He was a professional footballer and his goalkeeping ability was frequently proved in the slips. There were other young players making an impression. Brown, who also played football professionally and had been born in Nottinghamshire, was virtually a regular paceman and Sayer, a former Maidstone Grammar schoolboy, who had first played for Kent in 1955 and subsequently went up to Oxford, bowled rewardingly. He got into the side in August and topped the averages with 27 wickets at an average of 13.88. The best all-round form came from Pettiford, while Page missed his 100 wickets by 14 and Ridgway, in his benefit year, by only two. Halfyard hit the century mark again though (135) and his insatiable appetite for bowling which never left him wherever and for whomever he played was reflected in bowling nearly 300 overs more than anyone else.

At the end of the 1958 season Kent took the decision not to continue with the services of a full time coach. It was considered unnecessary in view of the close co-operation between manager and captain, so Lewis, after continuing to be responsible for coaching at the indoor schools during the inter and pre-season coaching and training at Canterbury switched to the duties of scorer for the first eleven during the season.

The wet summer of 1958 was followed by a 1959 season which revealed hard and generally fast wickets, with Kent often struggling to find the ability to bowl out sides to win matches. Injuries did not help, particularly to bowlers, with Brown out of action for six matches early in the season with a heel injury. Nottinghamshire, the county of his birth, must have wished he had remained an absentee because later in the season at Folkestone he achieved the feat of taking four wickets in five balls against them. Sayer was injured in only his second game of the season for the County and did not play again that summer. Halfyard and Pettiford also had their injury problems, but it still did not prevent the former from taking another 125 wickets, thriving on the bowling of over 1,000 overs in that dry summer.

There was a drop in Championship position, down to 13th, despite the efforts of the batsmen, who were in tremendous form, with the openers Wilson (1,808) and Phebey (1,737) again leading the way. The captain scored 1,613 in his restricted county programme. His 250 against Essex became a new highest ever score in a county game on the Rectory Field, Blackheath, beating the 207 by H. T. W. Hardinge there in 1921. Leary, the second Charlton footballer at Kent—Sid O'Linn, also from South Africa, had played earlier in the 1950s—scored 1,000 runs and so, for the first time, did Dixon, proving that a decision to return to first-class cricket the previous season was the right one.

Meanwhile there were runs promised in 1960 by Peter Richardson, who had been specially registered from Worcestershire but had to spend 1959 qualifying, doing so by scoring 799 runs in the second eleven with an average of 34.73. Born at Hereford where he was educated at the Cathedral School, he first played for Worcestershire in 1949 and became captain three years later. He had toured Pakistan in 1955–56, South Africa in 1956–57 and Australia in 1958–59. He had played in 28 Tests while with Worcestershire, so Kent were acquiring a batsman of top class. Also very much in their minds was the fact that he had the perfect experience to lead the side when Cowdrey was away on England duty.

Pettiford, who had played in England during the Second World War for the Australian Services team, was not offered terms at the end of 1959, his benefit season. A native of Sydney, he had played for New South Wales in 1947–48.

It was also the last season for one of the great Kent and England names: Evans, who had been awarded the CBE in the New Years Honours list. His record for County and country had been brilliant, and his popularity, particularly among the younger element in the crowd, was always at the highest level. His unlimited enthusiasm and vitality meant that whenever he was in the middle there always was a sparkle to the game. He was particularly keen to help young players and years later Knott was to write of the good advice he received from him. 'Keep going whatever might go wrong' was Evans' guidance—he was always looking for the next ball, the next moment in life. Evans' strength was also a major factor in his performance—on one occasion he was reported to have lifted the Hampshire and England bowler 'Butch' White, a fairly big man, by the elbows until his head was touching the ceiling. He followed in the footsteps of Ames by being elected an honorary life member of both the MCC and the Kent County Cricket Club.

In 1960 Kent were climbing again but only to tenth, and the weakness of not having a top-class spinner was

Alan Dixon, who was awarded his County cap in 1960, midway through a career as an all-rounder that saw him play 378 matches for Kent. He three times scored 1,000 runs in a season and three times took 100 wickets, but never achieved both in the same season.

bemoaned, as was the handicap of having a captain absent for half the season on Test duty. The annual report observed:

> The cares and worries of the England captaincy with the inevitable publicity and criticism, usually unjustified, weighed heavily on his shoulders and the County and the cricketing public seldom saw the Cowdrey we knew so well.

He did not manage 1,000 runs for Kent—scoring 759 for an average of 33—but six other players did, with the newcomer Richardson getting 1,087, despite a top score of only 99. Dixon, whose aggressive batting always entertained, again passed the 1,000 mark and so did Jones in his first full season.

Halfyard again proved to be the bowling workhorse, taking 123 wickets, but there were 80 from Brown, 60 from Dixon—all-round form from him—and Sayer took 39 wickets for an average of 23 after the Varsity match, winning a place in the MCC team to tour New Zealand. Sadly Ridgway did not always enjoy the best of health and retired at the end of the season, having obtained a permanent job in industry from which it was agreed he could be released if Kent should require his services. Since his debut in 1946 he had been the County's leading paceman, until recent years being the only bowler of real pace. How much better he might have been had he operated in harness with a bowler of similar pace and ability.

In the first season post-Evans, Catt, from Edenbridge, began behind the stumps in the County side. Disappointing form with the bat, however, let him down and when another Charlton player, Ufton, got his chance towards the end of June he was soon making useful runs and maintaining a regular place until the end of the season. Had either looked through the pages of the 1961 Kent annual which reflected on that 1960 season, he would have found the name 'Knott' in the report of the Kent Schools Cricket Association. He and a boy called Underwood were among seven from Kent capped in the South *v* Midlands match.

By 1961 the youngsters were with Kent in a semi-professional way, with Underwood topping the Club & Ground bowling averages, with his seven wickets costing 7.85 each, and at that level and in the second eleven were young players like Denness, Nicholls, Dye and Luckhurst, all embarking on their cricketing careers.

KENT *v* WORCESTERSHIRE

Played at Tunbridge Wells, 15–17 June 1960

KENT WON BY AN INNINGS AND 101 RUNS

KENT	**FIRST INNINGS**	
A. H. Phebey	b Gifford	16
P. E. Richardson	b Flavell	23
M. C. Cowdrey	c Broadbent b Pearson	17
R. C. Wilson	c Headley b Flavell	0
S. E. Leary	st Booth b Slade	23
P. H. Jones	c Broadbent b Slade	73
A. L. Dixon	c Dews b Pearson	17
A. W. Catt	st Booth b Gifford	0
D. J. Halfyard	st Booth b Gifford	0
A. Brown	b Gifford	1
P. Shenton	not out	7
Extras	b 7, lb 2, nb 1	10
Total		187

Fall: 1-41, 2-43, 3-43, 4-68, 5-104, 6-151, 7-154, 8-161, 9-179, 10-187

BOWLING	**O**	**M**	**R**	**W**
Flavell	18	8	25	2
Pearson	16	7	35	2
Slade	18	5	54	2
Gifford	17	5	63	4

WORCESTERSHIRE	**FIRST INNINGS**		**SECOND INNINGS**	
J. Sedgley	c Leary b Brown	7	c Richardson b Brown	2
R. G. A. Headley	b Halfyard	0	c Wilson b Halfyard	0
A. Spencer	b Brown	0	c Leary b Brown	4
D. W. Richardson	b Brown	0	b Halfyard	2
R. G. Broadbent	b Halfyard	0	c Catt b Halfyard	22
G. Dews	lbw b Brown	0	b Brown	0
R. Booth	b Brown	2	c Wilson b Halfyard	7
D. N. F. Slade	b Halfyard	9	c Leary b Shenton	11
N. Gifford	not out	0	c Brown, b Shenton	4
D. B. Pearson	b Halfyard	0	c Cowdrey b Halfyard	2
J. Flavell	b Brown	1	not out	0
Extras	b 1, lb 5	6	b 5, lb 1, w 1	7
Total		25		61

1st inns: 1-6, 2-7, 3-8, 4-9, 5-9, 6-9, 7-24, 8-24, 9-24, 10-25
2nd inns: 1-0, 2-6, 3-7, 4-17, 5-18, 6-40, 7-51, 8-51, 9-61, 10-61

BOWLING	O	M	R	W		O	M	R	W
Halfyard	9	4	7	4		13	2	20	5
Brown	8.1	5	12	6		8	2	22	3
Shenton						4.5	0	12	2

Umpires: T. J. Bartley and J. S. Buller.

This match was completed in one day—the first such in England for seven years. Jones, Halfyard and Brown were the heroes.

With little rain to interfere with that first-class season there were excellent batting wickets in Kent, produced in response to an MCC call for hard and fast pitches. It meant of course that the County had problems bowling sides out twice, and won only eight of their games—five of the 15 home matches only were victories—finishing 11th in the table. Cowdrey had assured supporters that his side would play bright and attractive cricket—and indeed their scoring rate was higher than any other County. Unfortunately the captain himself did not take as much part in the run-spree as he would have liked. He was missing as usual through Test calls and representative matches, before he was taken ill and did not play in the last five games. He still managed to score 1,239 runs, with a century in each innings against the Australians, the undoubted highlight of his season. It was the first time this feat had been achieved against an Aussie attack in England.

Richardson and Prideaux usually opened the batting and the former reached 2,119 runs in the season while Wilson, also a left-hander of course, was not seemingly deterred by dropping to No 3 or 4 as he scored 1,887 runs. Jones and Dixon both scored their 1,000 runs and took 77 and 71 wickets respectively. Brown reached 81 wickets, Sayer 44 in ten fewer matches and Halfyard 112, but the attack was criticised for failing too often in length and direction. There were actually 62 wickets gained by leg-spin with Leary, who had managed 1,440 runs despite his early return to the soccer season, taking 22, and Baker, in his second season on the staff, promising for the future by snaring 40 victims.

The wicket-keeping position had been settled for the 1961 season with Ufton keeping out Catt completely, and indeed his total of 90 victims was only one short of England wicket-keeper John Murray, whose 91 earned him the annual award of 100 guineas.

Things were stirring down in the second eleven, too,

Stuart Leary, one of the South Africans who played for Kent after the Second World War who were also outstanding footballers. Leary was centre-forward for Charlton and Queen's Park Rangers while also opening 381 times for Kent.

where Page had taken over as captain, having deputised the previous season when Ufton had moved up into the County side. Page was capable of imposing the right standard of discipline and creating the keen approach which could only be of advantage and a very enthusiastic young side won the second eleven championship. Constant, a young left-handed batsman, passed 1,000 runs in these matches for the first time in the history of the side. There was a record also for Prodger, who spent much of the season in the second eleven but registered a brilliant 170 not out against Essex in the Championship at Maidstone, and at Cheltenham against Gloucestershire excelled in the field. Brilliant in the slips—as a soccer goalkeeper often can be—he took eight catches in the match, a feat which has not been equalled by a Kent player since.

With the advent of the new opening batsmen, Phebey

found himself often down at No 3 or 4 and sometimes out of the side which in the absence of the captain he had led with skill and success. After 14 years loyal service he decided to retire at the end of the season to devote all his time to his business interests. He had played a very valuable role in the rebuilding of Kent cricket during the post-war years and he was to return subsequently to lend his experience to the County committee.

What Kent needed and still did not have in 1962 was an attack which could penetrate with either its pacemen or its spinners. Jones and Dixon, the spinners, were still handicapped by the covered wickets rule which prevented them from showing their ability on a wet wicket. Indeed there was criticism in the club's annual report both about this rule and the no follow-on rule. They made it more difficult to bring about definite results without resorting to freak declarations and contrived finishes. Surely, suggested the report, this could not be a good thing for cricket as a whole, advocating that both policies should be discontinued.

Cold weather in the opening week of the season saw the County at the bottom of the table but they recovered well, although the weather did not settle and Dover and Canterbury had their Weeks badly affected by rain—August Bank Holiday Monday at Canterbury was rained off for the first time for over 30 years. At least the County's performances and position had improved. There were hopes of a higher position than the eventual 11th but a nasty chain of snags arose. Cowdrey himself had games off because of illness, but recovered and proved it in the best possible way by ending his Kent season with two successive centuries. Then in August, in just over a week, the County was shorn of three key players. Leary, after another consistent season, which ended when he hit an unbeaten 74 to lead the five-wicket victory race against Gloucestershire at Canterbury, went home to South Africa. Meanwhile Kent journeyed to the West Country to play Somerset at Weston-super-Mare and Halfyard, who was two short of his regular 100 wickets for the season, was involved in a road accident on his motor scooter. It left him with a broken left leg and Kent without their leading bowler, for he still ended the season 41 ahead of his nearest rival. If that was not enough the side returned to Gillingham to be bowled out for 65 by Yorkshire and Jones had his jaw broken when he was hit in the face by Trueman.

So in 1962 it was same again—11th position—but all

Derek Underwood, scourge of batsmen for 25 years. A left-arm spinner whose pace at times was almost medium, and who was so unplayable on helpful wickets that he earned the nickname 'Deadly'.

change for the wicket-keepers, because Catt had got back in at the expense of Ufton and scored 905 runs, averaging 30.16. Within two more seasons, however, any discussion about who was the better wicket-keeper would be superfluous. For at the end of that season a young batsman-wicket-keeper, A. P. E. Knott, had accepted an engagement to join the staff.

The County was also looking now for a candidate to go in first with Richardson and they were interested in the form of Luckhurst, who having forced his way into the side reached 1,000 runs, a young Scot, Denness, who played more irregularly, and the left-handed Nicholls.

Where, though, were the up and coming bowlers? The answer was at hand, for coming through in the second eleven were Dye, a left-arm pace bowler, and Underwood, slow-medium left-arm. The latter, only 17, had taken 42 wickets at an average of 19, and was poised to explode on the first-class scene in 1963.

Just like Blythe, Freeman and Wright, so Underwood, once he broke into the County side, never looked back. He made his first-class debut a month before his 18th birthday and by the end of the summer had become the youngest player to take 100 wickets in a debut season. By the winter of 1970–71 he had reached his 1,000th first-class wicket, and he was only 25, an age when one of his illustrious predecessors, Freeman was beginning his career. In 1975 Underwood was to take his 200th Test wicket. His international career, spanning 86 Tests, ended when he was three short of 300 wickets. By 1981 he had taken his 2,000th first-class wicket. For Kent he was to master the tricky art of bowling in limited-overs cricket.

YOUTHFUL GENIUS: UNDERWOOD AND KNOTT

LIMITED-OVERS CRICKET and the impact of Underwood on the Kent, and eventually the England scene, provided two of the main talking points in 1963. Both were to become increasingly important as the years rolled by, for by 1972, the one-day game had taken such a grip that there were three separate competitions, in addition to the County Championship.

The first was the Gillette Cup, introduced in 1963 as a 65-overs a side match, subsequently reduced to 60, with no bowler being allowed more than 15 overs in an innings.

It was not a competition in which Kent were immediately successful but once they had won it in 1967 they eventually took all three limited-overs competitions in their stride, to take the title of undisputed 'kings' of the one-day game in the 1970s.

Kent, as a Club, was convinced that the new competition in 1963 was a resounding success, and opinion was almost unanimous that this type of cricket had come to stay. After the first round all ties were supported by crowds well above those of the Championship games, despite all of them, apart from the final, being played on Wednesday, which from past statistics was not the best viewing day. For the final at Lord's, the demand for tickets was so great that it had to be made an all-ticket match. Kent, however, did not get past the first hurdle. They were knocked out by the ultimate winners, Sussex, at Tunbridge Wells. Kent's first limited-overs match was played on 22 May, with Sussex reaching 314 for seven in their 65 overs, the left-handed Ken Suttle making 104. Kent's most successful bowler was Brown, who had three for 63 in his 15 overs and it was interesting to note, in view of successes in one-day cricket that were to come, that Underwood's analysis was 11-0-87-0. Kent put up a bold show in reply, despite making a dreadful start. After they lost two wickets for 19 runs, Richardson scored 127, an innings which earned him the Man of the Match Award. His support, apart from Cowdrey's 31, and 13 by Denness, was negligible until Underwood, going in at No 10, made the third highest score—28.

That was a good day in a summer which was one of the wettest on record for recent years. Despite that, Richardson still managed to score 1,977 runs for Kent, leading the race in all first-class matches of the season both to the 1,000 and 2,000 marks and being recalled by England for one Test against the West Indies. He also led the side in the absence of Cowdrey, who was not available until the last week in May, and then, after only a few games, broke his arm in the second Test at Lord's and was out of cricket for the season. In fact, he played only six matches for Kent, scoring 361 runs at an average of 36.10. Richardson, however, was always prepared to be aggressive, to take risks in an effort to get an outright win, and was often unluckily beaten by bad weather. Leary returned to football after Canterbury Week, again when he was in tremendous form with the bat, having scored 1,311 runs, while Kent's prayers for an opening partner for Richardson seemed to have been answered by the emergence of Luckhurst, who scored 1,501 runs for an average of 33.35. Wilson, now batting further down the order, between No 3 and No 5, also scored over 1,300 runs, and Denness, maintaining improved form, passed the 1,000 mark for the first time in his career.

He, Luckhurst and Nicholls, who made the highest score of the season—211 against Derbyshire at Folkestone—all had the distinction of scoring their maiden centuries that summer. The big problem when the season began was obviously the absence of Halfyard, who had not recovered sufficiently from his accident the previous year to be in the side. It was hoped that he might eventually be fit enough to resume, but that hope was never realised, he did not play a single game. Fortunately Brown, overcoming a new 'no-ball' rule, showed improved form with 86 wickets, but it was Underwood who made the big impact, taking 101 wickets in his first season, at an average of 21.12, the youngest player ever to pass 100 wickets. He made his debut in the third Championship match of the season, against Yorkshire at Hull, on 8 May, and picked up as his first victim in first-class cricket Yorkshire's Ray Illingworth, caught at cover by David Baker. He took four for 40 in 21 overs in that first innings, picked up five more in the next match against Northamptonshire at Dartford, had a match return of seven for 129 against Middlesex at Lords, and stayed in the side on a permanent basis. His initial impact was similar to those of Blythe and Freeman. He took the first of his many five wickets in an innings at Leicester (5-50); and his first ten in a match (10-113) against Surrey at Blackheath, with six for 88 in the second innings. He enjoyed five for 66 in 29.2 overs in his first meeting with the West Indians, at Canterbury in late August, when he numbered Seymour Nurse, Basil Butcher and Frank Worrell among his victims, and ended the summer at Bristol, with a very happy match aggregate of seven for 76. He left batsmen all over the country pondering on exactly what type of bowler he was. The Kent annual report said he could only be described as:

> . . . a slow, medium pace left-hand bowler, not quite the orthodox slow, left-hand type such as Blythe, Woolley and in more recent years, Lewis, but he has the great essential qualities of length and direction. He also has the ability to change his pace cleverly and on wickets giving him some assistance he definitely turns the ball away from the bat.

One swallow did not necessarily make a summer, it was suggested in the report, but it was certainly a most encouraging sign for the future.

This season Dixon switched from off-spin to medium pace and he opened the bowling with Brown, until he was injured in July and sidelined for the rest of the campaign. That gave a chance to the left-arm paceman Dye, who improved with each match and, bowling left-arm over the wicket, added variety to the attack.

The Kent team of 1963. Standing: C. Lewis (scorer), A. W. Catt, B. W. Luckhurst, D. W. Baker, M. H. Denness, D. L. Underwood, L. E. G. Ames (manager). Seated: A. Brown, P. H. Jones, R. C. Wilson, M. C. Cowdrey, P. E. Richardson, S. E. Leary, A. L. Dixon.

Catt had kept wicket throughout the season, and, probably bearing in mind the progress being made in the second eleven by the young wicket-keeper-batsman Knott, Kent decided to release Ufton who had been with the County for 18 years, and whose service throughout this time had been exemplary, particularly when he was helping in the second eleven. Other players released were Baker and Constant, who although batting prolifically in the second eleven, had never been able to take his chance in the County side. But he was to reach Test level as an umpire.

Moving in to the second eleven during that season, were a young Ashford cricket club batsman A. Ealham, and R. Burnett, who showed signs of following in the footsteps of his famous grandfather Frank Woolley. Bowling in a similar style to his grandfather, he had taken ten wickets in one second eleven match. Also, making his debut in the same side, and showing much improvement towards the end of the season, was a very tall, fast-medium bowler, N. Graham.

The County was still blessed with the chairmanship of Mr C. Stuart Chiesman, and grateful for his magnificent gift during 1963 of 15,000 shares in Chiesman's Ltd. The market value represented approximately £15,000 and was the basis of an endowment fund, the income from which would be used for the purposes of the Kent County Cricket Club, as may be directed by the donor or the trustees.

Mr Chiesman also chose the tea interval on August Bank Holiday, 1963, during the match between Kent and Hampshire, to honour Frank Woolley. He had presented to the club a beautifully carved plaque recording the records and achievements of Woolley and a vast crowd gathered around the pavilion to see Lord Nugent, President of the MCC, perform the unveiling ceremony. Lord Nugent said Woolley's name was known and honoured wherever cricket was played. In England, on tour abroad, he was always welcomed everywhere with respect and affection for his incomparable skill as a batsman, bowler and slip fielder and for his charming personality as a man. Woolley thanked all those responsible for the occasion and said that if he had given any pleasure, he was very glad, he had enjoyed every day of it. He would always remember this ceremony, as it had brought back happy memories of glorious days spent on the ground.

There was one other match during 1963, not competitive, which was to have an important bearing on the future of

Kent cricket—at Hesketh Park, Dartford, a three-day game between Kent and the Pakistan Eaglets. Kent were beaten by an innings and 84 runs, and in that Eaglets side was a young Pakistani, Asif Iqbal, who hit an unbeaten 74, coming in at No 7, as his side reached 414 for six declared. Then he opened the bowling and took four for 21 when Kent were bowled out for 100 in their second innings.

Cowdrey felt confident enough after the 1963 season to tell members at the annual general meeting before the start of the next campaign:

> We have now got a team of good cricketers. My biggest problem is to lead them on to the field and convince them that they can actually win something. Mostly they are young, immature and inexperienced, though we have a young Test cricketer or two on the horizon. But at last we stand a chance.

The County had always been saying that it needed a more penetrating attack to improve its championship position, and in 1964 it had two bowlers taking over 100 wickets in the same year for the first time since 1950. Underwood (101) did it again, and Dixon took 122 wickets, both of these bowlers deriving great support from pacemen Sayer (77) and Dye (63). The result was that Kent moved up to seventh in the table, their best season since 1947, and hopes of recapturing former glories were high again.

All this promise came after the season began with Halfyard still having problems with that leg injury. He played in only two games, while Brown broke down in the pre-season training period and had to have a cartilage operation, which kept him out for the summer. Fortunately, there was a change in the weather this season, with plenty of warmth and sunshine and good wickets. This helped to increase attendances by 15,000 paid entrants and receipts went up by over £3,000. Cowdrey was back—apart from ten matches which he missed through Test match calls—to score 1,562 runs and head the batting averages, while Wilson, in his benefit year, scored over 2,000 for the first time in his career. Richardson's aggregate dropped to 1,330 but he was compensated by a century before lunch against Hampshire at Canterbury, and a century in each innings against the Australians, repeating the feat of Cowdrey on the Aussies' previous visit in 1961. Leary also scored his 1,000 runs before returning to football but questions were already being asked about his future, bearing in mind that he was now past 30. He had to consider very seriously whether he could continue to serve both games, because cricket and football continuously without any break was arduous at any age. Luckhurst and Denness also scored 1,000 runs again, and late in the summer, after the university term, E. W. J. Fillary, the Oxford Blue, frequently opened the batting. Born in Sussex, at Heathfield, he had gone to school at St Lawrence, Ramsgate. He was also a leg-break bowler, taking three wickets in nine balls, finishing with five for 52 to speed Kent to victory over Middlesex at Lords. Then, on a very bad wicket at Dover against Yorkshire, he showed tremendous application and concentration in carrying his bat, scoring 28 out of a total of 146. The bowling, of course, proved the success story of the season, and the attack was spearheaded by Dixon, who took over the role of Halfyard, and bowled more than anyone else, 1,116.4 overs, mixing his off-breaks with his medium pace new-ball bowling. They were two entirely different styles, but he was able to change from one to the other without any loss of length or direction, and it was a tremendous bonus to the side. Underwood, meanwhile, was proving that on certain types of wickets, particularly those affected by rain, he could be a devastating match-winner, as was instanced by his nine for 28 against Sussex at Hastings. He was awarded his cap during the Australian game at Canterbury.

Just as Underwood had broken into the side the previous season, so in 1964 came a young man who was showing much promise and skill, both behind the stumps and as a batsman: Alan Knott. For Catt it had been a disappointing season, and Knott was given his chance at Folkestone at the end of June when he played against Cambridge University. He played in the second game of the week there against Leicestershire, and then after Catt had returned for eight games, Knott was back in the side at Wellingborough, on 8 August, and stayed there until the end of the season. Knott was to become one of cricket's 'greats' as a wicket-keeper-batsman and a character who did much to enrich a game which he served in a commendably dedicated manner. As soon as he made his debut the County were able to sit back and bask in the glory of producing yet another international wicket-keeper. He was to make his Test debut in 1967, claiming seven victims in the match, and altogether he made 95 appearances for his country. Like Evans before him, but in a very different way, Knott always had the knack of making spectators sit up and take notice when he was keeping or batting. With an extraordinary ability to improvise with the bat he had great success in that department, and at his best many people felt he could have commanded an England place purely as a batsman.

So well did Knott perform that Catt intimated to the committee that he did not want to be considered for re-engagement in 1965, because he would be moving to start a new life in South Africa. Another departure was Jones, who had been on the staff since 1952. He took up a post outside cricket, but said that he would be willing to play in the occasional second eleven game if required. The biggest tragedy of all was the decision of Halfyard, very reluctantly made, that he could not continue playing first-class cricket. He had made tremendous efforts to get himself physically fit from the injuries received in his accident $2\frac{1}{2}$ years earlier, but his broken leg had never recovered sufficiently to allow him to bowl with his old vigour and speed, and he had been left with a permanent limp. In thanking him for his past services, the County awarded him a testimonial in 1965, and Halfyard, eager to stay in the game he loved, decided to become a first-class umpire, before fighting his way back to play for Nottinghamshire and for several of the Minor Counties.

Meanwhile, Woolley was back at the St Lawrence ground at Canterbury again in 1964 to join in honouring Leslie Ames, because the Chairman, Mr Chiesman, had presented a plaque commemorating his cricketing deeds, which was placed on the opposite side of the pavilion door to Woolley's. It was unveiled by Gubby Allen, the President of the MCC, during the tea interval on August Bank Holiday, and Allen said he was happy to return to perhaps the most beautiful ground in the world to do honour to a great Kent and England cricketer. Ames' record was sure of a place in cricket history, being equally important for the manner of his achievements and the example he set. There was never a finer tourist or more modest a cricketer, and no-one more able to laugh in the face of adversity. Ames said he had had the pleasure of playing in Test cricket under Allen's captaincy, and faced up to his fast bowling many times. He had also been honoured to serve as a Test selector under Allen's chairman-ship. It was a memorable occasion for him, although the records only told half the story, the other half being the immense fun and enjoyment he had derived from his cricket.

There was another unusual ceremony in 1964, on 23 June,

when the Club conferred honorary life membership on HMS *Kent*. On board the ship the President of the Club, Mr H. L. Cremer, presented an honorary life member's pass to Captain A. M. Lewis. Mr Noel Boucher, who was President of the Club in 1963 and who was instrumental in organising the presentation, also gave the ship a suitably inscribed plaque, bearing the name of the Kent County Cricket Club. In return, the Captain presented to the Club a ship's plaque, which hung in the pavilion at Canterbury. To commemorate the fact that HMS *Kent* was commissioned during his year of office as President of the Kent County Cricket Club, Mr Boucher made a personal presentation to the ship's officers of a piece of Armada plate. The life membership of HMS *Kent* was to stay in existence for 20 years, until the ship was paid off, and as a gesture, the Armada plate was presented to Kent County Cricket Club.

Up two more places to fifth—that was the progress in 1965, which produced one of the worst summers for some years. Indeed there were high hopes of Kent doing even better, because having beaten Somerset at Canterbury on 11 June, when Dixon and Underwood had excelled with their spinning partnership in the second innings, Kent struck a bad

Colin Cowdrey hitting to leg with elegant ease against Australia during the 1965–66 tour. Mike Smith is the non-striker.

patch. They failed to win any of their next ten Championship matches, losing three of them in succession. They finally recovered their composure and their winning ways by beating Middlesex in the second game of Canterbury Week, going on to win five of the last nine games, with only one defeat.

The annual report was critical of the side's approach, saying it should have been more positive, and too often the rate of scoring was allowed to get behind the clock, pointing out that excessive caution rarely paid. The report was also critical too of the complaint that had been made many times on home grounds, about the rather slack way in which batsmen went out to the wicket. On many occasions it appeared that there was a considerable delay before the incoming batsman left the pavilion, and that contrasted sharply with the opposing batsmen, most of whom were crossing on the field. It was a matter which was receiving the attention of both the committee and the captain, the report added.

For the third successive season Kent fell at the first hurdle in the Gillette knock-out competition. This time defeat was at the hands of Hampshire, by 23 runs at Portsmouth, and that was disappointing, not only from the team's point of view, but also from the members'. Obviously Kent had to get their game geared to the requirements of the new knock-out competition, which it was appreciated had come to stay, and a more successful approach had to be ensured in the future.

Cowdrey was back in top form, however, in 1965, heading the Kent batting averages, and indeed those of the whole country, scoring over 2,000 runs.

When he was not in the side, Wilson took over as skipper because Richardson had a poor season, scoring under 1,000 runs for the first time since he had joined the County, and playing in only 21 of the matches.

This meant that Kent's opening batting combinations were permed again, but by the end of the season Denness and Luckhurst had settled happily into the No 1 and 2 spots which they were to occupy so successfully for many years. Both scored more runs than ever before, over 1,500 each, and were as good an opening pair as any in the country. For Leary it was a different season—it was the first time that he had played full-time for the County and not returned to football after Canterbury Week. He had a disappointing end to a summer which nevertheless brought him 1,252 runs. Underwood's form was sustained, although he fell 12 short of his hundred wickets, but Dixon passed the hundred mark again (117), and was joined by Brown (114), who gave the side a great boost by showing that despite a year away following his cartilage operation, he could still spearhead the attack. What he lost in pace, he gained in greater accuracy and ability to move the ball off the wicket, particularly the new ball. With nearly 800 runs Dixon was now in the true all-round class, but while he was bowling his medium pace, it was difficult to play both Sayer and Dye in the side. Dye played in 18 matches to Sayer's 11, and although it was disappointing for the one who was left out, it had to be realised that to develop a Championship-winning side, top class replacements needed to be available, particularly in the fast bowling department, where there was a greater risk of people breaking down. Graham also came into the pace bowling category, playing in several of the matches and doing well. If the first of the two tourist matches—against the New Zealanders at Maidstone—had produced some splendid batting, with Denness scoring 86 and 82 and J. R. Reid 165 for the New Zealanders, then the second tourists' match, against the South Africans at Canterbury, surpassed it with the form of the left-handed Graeme Pollock, who scored a brilliant double-century. The South Africans had travelled down to Canterbury the previous night after winning the Test series at the Oval and Pollock, shaking off the celebrations of the night before, thrashed the Kent attack to all parts of the ground. It was a memorable innings and one which had the older members talking animatedly about Frank Woolley.

Richardson, having suffered a poorer season than usual, accepted an offer of employment outside cricket and decided to retire. He was sadly missed because his batting inevitably had brought a sparkle and impetus, and his experience proved invaluable. He was presented by the committee, on behalf of the Club, with a silver salver and cheque. There was no doubt that Richardson left cricket before his time, because he would have been a great success both as a batsman and as a captain in the spate of limited-overs cricket that was to follow.

During the season the Chairman completed a hat-trick of plaque unveilings during Canterbury Cricket Week and this time it was the late 'Tich' Freeman who was honoured.

Sadly, he had died earlier in the year, but his son Percy and many of his contemporaries were present at the ceremony performed by Lord Cornwallis, once captain of the side in which 'Tich' played. Lord Cornwallis said it was 'Tich' Freeman's great accuracy and stamina which enabled him to hold so many cricketing records—it was doubtful if anyone would ever better his 1928 feat of 304 wickets in a season, though he thought if 'Tich' had been playing at that time he might easily have obtained 400 wickets in a season. The majority of present day batsmen failed to use their feet and 'Tich' would have tied them up completely.

There was little improvement in the weather in 1966 when Canterbury Week proved to be the worst in living memory, only 4,000 people paying for admission. The ground had never been in such an appalling condition, with cars often nearly axle deep in mud. The Maidstone Week was almost as bad, with only one day when rain did not intervene. The total gate attendances for Championship games were the lowest on record, only 37,000 paying for admission against 61,000 the previous year, and an average of 73,000 over the previous ten years. Wickets, too, caused problems throughout the country and Kent were not entirely free from criticism because those at Dartford and Blackheath were not up to first-class standard. At Dover there seemed to be a big improvement, but it was over-watered a few days before the match and the game only lasted two days. The County's annual report noted that pitches steadily deteriorated year after year although counties were implored by the MCC to prepare better wickets. Whatever the answer was to the problem it was quite certain that the country would not produce Test Match cricketers of the requisite class by playing on inferior wickets. There was also a new rule in 1966 with an experiment which limited the first innings of each side to 65 overs. While many spectators approved, the majority of cricketers were against it, saying it was not always prudent to bowl the opposing side out, but preferable to bowl negatively to prevent the batsmen from scoring quickly. Again a side genuinely bowling the opposition out in less than 65 overs and then overtaking their opponents score for the loss of only a few wickets immediately had to surrender the advantage gained.

The Gillette Cup again proved disappointing for Kent. Having won their first match in the competition by knocking out Suffolk in the first round with the captain scoring a century, Kent were beaten in the second round by Hampshire at Southampton. It was a game they had looked almost certain to win, and indeed, champagne had been on ice in the dressing room.

In the Championship it was a different matter because the County finished fourth, their highest position since 1947 and one place up on the previous season, giving hopes that the title could soon be within their reach. Luckhurst and Denness both scored over 1,500 runs but the middle order batting was not as reliable. The captain, Wilson and Leary all had their most disappointing seasons for many years with Wilson the only one of the trio to reach 1,000 runs (in the last match of the season). With Prodger and Nicholls also unable to score consistently an extended trial was given to Ealham, in his first season on the staff.

Underwood, who made the first of his 86 Test appearances, had a great season. He obtained more wickets than anyone else in the country, 157, and finished top of the national averages—the first Kent cricketer to do so since Blythe in 1914. His total of 144 for Kent was the highest for the County since 1935, when Freeman topped 200. Dixon, who led the side in the absence of Cowdrey, was the next most successful bowler with 115 wickets, and the pace attack was shared by Sayer, the most consistent, Brown, Dye and Graham. The fielding and catching gave much pleasure to spectators and Ealham, in his extended trial period, proved himself a reliable fielder, particularly with his catching in the deep. Meanwhile, showing encouraging form in the second eleven was the all-rounder from Barbados, Shepherd, who had to spend the 1966 season qualifying. He scored 873 runs and took over 50 wickets and his fielding was of the highest standard. He had been spotted playing in Barbados when the Kent side had toured there the previous winter, and manager Leslie Ames persuaded him to join Kent. He and his great friend Keith Boyce travelled to England together, with Boyce joining Essex.

It was the final full season for Wilson although he played on for part of the 1967 campaign. Not only had his batting been so consistent for the County over so many years, but he had also stepped back into the shoes of Cowdrey when the captain was away on Test duty. Wilson had first played for the County in 1952, being awarded his cap two years later and his fair hair, cheerful countenance and stocky figure had provided a consistent feature of the Kent scene. He was serene

Brian Luckhurst, a great servant to Kent both on the field and later as an administrator. A sound opening batsman, he played 21 times for England.

and compact, but could be pugnacious and powerful, and overcame the difficulties that beset the left-hander who was short of reach. He was one of the strongest players off the back foot in the game and his square cut left fielders standing. Only an outfielder of his own high calibre could have lived in the area of third man when he was middling them. He had the ability to pick the right shot for the right ball and contributed many fine innings against the clock. His fielding, of course, won him the plaudits of crowds everywhere. Pick-ups on the boundary at speed were appropriate for a man who had been a left-winger with Bowaters when he gained a Kent Amateur Cup winners medal.

SUCCESS AT LAST

THE LIGHT HAD BEEN SEEN at the end of the tunnel for a few seasons now and it was time in 1967 for Kent to emerge and begin to reap the benefits of the patient team-building which had been undertaken for over 20 years. The plan had been to produce a side which would be successful and which would endure for some 10 years, and this had been achieved. Despite the departure of Bob Wilson at the end of the 1967 season and of Peter Richardson the previous summer, the team could cope—and responded with the County's first trophy success since 1913. True it was not the Championship title but it was the next best thing—the Gillette Cup.

That memorable success at Lords in early September, attracting the attention of the County in a very marked manner, provided the boost to confidence which was to see the side make very strong bids for further success over the next three years. It also helped to equip them for the demands of a new Sunday limited-overs competition which was to start in 1969. Looking down the roll of the playing staff it was evident that the resources existed for the push towards even greater glory.

Meanwhile the Gillette Cup and runners-up position in the Championship in 1967 were enough to be going on with and it was a season to savour with much satisfaction. Not since 1928 had the County occupied such an exalted position in the Championship table and as far as the limited-overs competition was concerned they had never beaten another first-class county since it had been inaugurated in 1963.

The county's trail to Lord's began at Brentwood on 13 May, when they beat Essex by 42 runs. Denness (30) and Luckhurst (66) put on 68 for the first wicket before Cowdrey played an innings of 66 which won him the 'Man of the Match' award as Kent reached 239 for eight. Essex began well enough but struggled subsequently against Graham (4–19) and Underwood (3–21) and were all out in 56 overs for 197. The next round took Kent to The Oval where on a sensational morning Surrey collapsed against Dixon and were all out just after lunch for a measly 74. Only two players had reached double figures as Dixon, who was brought on as first change, ran through the Surrey batsmen. He finished with seven for 15 in his 12 overs, seven of which were maidens. They were figures which were to stand as a record in the competition until beaten 20 years later, appropriately by one of his colleagues, Derek Underwood, who did not need to bowl that day at The Oval. Dixon's destruction earned him the 'Man of the Match' award and although Kent lost four wickets for 41 runs Luckhurst and Ealham steered them to victory. The stage then switched to Canterbury for the semi-final against Sussex, when a crowd of nearly 17,000 saw Kent display tremendous batting form. They lost Denness early but Luckhurst, Shepherd and the captain all reached the 70s as a total of 293 for five was achieved. It was always going to be too much for Sussex as Kent's fielding and catching backed their all-round bowling strength and Cowdrey won his second 'Man of the Match' award of the summer.

So on to Lords with the Kent pavilion decorated by garlands of hops, for Denness (50) to play the innings of the day, winning the 'Man of the Match' award, as he and Luckhurst put on 78 for the first wicket. Luckhurst, who had broken a bone in his left hand during Canterbury Week, had missed the last six Championship games, but although not 100 per cent fit he played in the final and scored a valuable 54. Kent reached 138 before they lost their second wicket, but then slumped badly to 193 all out off 59.4 overs. Somerset replied with 51 without loss off the first 17 overs by the tea interval and then Shepherd pulled a thigh muscle while fielding and could only bowl at a reduced pace, which he did well enough to contain the batsmen. Kent held all their catches and finally bowled Somerset out for 161 off 51.4 overs to win by 32 runs. The cup was presented to Cowdrey, by the President of the MCC, Sir Alec Douglas Home, amid much rejoicing by the jubilant Kent fans. Later in the year, on 27 November, Edward Heath entertained the winning team, together with club officials, to dinner at the Carlton Club. Before the dinner everyone had assembled at the House of Commons and listened to a debate from the Strangers Gallery. It was a memorable evening.

In the Championship, Kent made the winners Yorkshire fight to the bitter end and the race was so close that after completing their programme Kent led the table, with Yorkshire to play Gloucestershire in the final game of the season. To be sure of winning the title Yorkshire needed only to win on the first innings. This they did, going on to win the match by an innings.

GILLETTE CUP FINAL
KENT *v* SOMERSET

Played at Lord's, 2 September 1967

KENT WON BY 32 RUNS

KENT

M. H. Denness	c Clayton b Alley	50
B. W. Luckhurst	c Atkinson b Alley	54
J. Shepherd	c Virgin b Rumsey	30
M. C. Cowdrey	c Robinson b Palmer, K.	1
S. E. Leary	c Clayton b Palmer, R.	1
A. Knott	run out	21
A. Ealham	run out	17
A. L. Dixon	b Alley	0
A. Brown	c Barwell, b Palmer, R.	1
D. L. Underwood	b Palmer, R.	7
J. N. Graham	not out	0
Extras	b 1, lb 8, nb 2	11
Total (59.4 overs)		193

Fall: 1-78, 2-138, 3-141, 4-145, 5-147, 6-148, 7-150, 8-177, 9-187, 10-193

BOWLING	O	M	R	W
Rumsey	12	1	28	1
Palmer, K.	12	3	37	1
Palmer, R.	10.4	0	53	3
Atkinson	7	1	25	0
Alley	12	4	22	3
Burgess	6	2	17	0

SOMERSET

R. Virgin	c Graham b Dixon	17
P. J. Robinson	c Knott b Shepherd	48
M. Kitchen	c and b Dixon	15
T. E. Barwell	run out	24
W. E. Alley	c Brown b Shepherd	8
G. Burgess	c Knott b Brown	27
C. R. M. Atkinson	c Luckhurst b Underwood	1
K. E. Palmer	c Luckhurst b Underwood	0
G. Clayton	b Underwood	8
R. Palmer	c Leary b Graham	2
F. E. Rumsey	not out	1
Extras	lb 8, nb 2	10
Total (54.5 overs)		161

BOWLING	O	M	R	W
Graham	12	4	26	1
Brown	9.5	3	20	1
Underwood	10	2	41	3
Shepherd	12	2	27	2
Dixon	11	2	36	2

Umpires: W. F. Price and J. S. Buller.

Kent's first major trophy success for 54 years. Mike Denness was made Man of the Match.

Ironically it was the defeat sustained at Yorkshire's hands in the second match of Canterbury Week which probably put paid to Kent's title hopes. Only two points were gained in the Week, attended by some 40,000 spectators. The Yorkshire game contained all the necessary ingredients for a dramatic match, although the end result was not good from Kent's viewpoint. Both sides were weakened by Test calls— Kent were without Cowdrey, Knott, who that season embarked on a trail which led to 95 Tests, and Underwood. Godfrey Evans was called out of retirement to keep wicket at the age of 46! On three other occasions the left-arm spin bowler and left-handed batsman P. H. Jones was also summoned from retirement to help out—warnings, if any were needed, that the County had to sustain its reserve strength to live happily at the top. The return of Evans naturally delighted the older spectators, and indeed the younger ones who had not had a chance to see him in action. He had to bat, scoring ten, before he kept wicket. Kent suffered an early blow when Luckhurst was struck on the hand by Trueman and suffered a broken bone. Kent fought back when Yorkshire batted, with Evans snapping up the first of his two catches to break the Tykes' opening stand at 48. They were bowled out for 225, a first innings lead of just two, after Dixon had taken nine for 73. One of his victims was Trueman, whose lusty hitting came to an end when the substitute fielder Alan Ealham sprinted round the boundary from long on to take a brilliant catch on the boundary rope. The Kent second innings was a disaster as they were dismissed for 100, with only Wilson offering serious resistance to score exactly half the runs, and Yorkshire won comfortably by seven wickets before lunch on the third day.

Earlier in the year, at the Club's annual general meeting, Cowdrey had said: 'If one of my fast bowlers can give me 100 wickets then Kent have a good chance of winning the

Championship.' Well, Norman Graham finally obtained his 100 wickets in the last match of the season, a great one for him, and Cowdrey's forecast very nearly came true. Graham, 6ft 8in tall, came third in the national bowling averages, with Underwood top for the second year in succession. Once again he had taken 100 wickets in the season reaching a total of 128.

The failure to win the Championship may have been due to the batting, which looked adequate but all too often disintegrated in the middle. Shepherd, in his first season, scored 950 runs and took 54 wickets and confirmed that here was a cricketer who would give Kent great service. With him and Dixon in the side Kent possessed two all-rounders of quality, and Dixon failed by only six wickets to reach the 100 mark. The weather was far better, apart from May, and attendances were the best for many years, reflecting the improved performance of the side. They rose to 75,438 compared to 38,593 the previous year as the County continued to show a slight increase in membership with the figure rising to 5,830. Sunday cricket was introduced for the first time, proving an overwhelming success. Capacity crowds watched the play at Folkestone, Maidstone, Canterbury and Gillingham and the County decided in 1968 all weekend games would feature Sunday play. Again there was a problem over the deterioration of wickets, with only Gravesend, Blackheath, Canterbury and Folkestone escaping criticism. The Club made it clear that if it was to continue to play cricket in various parts of the County, which had always been its policy and, it was hoped, always would be, it was vital that the wickets for the games were prepared to first-class standard.

Leary had record benefit receipts for the County of over £9,000 and his game against Leicestershire at Canterbury, blessed with fine weather and an excellent attendance, realised £2,957. He also featured in a Kent XI v International Cavaliers game at Canterbury when the Cavaliers included such famous names as Gary Sobers, and although no charge was made at the gate the sum of £750 was realised.

For 1968 there were more changes in the County Championship, which proved important for Kent. For a win ten points were awarded, plus any points scored in the first innings, which were awarded only for the first 85 overs and retained whatever the result of the match. Batting points were gained as follows: one for passing 175, two at 200, three at 225, four at 250, five at 275 and so on. For each two wickets taken by the fielding side in the first 85 overs there was one point, leading to a maximum of five if all ten wickets fell. In the event of a tie each side scored five points, plus any first innings points scored; if the scores were equal in a drawn match the side batting in the fourth innings scored five points plus any points scored from the first innings. The side which had gained the highest aggregate of points at the end of the season would be the Champion county, and if two or more sides were equal on points the side with most wins would have priority.

Those changes in the system made their impact for Kent in the first season when, for the second year in succession, they were runners-up in the Championship to Yorkshire. In fact Kent won more games than any other county, but Yorkshire had a clear lead of 14 points. So was it the new bonus points system which cost Kent the title or their failure to take advantage of it? They scored five fewer batting points than Yorkshire and 19 less in bowling. Still the side had proved that it had the ability to stay in a title-challenging position during a summer when the lack of bonus points was not the only problem. They suffered probably more than any other county from Test calls, while injuries also took toll of the side's playing strength. Cowdrey missed 15 games through England duty or injury, while Underwood and Knott missed nine and ten games respectively because of Test demands. Asif, Luckhurst, Denness, Dye, Graham, Woolmer and Johnson all had injury problems.

It was the first season in the Kent side for Asif, the young Pakistan Eaglet of 1963, and he made a big impression with the fans, scoring over 1,200 runs in exciting style. Unfortunately back trouble restricted him to bowling only 49 overs during the summer. Denness and Luckhurst maintained their reputation as an opening pair probably without equal in the country, and Shepherd scored over 1,000 runs for the first time and captured 96 wickets with his medium-paced bowling. But for missing three games in the middle of the season he surely would have become the first Kent player to complete the 'double' since L. J. Todd in 1936.

It all added up to a difficult season for Dixon, who led the side in Cowdrey's absence, and although not enjoying his usual all-round success, he stuck to his responsibilities and kept the side in the hunt for honours.

Knott scored 1,000 runs for the first time in all games, and

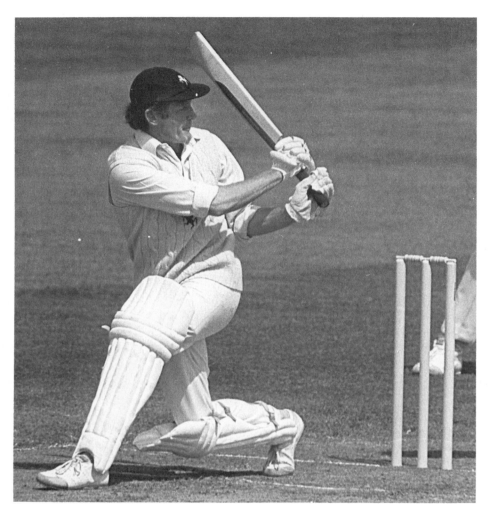

Mike Denness, fine forcing batsman and captain of Kent from 1972 to 1976. During this time he also captained England. He lost both captaincies, and many feel he was not treated kindly by his county.
(Courtesy of Patrick Eagar).

when he was away on Test duty the left-handed batsman Nicholls kept wicket adequately.

Ealham, Johnson and Woolmer all had chances in the side and their performances augured well for the future, but the main problem was still a lack of consistent penetration from the pace attack. Graham, one of the injury victims, had to be content with 60 wickets, with his colleagues in the fast bowling department—Dye, Brown and Sayer—sharing 87 victims. It was still Underwood, with 91 Championship wickets leading the way, hotly pursued now by Shepherd (85).

There was an improvement too in wickets throughout the County, with the exception of Gillingham. The Dover wicket was one of the best, as Sobers would testify after his magnificent century in 73 minutes had enabled Nottinghamshire to beat Kent in a run-chase. In fact Gillingham staged its last County Championship match in 1968, probably much to the dismay of Underwood, who followed his match return of nine for 73 there the previous year against Glamorgan with 11 for 74 against Hampshire. Luckhurst had scored 111 out of Kent's first innings total of 223, and by the end of the game Underwood was virtually unplayable. Despite a suggestion by a Hampshire player that the best remedy for the wicket would be to dig it up, Sunday games in the John Player League were allocated in 1971 and 1972 before Kent finally stopped playing on the ground altogether. It was unfortunate that in the Medway towns, with probably the biggest catchment area in the County, no suitable venue could be found for county cricket. With the three-day Championship programme reduced from 28 to 24 games the County expected to have to alternate between Folkestone and Dover for a cricket week.

Membership had risen in 1968 to 6,734, obviously reflecting the tremendous interest now being accorded the side with success, achieved the previous year in the Gillette Cup, seemingly just around the corner in the Championship.

Just after the season ended, on Sunday 15 September, the chairman and members of the club and of Otford Cricket Club paid tribute to one in a great line of Kent wicket-keepers, Fred Huish, who kept wicket between 1895 and 1914. In the village churchyard at Otford, where he was buried in 1957 at the age of 87, there now stands a memorial stone donated by Miss Frances Blackburn which was dedicated on that Sunday by the Bishop of Tonbridge, the Rt Rev H. D. Halsey.

Before the start of the 1969 season, in March, the club suffered a shattering blow with the sudden death of its Chairman, Mr C. Stuart Chiesman. He had been a committee member for 18 years and Chairman for the last ten. Throughout this long association with the club he had not only proved himself to be a wise and energetic chairman, but he was a great benefactor, having set up the Stuart Chiesman Endowment Trust in 1962 with a gift of 15,000 Chiesman shares and a further gift of 1,000 shares worth £1,000 towards the Centenary Appeal. In addition to being head of

Chiesmans, he was an underwriter at Lloyds and a director of Lombank. From 1967–68 he was High Sherriff and his interest in charitable causes included the Kent County Playing Fields Association and the Textile Benevolent Association, which endowed beds and wards in many convalescent homes—the new wing at the Association's home at Kingsgate being named after him.

The main talking point of the 1969 season was the introduction of cricket's second one-day competition, the Players' County League, played on Sundays. Both sides were allotted 40 overs for batting, with each bowler allowed a maximum of eight overs and their run-up limited to 15 yards. If weather intervened there were conditions laid down for a result to be obtained and the only way in which the match could not be won or lost was if rain washed out play completely (or, of course, if it was a tie). The new competition was met with fierce opposition from many, who felt that it just was not cricket as they knew it, and that it would hamper the breeding of cricketers up to international level. Whatever the rights and wrongs of the arguments, the new competition immediately attracted support through the gate and it has to be faced that if the one-day game generally had not been introduced this history might have taken less time to read.

Certainly the Kent public were not inclined to follow the 'Never on Sunday' arguments and as their side finished fourth in the table in that first season, 22,000 people paid to see their eight home game. The first ever Sunday League game in Kent was at Canterbury on the opening day of the Sunday season when Hampshire were the visitors. Although Luckhurst, who became one of the County's highest scoring Sunday batsmen, was dismissed without a run on the board Asif and Knott scored half-centuries. Revelling in the new challenge, with the opportunity it provided for their own expertise in improvisation, they soon settled down as Kent reached 211 for six. Hampshire never mounted a serious challenge and Underwood, who became the County's leading wicket-taker in the competition, got off the mark with four for 26 and Shepherd, for whom the Sunday game provided a great stage for his all-round capabilities, took three for 19. The winning streak was sustained for the first four games and this had much to do with the Kent crowd's instant liking for the new competition.

In the Championship, although everyone had been saying

'This is the year' Kent dropped from second to tenth, their lowest position since 1963. Injuries and Test calls, the old story, had such a damaging effect that after the first two matches of the season the side was never again at full strength. The most damaging blow was felt as early as 25 May, with a serious injury to the captain. Playing in the fourth Sunday game, against Glamorgan at Maidstone, he was forced to retire hurt on 39 after snapping an Achilles tendon in his left foot—an injury which was not only seen but also heard when the tendon was ruptured. He underwent an operation and did not play again that season. Meanwhile England duty robbed Kent of the services of Knott in 11 games, Underwood in nine and Denness in three. The side was also without the all-round qualities of Shepherd because he was with the West Indies party touring England. Then he sustained a back injury during the final Test and was unable to play for Kent until their last two games of the summer. Asif also had his share of injury problems, missing the last six games with a groin muscle problem. So the only consoling feature was that the younger players had even more opportunities again. Although not sustaining his promise as an off-spinner, Johnson, going for his shots, batted most encouragingly and his ability as a slip fielder shone through and was much appreciated in the absence of Cowdrey.

The injury to Cowdrey had Kent looking towards the future again. Dixon, who was enjoying a successful benefit season, had been deputising for Cowdrey previously, but was himself currently sidelined by illness. When he returned to the side it was decreed that Denness, who with Luckhurst again dominated the batting, should continue as captain.

After the end of the season, in which the second eleven, under Colin Page, had won their championship, thoughts turned even more towards the Club's Centenary appeal in 1970. It had committed itself to spend £60,000 for additions and alterations to the pavilion, but required something like £80,000 to achieve all its aims. By the end of 1969 the advance takings situation was distinctly satisfactory, with £17,000 already banked.

CHAPTER ELEVEN

CHAMPIONS AGAIN

FOR THE CLUB 1970 was to be a memorable year indeed. It was
celebrating its centenary and had appealed for money for the
reconstruction and alteration of the pavilion. New dressing
rooms were built and the whole project was completed by
the start of the new season which, on the St Lawrence
Ground, was 30 May, for the Gillette Cup tie with
Worcestershire. Lord Harris was the County's President—
his father had skippered Kent from 1875 to 1889—and the
stage was set for the side to produce the results which would
complement such an important year. Colin Cowdrey was fit
again after his serious Achilles tendon injury of the previous
season, but he and the team could not have had a more
disastrous start. The first two Championship matches were
lost and Cowdrey went on to total only 152 runs in 13
innings. With Test calls likely to be as demanding as ever,
Kent had needed a good start when the side was at full
strength. In those first seven games they managed one
victory, with only 13 batting points, and were fourth from
bottom. Defeats included one by Warwickshire at Gravesend
where Underwood had a match analysis of 14 for 213, but
had to contend with a quite magnificent display of batting by
the West Indian Rohan Kanhai. Cricket lovers had seen
many fine innings on the famous Bat and Ball ground but
none could have been much better than that of Kanhai. On
what the County's annual referred to as a 'sub-standard
wicket' he straight drove his first ball from Underwood over
the pavilion for six, and went on to score 107 out of 177.

For Cowdrey personally, things improved during the
Tunbridge Wells Week when he scored a century in each of
the two matches on the Nevill Ground. Yet there was a
disappointing defeat by Sussex in the Gillette Cup at
Canterbury and at the start of Maidstone Week in early July
the side was at the bottom of the Championship table.
Secretary-Manager Les Âmes, never afraid to speak his mind,
was just the person to put the matter to rights and he held a
dressing-room conference on the Mote Park ground, where
the very disappointing form and approach of what was on
paper a very talented side, was carefully and fearlessly
analysed. High on the agenda was the very vital subject of
batting bonus points. To everyone's credit the lesson was
learned with immediate effect. The remaining 13 games of
the season were traversed without defeat; in four of the seven

wins over 20 points were achieved, a record 23 in the last home game of the season against Leicestershire at Folkestone. Six batting points were obtained in the drawn game with Derbyshire at Maidstone; six more in the second match of the week against Hampshire, which a Kent side weakened by Test calls won handsomely.

With Cowdrey on England duty, Denness led the side in fine style. An unselfish batsman, he showed how to respond to the need for faster scoring, while Asif was by nature a ready supporter of such a cause. It was this combination that spearheaded the remarkable one-wicket victory over Glou-

Asif Iqbal in full flight. Asif was one of the most popular cricketers and captains of Kent. His masterly innings in the losing Gillette Cup final of 1971 will long be remembered. (Courtesy of Patrick Eagar).

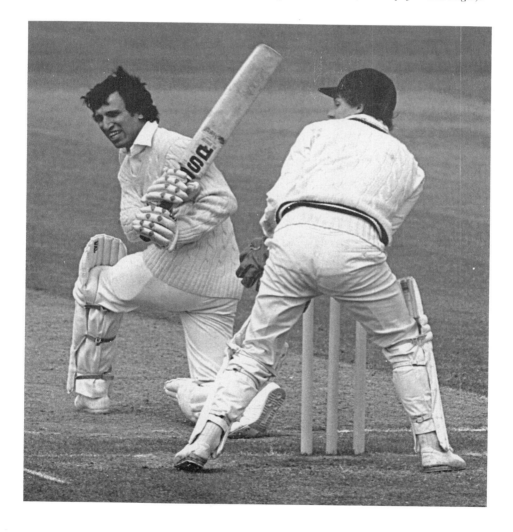

cestershire at Cheltenham midway through August. Kent scored 340 for nine on a bad wicket to win the game, and it could hardly have provided a better stimulant for the final lap because Kent were now very much in the Championship race. No-one was more optimistic about their chances than Asif. When Cowdrey suggested it was a pity the season couldn't be extended because Kent might then win the title, Asif was astonished. He said: 'I've already told Mike Denness we shall win it in our last match at The Oval.' He sustained that view, then applied his superb talent to achieving it. He scored a century in a magnificent win over the old Blackheath 'enemy' Surrey. It was achieved by 12 runs, with Pat Pocock brilliantly caught on the long off boundary by Asif off the fifth ball of the penultimate over, going for a six. The bowler was Graham Johnson, whose first full season yielded him over 900 runs with the bat. His 12 wickets in that match at Blackheath were vitally important too, not merely for the Championship challenge but because his off-breaks were to become a more permanent feature of his cricket with the retirement at the end of the season of Alan Dixon.

From the Rectory Field, Blackheath, the scene switched to Folkestone's Cheriton Road ground for a never-to-be-forgotten Week of excitement, drama and superb entertainment. That great West Indian all-rounder Gary Sobers threatened to re-write the script. On a perfect wicket he scored a masterly century, and in his second innings stroked 44 out of 53 in 35 minutes to set Kent 282 to win in three hours. Denness and Luckhurst provided the ideal start with a century opening stand at just under five an over. Then Denness and Asif hit 94 in 52 minutes and 112 were needed from the last 20 overs. Wickets fell as the target was gradually reduced and finally Knott, cool, calm and collected in the mounting tension, hit three fours to steer his side home with eight balls to spare.

Another good wicket for the second match of the Week at the seaside promised well for the visitors Leicestershire until John Shepherd, who had a busy and remunerative bowling season, broke through with four wickets for nine runs in 21 balls. Leicestershire were dismissed for 152, leaving the Kent batsmen to show their appreciation of the wicket by building a mammoth total of 421 for seven declared. Leicestershire lost three wickets overnight and on the final day Underwood was the deciding factor in an early and conclusive victory by an innings and 40 runs achieved just before lunch.

Yet when the Week had started at Folkestone both captain

and manager had not been happy to note two superb batting wickets. It seemed though that Ames had caught some of Asif's optimism. He told Cowdrey: 'Still, if you lose the toss twice you might just have a chance of coming from behind on the final days of the matches'. How right he was, as the visiting captain called correctly on each occasion. The match against Nottinghamshire produced a particularly thrilling victory, with some corruscating batting from Luckhurst, Denness and Asif. (See scorecard overleaf.)

Four days of inactivity followed before Kent made the short journey to The Oval knowing that bonus points would probably give them the title. Naturally Surrey were put in to bat when a start, delayed by rain, was eventually possible at 2.50 pm. By the next morning, when Surrey declared at 151 for nine, Kent had four bowling points. Like Surrey, Kent lost two early wickets but Luckhurst and Cowdrey retrieved the situation; and the captain celebrated with a century the title success for which he had waited so long, and which the County had not recorded for 57 years. Those eight bonus points virtually clinched the issue, and in the event the margin at the top of the table was 17 points.

On the final day at The Oval the Prime Minister, Edward Heath, joined the players in a celebratory glass of champagne, no doubt revelling in the triumph of the Club he had supported since as a schoolboy he used to cycle from his Broadstairs home to watch Kent at Canterbury. It was on that day too that Cowdrey, asked about his future, replied spontaneously that he would retire from the Kent captaincy at the end of the 1971 season.

It was very nearly a first-eleven double, for the runners-up spot had been attained in the John Player League where Leary, who lost his place in the County side in the second half of the season, virtually won several Sunday games off his own bat. In only its second season the Sunday competition had certainly captured the imagination of the Kent fans. The paid attendance on 36 home days in the Championship was 29,328, while eight Sunday games were watched by 25,151.

Kent experimented with a Sunday game, not repeated, at the Midland Bank ground in New Beckenham, trying desperately to find a new venture in the Metropolitan part of the County. Rain washed out the game which ended in confusion and caused the rules of the new competition to be amended. Lancashire reached 202 for seven and Kent were 58 for one off nine overs when rain intervened. It was ruled that Kent had won on faster scoring rate.

KENT v NOTTINGHAMSHIRE

Played at Folkestone, 29, 31 August and 1 September 1970

KENT WON BY THREE WICKETS

NOTTINGHAMSHIRE	**FIRST INNINGS**		**SECOND INNINGS**	
M. J. Harris	run out	53	b Shepherd	11
J. B. Bolus	c Denness b Dye	43	c Denness b Underwood	73
B. Hassan	c Knott b Woolmer	55	c Shepherd b Dye	0
M. J. Smedley	b Shepherd	92	c Knott b Underwood	23
G. A. Sobers	not out	123	b Johnson	44
G. Frost			not out	49
R. A. White			b Johnson	3
Extras	lb 6, w 1, nb 3	10	b 6, lb 5, nb 1	12
Total	for 4 wkts dec	376	for 6 wkts dec	215

M. N. S. Taylor, D. J. Halfyard, P. Plummer, D. Pullan did not bat

1st inns: 1-80, 2-110, 3-173, 4-376
2nd inns: 1-16, 2-21, 3-71, 4-124, 5-206, 6-215

BOWLING	**O**	**M**	**R**	**W**	**O**	**M**	**R**	**W**
Dye	22	2	88	1	11	3	29	1
Shepherd	27	4	91	1	15	8	29	1
Woolmer	20	3	67	1	6	1	23	0
Underwood	22	7	64	0	28	10	63	2
Johnson	17	2	56	0	14.1	2	48	2
Asif					3	0	11	0

KENT	**FIRST INNINGS**		**SECOND INNINGS**	
M. H. Denness	c Pullan b Taylor	2	b Taylor	90
B. W. Luckhurst	not out	156	c Plummer b White	58
G. W. Johnson	c Smedley b Halfyard	0	c Hassan b Sobers	0
Asif Iqbal	c Plummer b Halfyard	10	b Sobers	56
M. C. Cowdrey	c Sobers b Halfyard	4	c Hassan b Sobers	18
A. Ealham	b Harris	57	c White b Taylor	11
J. N. Shepherd	lbw b Sobers	47	lbw b Taylor	22
R. A. Woolmer	not out	26	not out	2
D. L. Underwood	c Pullen b Taylor	1	did not bat	
A. P. E. Knott	did not bat		not out	12
J. C. Dye	did not bat		did not bat	
Extras	b 1, lb 2, w 1, nb 3	7	lb 8, nb 6	14
Total	for 7 wkts dec	310	for 7 wkts	283

1st inns: 1-2, 2-6, 3-7, 4-13, 5-27, 6-140, 7-245
2nd inns: 1-103, 2-197, 3-221, 4-253, 5-262, 6-268, 6-268, 7-269

BOWLING	O	M	R	W	O	M	R	W
Taylor	25	7	62	2	23	2	107	3
Halfyard	30.2	9	85	3	5	0	31	0
White	3	2	8	0	5	0	28	1
Plummer	13	1	46	0				
Sobers	15	2	49	1	19.4	2	103	3
Harris	9	1	53	1				

Umpires: H. Bird and A. E. Fagg.

With this victory, Kent established themselves as potential champions in 1970. Kent's target of 282 was achieved in two hours plus 20 overs with eight balls to spare, Knott hitting three fours from the four balls he received. Ealham was awarded his county cap.

For the second successive year the second eleven won their Championship, and the County's policy of producing young players to come through the ranks into the first eleven was reflected in the award during 1970 of caps to Johnson and Ealham and, in the final celebratory day of the season, to Woolmer.

Success is never easily or cheaply forthcoming. That was to be seen from the County's balance sheet—for the second successive year there was a loss. It was due to three factors—the ever-increasing running costs, the loss of revenue from Test Matches following the cancellation of the South African tour and, as pertinent reason as any, the large playing staff of 21. The committee wisely considered that this size of playing strength needed to be maintained because of the continual demand on its top players of international calls.

The 1970 season was the last and probably the proudest for Dixon, who retired after 20 years' valuable service. He had given all-round service, batting and bowling both medium-pace and off-spin. He had led the side on occasion during the absence of Cowdrey, and was a popular figure with players and supporters alike. Always of cheery personality, he was a cricketer who entertained, who could bring a game to life with an aggressive innings or with a remarkable piece of fielding, for he excelled in that department, particularly in the covers. For most of his playing career he was a hard-working member of a not very successful side. Otherwise he would probably have enjoyed even more success and it must have been frustrating for many of his fans that he retired before limited-overs cricket really got into its stride. What a variety of roles he could have played so successfully in the one-day game!

Kent, County Champions, 1970. Standing: L. Kilby (physiotherapist), R. A. Woolmer, J. N. Shepherd, A. Brown, J. N. Graham, J. C. Dye, G. W. Johnson, Asif Iqbal, J. C. T. Page, C. Lewis (scorer). Seated: D. Nicholls, A. P. E. Knott, D. L. Underwood, M. H. Denness, M. C. Cowdrey, L. E. G. Ames (manager), S. E. Leary, B. W. Luckhurst, A. G. E. Ealham.

THE SWEET AND SOUR REIGN OF DENNESS

THERE WAS NO REPEAT Championship performance in 1971, as Kent had to be content with fourth place. They slipped from second to seventh in the John Player League, but gave their supporters and cricket in general a performance of which to be proud at Lord's in the Gillette Cup final. They lost, by 24 runs, a match which two people more than anyone else will always remember. Asif, on 89 and seemingly winning the game, hit a ball from Jack Simmons hard and high into the covers where Jack Bond leaped to pull off a fabulous catch. The last three wickets went down quickly leaving Asif, still in tears, to gain consolation with the 'Man of the Match' award.

The Championship season had started well enough with an opening victory by an innings and 92 runs against Yorkshire at Bradford. Cowdrey, in his last season as captain, was in tremendous early form. Unfortunately illness prevented him from playing again after the end of June and with Knott, Luckhurst and Asif all away for part of the season on international duty Kent did well to stay in the race for so long.

Apart from Test calls, and Cowdrey's illness, there were a variety of injury problems and on one occasion the squad did not need to be selected—there were only 12 fit players available. Johnson, who had scored 885 Championship runs the previous season, had to overcome the handicap of a chipped bone in the ankle just before the season started. Shepherd often was plagued by back troubles while Graham, who was the second most successful bowler, 32 wickets behind Underwood, missed several matches because of injury. Denness, having got rid of tooth trouble at the start of the season, then damaged a wrist, which troubled him for the rest of the summer, but being plunged again into the role of captain in place of Cowdrey he indulged in a purple patch. His first nine innings in his acting role yielded 492 runs, and he always set the perfect example in quick scoring.

With Luckhurst and Knott frequently on Test duty, the left-handed Nicholls grabbed his chance to shine in both their roles. He had always deputised behind the stumps for Knott, now he took over opening the innings as the Denness-

Luckhurst combination broke up. He scored over 1,000 runs in a season for the first time and so did Ealham, who was always ready to answer the call for aggressive batting.

Those attendance statistics revealed for the 1970 season, showing the interest in the Sunday game, were repeated in 1971 with the gap between 38 home days Championship cricket and eight Sunday games being narrowed to just over 3,000. It showed the Sunday support that was available and it was to be rewarded very quickly. It was a unique season in that the County's two pacemen Brown and Sayer, shared a benefit. It was well deserved, for between them they had given the County 29 years of service and taken together some 1,350 first-class wickets. Their manager Les Ames summed up their achievements when he said: 'It is the service

Alan Ealham, a popular cricketer who captained Kent for three seasons, including 1978 when the Championship was won. His fielding and throwing were outstanding.

of stalwarts such as these which has laid the foundations on which the present County Champions have been built.' The pair had been firm friends for many years, not only through respect of each other's ability but through a mutual appreciation of a situation in which they often found themselves competing for the same position.

With the advent of the Trinidadian all-rounder Bernard Julien, who batted right-handed and bowled left-arm fast, with an added ability to bowl spin as well, the end of the season saw the departure of Dye.

Leaving with Dye was Stuart Leary, one of the most popular cricketers who ever played for Kent and who had given 20 years' loyal service. He returned to his native South Africa after making 379 appearances for the County. A right-handed middle-order batsman, he could adapt to any situation as he had shown in the new Sunday League competition where he relished the challenge of hitting sixes. He loved to bowl his leg-breaks when he could get the chance and he fielded brilliantly, particularly close to the wicket on the leg side. He was one of the last all-round sportsmen who played cricket in the summer and soccer in the winter. His football was played almost exclusively with Charlton Athletic—he finished his career briefly with Queen's Park Rangers—and might well have played for England in attack but for the fact that he was South African born. It was a decision that puzzled him—and many of his legion of friends and supporters—because he had done two years National Service in the Royal Air Force.

Unlike Dye and Leary, Cowdrey, although he had resigned from the captaincy, intended to continue as a player under the new skipper Denness. It was the end of the longest period of captaincy, 15 years, since Lord Harris (1875–1889) and he had seen Kent rise from a very ordinary side in 1957 to one that had won the Gillette Cup in 1967, the Championship in 1970 and given notice that further honours were at hand.

Paying tribute to Cowdrey's period of captaincy, Ames wrote:

He took over when the fortunes of the Kent XI were at a low ebb. All the pre-war members of the team had retired and there had been a lack of promising cricketers emerging. There was no magic wand that he could wave, but gradually year after year through his own enthusiasm, example and dedication, the fortunes of the County improved, and for the last six years there has been no better side in the land.

By the time the new season started in 1972, Cowdrey had been honoured with the award of the CBE and his successor as captain, Denness, had four trophies at which to aim, for this was the first season of the new Benson & Hedges Cup. It was another one-day competition, of 55 overs each side, with 20 teams divided into four zones. Each team played all its zonal opponents once and the top two teams in each section qualified for the quarter-final knock-out stage. The club's 1972 annual editorial said:

> The County is indeed fortunate in having Mike Denness to take over the captaincy. He has already proved his capabilities as a cricketer and as a leader and with his charming manner should have no difficulty in following in the footsteps of one of Kent and England's greatest cricket captains.

Even the most ardent Kent fan would not have dared to predict the success that Denness and Kent were to enjoy. For he was embarking on a spell of captaincy that was to prove by far the most successful in the County's history.

Denness, a Scot, born in Ayr, had played cricket for the country of his birth and might well have won caps at rugby, for he had played stand-off for Glasgow against Edinburgh in the inter-city schools match. Kent first expressed their interest in him in 1960, in competition with Warwickshire, and he played for the Arabs against the Royal Navy at the old Nore Command ground in Chatham, at the instigation of E. W. Swanton, cricket writer and broadcaster and subsequently a member of Kent's General Committee and President of the club. A month's trial followed in 1961; Denness joined the Kent staff in 1962, making his first-class debut against Essex at Dover that season. Subsequently he had built a reputation as a batsman of natural ability, a fine stroke-player and a man who believed in an aggressive and entertaining policy. A brilliant fielder, he had been leading the County intermittently since 1969 but now appreciated that on a full-time basis he would be accepting complete responsibility.

As he was a person who believed in leading from the front, Kent were assured of having a captain willing to go for quick runs at any stage of the match, whether bonus points, a declaration, or a winning target represented the challenge. He was the ideal captain for the one-day game. In the first three years of its existence Kent had not won the John Player League title. They were a side well equipped to do so and it was one of the targets the new captain set for himself and his side.

The first limited-overs competition in which he was engaged as captain was the Benson & Hedges Cup, and Kent disappointed by failing to qualify for the quarter-finals.

One of their defeats in the qualifying game was by Surrey at Blackheath, the last county match played at the Rectory Field, the home, of course, of Blackheath Rugby Football Club. It was appropriate that Surrey should have provided the opposition on that last occasion because the venue had seen so many battles between the two counties. In 1958 the Kent v Surrey game had attracted 15,420 at a time when the good times for crowd figures had ended. As many county grounds had found, particularly since the introduction of limited overs cricket, facilities were important and car parking doubly so. That had been there in abundance at the Rectory Field until the sale of the land behind the rugby stands.

Kent lost by seven runs to Lancashire at Old Trafford in the semi-final of the Gillette Cup but by that stage they were involved in title races in the remaining two competitions. Finally, in the Championship Kent had to be content with the runners-up spot and things did not look any more promising in the Sunday struggle. Of the first ten matches Kent had won five, had one abandoned and lost four—one of the defeats being an unbelievable conclusion at Folkestone on 11 June when Middlesex triumphed by one run. Having bowled out Middlesex for 127 Kent reached 126 for six only to lose their last four wickets without scoring again. Kent's Secretary Manager, Leslie Ames, had already made out the winner's cheque and had to tear it up and start again. Middlesex and England batsman Peter Parfitt likened the victory to getting the gold out of Fort Knox. Denness was not amused. Indeed he was distinctly angry and as he and his side managed only one win in the next four games they left themselves the ultimate challenge of winning the last six games, including one against the pacemakers, Leicestershire. Surrey were comfortably accounted for at The Oval by 78 runs. Then it was Leicestershire—at Gillingham—and Kent won this vital game by five runs. Comfortable victories followed—by seven wickets against Glamorgan at Cardiff; by nine wickets against Yorkshire at Folkestone (no mistakes that time); and by six wickets against Derbyshire at Derby.

So the stage was set for the final act—for one of those big occasions at Canterbury which were to become such a feature of cricket on the St Lawrence ground during the glorious 1970s. A crowd of 12,000 saw Worcestershire reach 190 for five in their 40 overs. Gradually Kent whittled down the target until they got there by five wickets with two overs to spare to the delight of the fans who massed in front of the pavilion, waving banners with such slogans as: 'AS IF Kent could KNOTT win.' In the midst of the celebrations on the balcony of the dressing room, Denness presented Bernard Julien with his county cap.

So the new captain had his hands on a trophy in his first season. Kent had won their second competition in three years and the Club's membership had escalated to a best-ever figure of 7,183, with the side enjoying the added bonus of invariably performing in front of a loyal and enthusiastic following.

Crowd Scene at Canterbury in 1972 following Kent's victory over Worcestershire to win the John Player League.

KENT *v* WORCESTERSHIRE

Played at Canterbury, 10 September 1972

KENT WON BY FIVE WICKETS

WORCESTERSHIRE

G. M. Turner	c Nicholls b Shepherd	7
R. G. A. Headley	c Julien b Shepherd	66
P. J. Stimpson	c Shepherd b Asif	1
J. A. Ormrod	c Knott b Asif	69
K. Griffith	not out	7
D. E. R. Stewart	b Underwood	7
G. R. Cass	not out	19
Extras	lb 12, w 1, nb 1	14
Total	for 5 wkts	190

N. Gifford, V. A. Holder, A. P. Pridgeon and B. M. Brain did not bat

Fall: 1-25, 2-34, 3-107, 4-146, 5-164

BOWLING	O	M	R	W
Julien	8	2	20	0
Asif	8	0	39	2
Shepherd	8	0	22	2
Woolmer	8	0	34	0
Underwood	8	0	61	1

KENT

B. W. Luckhurst	run out	67
G. W. Johnson	c and b Pridgeon	22
D. Nicholls	c Stewart b Brain	46
B. Julien	lbw b Brain	11
Asif Iqbal	not out	21
M. H. Denness	c Cass b Holder	1
A. Ealham	not out	4
Extras	b 8, lb 9, w 1, nb 1	19
Total	for 5 wkts	191

A. P. E. Knott, R. A. Woolmer, J. N. Shepherd and D. L. Underwood did not bat

Fall: 1-43, 2-151, 3-151, 4-180, 5-181

BOWLING	O	M	R	W
Holder	7	1	32	1
Prigeon	8	0	32	1
Gifford	8	1	28	0
Griffith	8	0	48	0
Brain	7	0	32	2

Umpires: J. Langridge and K. E. Palmer.

The final John Player League match of the season. By recording their sixth successive victory, Kent took the title for the first time. A crowd of 12,000 saw them win with two overs to spare.

It had been a gallant late run, too, in the Championship race. Only one win had been registered at the halfway stage, but then the side won five of its last seven matches. The former captain Cowdrey played mainly in the three-day game where he gathered in two more centuries and proved how his reliability could be so useful when the middle-order batting looked brittle. To win Championship matches Kent had to come from behind. Early in the season they were continually batting first and being held to a draw or losing. In their seven Championship victories they only once batted first.

Johnson, recovered fully from the ankle problem of the previous summer, often opened the innings with the successful Luckhurst and emerged as a consistent and attractive striker of the ball in limited-overs cricket. Julien enjoyed his second season in England much more than his first, showing marked all-round improvement. He featured in, dominated in fact, a thrilling match-winning stand with Asif at Dover when Northamptonshire were beaten by five wickets. Kent scored 195 for five in 30.2 overs with Julien scoring 90 out of 132 added in an hour with Asif, who was feeling unwell! Knott, keeping wicket consistently well, displayed the aggressive approach to batting that he enjoyed. It provided some wonderful entertainment, particularly in the match against Surrey at Mote Park, Maidstone, where he joined the distinguished list of the County's batsmen who have scored a century in each innings (127 not out and 118 not out).

Improvements on the St Lawrence ground continued. New seating had been provided in the concrete stand and work started during the winter on repairs to the iron stand which was also re-designed to accommodate eight private boxes. The old scoreboard on top of that stand was replaced by a modern unit, the result of a gift of £2,000 by Mrs V. M. Gough-Cooper, one of the club's keenest supporters. She had also given £3,000 for the establishment of the Kent Cricket Youth Trust for the development and encouragement of the game.

With big crowds flocking to the one-day games, particularly on Sundays, the Club had dropped three of its grounds—Gravesend, Blackheath and Gillingham. Conditions there for players and spectators were not reckoned to be up to modern requirements, with car parking space one of the main problems.

St Lawrence Ground, Canterbury, showing the famous tree which stands within the playing area.

Fund-raising efforts continued with the 'Hosts' scheme remaining a popular form of sponsorship by individuals and firms, who footed the bill for players' 'lunches and teas' at all home games. There was a contribution to the Club of £4,000 from its supporters' club, where an enthusiastic band of collectors who organised the daily draws, raised nearly £2,000. The club's accounts showed a surplus of £18,000, a figure boosted by the successful playing season and the benefit felt from the very profitable Test series against Australia. What a successful season it had been—even Canterbury Week, when the President, Mr Oliver Grace, presented Colin Cowdrey with a clock and cheque to mark his 15 years of captaincy, was memorable. Not only did Kent win both matches but the weather was fine for six days—a combination which even the oldest members scratched their heads to recall.

Having started the 1973 season with a very comfortable 45-run victory over Middlesex at Canterbury in the Benson & Hedges Cup, Kent moved on to win a Championship 'Battle of Hastings' in tremendous style—by an innings and 161 runs. Denness began his new three-day season with a century off the Sussex attack and Underwood, for whom the Hastings ground was always the happiest venue, took eight for nine in 10.1 overs on a rain affected pitch to polish off the opposition.

The Kent fans were buoyant. Having tasted success in 1972

they were clearly expecting similar glory in 1973. The first objective was qualification for the quarter-finals of the Benson & Hedges Cup—duly achieved with a crushing 100-run victory over Surrey at The Oval after a 15-run loss at Hove against Sussex. Three wins out of four in the zonal games sent Kent into the quarter-final where Hampshire were beaten by 11 runs at Southampton. Next Essex were vanquished by 46 runs to set up a final against Worcestershire at Lord's.

Meanwhile there was considerable tension building up over the progress of Colin Cowdrey towards his 100th hundred. Starting the season on 98 he looked certain to reach 99 against New Zealand at Canterbury on 8 May—only to be adjudged leg-before to the left-arm paceman Richard Collinge when four short of his century. When the side was at full strength Cowdrey was batting at No 5 or No 6, not the best position from which to build a big innings, especially with the strength of the batting above. In the first match of Maidstone Week he arrived at the crease at No 6 with two wickets having fallen at the same total, 174, but his captain Denness going well. Somerset had been bowled out for 163 so Kent could concentrate on building a big lead the pair figured in a stand of 241, with the captain making 178 and Cowdrey 123 not out, recording his 99th century.

In the following match of the Festival Week at Mote Park, Kent, replying to a Surrey total of 367 for six dec were 124 for five when Cowdrey went in at No 7—just before the lunch interval on Thursday 5 July. Some ten minutes after tea, in rain, Cowdrey pushed a ball on to the offside and the fast running Asif called him through for the quick single to give him that 100th hundred.

Cowdrey admitted when he saw 99 on the scoreboard that his heart was beating faster than the medical profession would have liked. In a mid-wicket conversation with Asif the Pakistani had said: 'Just keep your eye on the ball and push it anywhere and I will run.' Cowdrey did not think there was a chance of a single when he pushed the ball towards cover but said: 'Before I could make a decision Asif was almost arriving in my crease. All I had to do was to scramble to the other end somehow. What a magnificent partner to have at that moment.' Denness declared immediately with the unbroken stand worth 202 and the crowd gve Cowdrey a magnificent welcome as he returned, smiling very happily, to the pavilion and eventually a champagne reception. It was a celebration in which the press box joined because the next morning Cowdrey sent a bottle of wine with an appropriate card for each member of the press box who had seen his 100th century—even including the correspondent who had him hitting the final single to leg instead of off.

So Cowdrey became the third Kent player to have achieved the feat—Frank Woolley had registered 145 centuries between 1906 and 1938, the 100th being recorded in 1929, and Leslie Ames scored 102 centuries between 1927 and 1950, the year he reached the 100th. Cowdrey's first century had been for Free Foresters against Oxford University at Oxford in 1951 and he was on course for an even faster completion of the 100 centuries for he scored his 90th in August 1968 against Middlesex at Lord's. However the 1968–69 MCC tour to South Africa, for which he had been appointed captain, was cancelled. Then he missed half the 1969 season because of a bad achilles tendon injury and half the 1971 season through a pneumonia virus.

Colin Cowdrey, Frank Woolley and Les Ames. Between them they made 354 first-class hundreds and 225 appearances for England.

From the end of Maidstone Week to the Benson & Hedges final at Lord's it was just 15 days and a packed-to-capacity

ground saw Kent lose two wickets for 23 runs, Johnson and Denness. Luckhurst and Asif then added 116 and with Cowdrey contributing what he called a 'cheeky' 29 Kent had a total of 225 for seven to defend. At 98 for five Worcestershire looked out of it but D'Oliveira and Gifford added 70 in 12 overs to keep the Kent fans on the edge of their seats. That is until Asif dismissed them both, and with a return of four for 43 to add to his 59 left the Gold Award adjudicator in no doubt that it should be his property. What a triumphant return it was to a Lord's final for the Pakistan all-rounder, who two years earlier had been in tears as Kent lost that exciting Gillette Cup final with Lancashire. While many of their supporters were probably still downing the celebration drinks, Kent moved on to Brackley the next day to crush Northampton by 190 runs in the John Player League.

It was their tenth victory in 12 games and seemed to be warning their huge following that another trophy was on the way. They only needed to win two of the last four games—one was abandoned and the final match ended in a seven-wicket defeat by Lancashire—to carry off the title for the second successive year.

So in 1973 it was two trophies out of four, plus fourth place in the Championship, but a disappointing end in the quarter-final stage of the Gillette Cup. Until that defeat there had been talk of the 'grand slam', but as if to compensate the side carried off the Fenner Trophy at Scarborough in September.

Leadership, the team spirit of which the captain spoke so highly and the strength in depth of the playing staff contributed much to the exciting season. For yet again there were handicaps. Knott, Underwood and Luckhurst all received Test calls and Julien, having shone with fine all-round form, left the county scene halfway through the season to help contribute to England's downfall at Test level at the hands of the West Indies. Johnson opened the batting regularly and rewarded himself and the County with 1,000 runs in a season for the first time and Shepherd, who, like Cowdrey, Knott and Woolmer, would surely have batted much higher in any other side, added some superb hitting to his marathon bowling spells. In one Sunday match at Canterbury, Shepherd thrashed four sixes in one over from his fellow Barbadian Hallam Moseley. One straight drive sent the ball soaring into the top tier of the Frank Woolley stand—a feat only achieved twice before in the long memory of Manager Leslie Ames.

A marvellous season for the captain Denness was crowned when he became captain of England. His appointment to lead England in the remaining one-day internationals against West Indies, then to take the side to the Caribbean during the winter, came during the first game of Folkestone Week. Ironically the second match of that week was against Leicestershire, skippered by the man Denness succeeded— Ray Illingworth. So Denness became only the fifth Kent player to captain England.

Back home again in 1974 Denness was still leading England and with Underwood and Knott on Test duty, Asif with the Pakistan side and Bernard Julien out injured for most of the season, Kent were scarcely at full strength for any decent period of time.

Julien's was probably the worst blow—for player and for County. Having stamped his undoubted talent on the Test scene the previous summer, he found himself hampered by an ankle injury at the start of the campaign. He played only nine one-day games and four Championship matches and what promised to have been a great season from the Trinidadian all-rounder was over. It meant that Graham, Shepherd and Woolmer had to shoulder the main burden of the attack and often Shepherd had to share the new ball with Graham for another left-arm paceman, Richard Elms, sometimes could not display the form to justify a place. So it was not an easy task for Luckhurst when he had to captain the side in the absence of Denness, for injuries also made an impact and young players were drafted into the side. In limited-overs cricket Luckhurst reached new peaks—two centuries in the Gillette Cup and one in the Benson & Hedges Cup, and in the John Player League he six times passed 50 with a top score of 97. Although the three-day game revealed some batting inconsistencies, Cowdrey hit five centuries and Woolmer, appreciating the chance to bat regularly at No 5, responded with three hundreds.

Despite all the handicaps it was still a season of success. The Gillette Cup was won, and third place was achieved in the John Player League. The Benson & Hedges Cup, however, ended with defeat in the quarter-final, and in the Championship the side dropped from fourth to tenth. The annual report somewhat inaccurately rated it the lowest position for 11 years—in fact the side was tenth in 1969—and although accepting the extenuating circumstances, warned: 'Our failure to win matches in the most important of the county competitions should prevent any complacency regarding our standing in English cricket.'

The annual report did not let it end there. It continued:

Kent's performance in the County Championship may deserve criticism in the light of our success in the limited-overs matches. In this cricket the Kent team excels, every player giving the impression that he is especially trained for the particular part he has to play and every player, of course, putting every ounce into it. When the team returns to the Championship matches, more often or not with three or four of their leading players away playing in Test Matches and their opposition at full strength, the smaller attendance makes for a less vital atmosphere. The Championship matches require a side to bowl their opponents out, rather than to contain them; here we often fall short.

Of course, success in the Championship was desirable, but on the opposite page in that annual report was spelled out the financial success enjoyed through the three sponsored limited-overs competitions which enabled the club to show a surplus in its accounts of £3,348.

That success in the one-day game also must have had an important bearing on membership. Indeed it rose to over 8,300, and if that growth continued the Club accepted it might have to consider limiting new recruits, if only because of the impossibility of providing them with adequate accommodation anywhere but at Canterbury. On the St Lawrence Ground the conversion of the top tier of the Leslie Ames stand into eight more boxes had been successfully achieved.

For Kent, the aim to win a major trophy in 1974 was even keener because it was the final season for Leslie Ames as Manager. He had resigned as Secretary a year earlier to be succeeded by Eric Attenborough and it was fitting that his summer should end with a Gillette Cup win at Lord's.

After two big victories against Minor County opposition—Buckinghamshire and Durham—Kent enjoyed a comfortable win over Leicestershire and a tight three-wicket success over Somerset in the semi-final.

All those matches had been played at Canterbury, so the first time the team had to travel was to Lord's for the final against the old one-day enemy Lancashire. Rain prevented any play on the Saturday and on the Monday, in a low-scoring game, Kent won by four wickets, steered home by Knott and Woolmer. Knott was named 'Man of the Match', having received a similar honour in the semi-final, which was his first such award.

No-one was more delighted, nor more deservedly rewarded by this latest trophy success, than Ames, whose second 'innings' with the County ended in triumph. He had taken over as cricket manager in 1957, and became Secretary as well, three years later. During those administrative years, he had managed an MCC under-25 side, a full MCC tour to the West Indies and Pakistan, served on the Test and County Cricket Board, and on the Cricket Council.

His success as an administrator was based on respect. He received it from all sides—committee members, players, members, fans. He was respected because he knew the game so well, because he analysed in a simple, direct manner and because he had the great assets of any leader—strict impartiality. In all his dealings he was scrupulously fair. He had no favourites—everyone was treated alike, with generous praise when it was deserved, with constructive criticism when need be. On one occasion he was scathing in his criticism of a Kent batsman in failing to score quickly enough. He said so in front of a journalist, whom he was talking to 'off the record'. Unfortunately, the confidence was broken and a very full story appeared in a national newspaper on the following day, with plenty of quotes from Ames. The player concerned was upset and took an early opportunity to meet the manager. Ames, as usual, was straight to the point. 'I'm sorry that what I said got into the paper, but I stand by every word of it,' he told the player.

Ames' successor was Colin Page, who had already given 26 years' service to the County as player and administrator. Many of the first-team players had grown up with him or under his guidance as they graduated through the ranks to the County side. Page found himself in much the same position as Denness had three years earlier when he took over from another legend in Kent cricket history, Cowdrey.

There were other changes behind the scenes. Bert Crowder, who had been assistant secretary to Ames for 14 years, had retired, too. David Clark, one of the game's top administrators, had retired from being chairman of the County's general committee for health reasons, and his place was taken by Walter Brice, a prominent businessman in the

County, and President of the Club in 1973. Meanwhile, Mr Clark remained as the County's representative on the TCCB, and on the Club's general committee, and cricket sub-committee.

In his last year as Manager, Ames had seen Kent win the Gillette Cup. Unfortunately, in 1975, the year of his Presidency, the trophy cupboard was bare. For the first time since Denness assumed the captaincy, nothing was won. He also lost the job of leading England after the first Test, having captained in 19 Tests, a figure exceeded only by Colin Cowdrey (24) of the four other Kent players who led England. So he had to endure again in 1975 the considerable demands on Kent players from the national side, and Kent stumbled out of the Benson & Hedges Cup, failing to qualify for the quarter-finals, and fell at the first hurdle of the Gillette Cup. In the John Player League, it was third again, and in the Championship, it was up to fifth from tenth.

The season marked the end of first-class cricket at the beautiful Crabble Ground at Dover, with Asif (107 not out in 144 minutes) recording the last first-class century on the ground, having already done the same at the Rectory Field, Blackheath. A natural amphitheatre, the ground had inspired all the leading cricket writers with its beauty, and its pavilion built into the side of a hill, making that walk back from the crease, particularly after a short stay, a very tiring journey for members of the team in the top dressing room, usually Kent.

One of the highlights of the season was the defeat of the Australians for the first time since 1899. They were beaten by four wickets at Canterbury, when Cowdrey (151 not out) and Woolmer (71 not out) engaged in a thrilling stand, which was interrupted when Woolmer had to go off for treatment to an arm injury. Kent scored 354 for six at a run a minute to win the game, and it was one of Cowdrey's finest innings, batting against the clock and establishing complete mastery over an Australian attack spearheaded by Dennis Lillee.

The annual report condemned Kent's overall performance as 'extremely disappointing' and amazingly there were, as the season progressed, definite but very *sotto voce* mumblings about the Kent captain. Certainly they were never allowed to manifest themselves publicly, but they provided a backcloth to a 1976 season which was to be one of the most staggering in the Club's history.

Colin Cowdrey had said that he did not wish to be

KENT *v* AUSTRALIANS

Played at Canterbury, 25–27 June 1975

KENT WON BY FOUR WICKETS

AUSTRALIANS	FIRST INNINGS		SECOND INNINGS	
R. B. McCosker	c Nicholls b Shepherd	58	c Ealham b Johnson	26
A. Turner	c Luckhurst b Shepherd	156	not out	25
I. M. Chappell	c Rowe b Woolmer	27	b Johnson	0
B. M. Laird	st Nicholls b Underwood	27	not out	63
K. D. Walters	lbw b Underwood	50	lbw b Underwood	21
G. J. Gilmour	c Woolmer b Julien	30		
D. K. Lillee	b Underwood	0		
R. D. Robinson	b Johnson	36		
A. A. Mallett	not out	8		
A. G. Hurst	} did not bat			
J. D. Higgs				
Extras	b 2, lb 16, w 1, nb 4	23	b 3, lb 2	5
Total	for 8 wkts dec	415	for 3 wkts dec	140

1st inns: 1-121, 2-230, 3-273, 4-300, 5-367, 6-377, 7-377, 8-415
2nd inns: 1-55, 2-55, 3-88

BOWLING	O	M	R	W	O	M	R	W
Julien	18	3	80	1				
Elms	8	0	42	0				
Shepherd	18	4	70	2	7	0	18	0
Woolmer	22	5	85	1	4	1	10	0
Johnson	16	2	48	1	24	4	65	2
Underwood	24	5	67	3	21	9	38	1
Rowe					2	0	4	0

KENT	FIRST INNINGS		SECOND INNINGS	
B. W. Luckhurst	c Robinson b Gilmour	2	lbw b Hurst	40
G. W. Johnson	c Mallett b Gilmour	19	b Gilmour	11
M. C. Cowdrey	c Robinson b Gilmour	22	not out	151
R. A. Woolmer	c Robinson b Hurst	4	not out	71
A. G. Ealham	lbw b Hurst	41	c McCosker b Lillee	0
D. Nicholls	b Higgs	16	c Robinson b Lillee	39
J. N. Shepherd	c Walters b Higgs	38	lbw b Lillee	2
B. D. Julien	st Robinson b Mallett	41		
C. Rowe	st Robinson b Higgs	3	c Robinson b Gilmour	30
R. B. Elms	st Robinson b Higgs	0		
D. L. Underwood	not out	0		
Extras	b 4, lb 6, nb 6	16	lb 7, nb 3	10
Total		202	for 6 wkts	354

1st inns: 1-3, 2-39, 3-44, 4-58, 5-96, 6-137, 7-164, 8-186, 9-202, 10-202
2nd inns: 1-39, 2-77, 3-116, 4-242, 5-246, 6-295

BOWLING	O	M	R	W	O	M	R	W
Lillee	8	1	28	0	22	3	95	3
Gilmour	13	5	40	3	21.5	2	92	2
Hurst	15	4	44	2	13	0	48	1
Higgs	15	6	49	4	12	2	67	0
Mallett	5.1	1	25	1	13	3	42	0

Umpires: D. J. Constant and B. J. Meyer.

Kent's victory was their first over the tourists for 76 years. Against an Australian attack spearheaded by Dennis Lillee, Colin Cowdrey, at the end of an illustrious career, played what was arguably his finest innings for the County when they were asked to score 354 to win at more than a run a minute. Cowdrey was given tremendous support by Bob Woolmer as the tourists' attack conceded 107 off the last 20 overs.

considered for the side in 1976, and indeed he played in only one game. Following the announcement of his retirement during the 1975 season, he had been approached by Sussex to join them, for three years. Obviously they saw in him an ideal person to provide encouragement and an example for their younger players, who could have benefited immensely from listening to and watching him. He considered it seriously, but his final verdict was the time had really come to retire. After the failure to win anything in 1975, the Benson & Hedges Cup zonal games provided the immediate challenge, and all four were won. With reasonably comfortable wins over Nottinghamshire in the quarter-final, and Surrey in the semi-final, Kent had booked a return passage to Lord's. Three days before the final, came a disappointing 57-run defeat by Sussex at Canterbury in the second round of the Gillette Cup. There were no mistakes in the Benson & Hedges final when Worcestershire and England all-rounder Basil D'Oliveira limped off after bowling only four overs with a bad hamstring injury. Kent, put in to bat, reached 236 for seven, a total which always looked too much for Worcestershire despite a gallant innings by D'Oliveira, who made 50, batting virtually on one leg. Graham Johnson, for his top score of 78, and four catches, three of them in the deep, won the 'Man of the Match' award.

So it was a return to trophy-winning form, and the next objective was the John Player League. The victorious cup holders travelled down to Folkestone the next day knowing that with five wins and five defeats in the Sunday competition, there was no room for anything but victory. A 48-run win over Derbyshire put the side on the right road, and the next two matches were won before the confrontation

Alan Knott brings off another spectacular catch, the victim this time Australia's Rodney Marsh off the bowling of Ian Botham, Headingley 1977 (Courtesy of Patrick Eagar).

with Somerset, one of their closest rivals for the title, at Taunton. The game was lost by eight runs, but a three-wicket win over Glamorgan at Canterbury in the penultimate match, set the scene for the spectacular climax on Sunday 5 September at Maidstone, when the opponents were Gloucestershire. Leicestershire and Essex had finished their programme with 40 points each; Somerset, also on 40 points were playing Glamorgan at Cardiff, and Sussex, also on 40 points, were at Edgbaston playing Warwickshire. Kent, with 36 points, had to win and ensure that their run rate was better than Essex, because both sides had five away wins. Provided Kent won, and their rivals lost, they were better placed because Leicestershire, Sussex and Somerset had each recorded only four away victories. In the event, Kent's final run rate was 4.988 against Essex's 4.560.

A helicopter bearing the trophy hovered between Maidstone, Cardiff and Birmingham as Kent piled up a massive 278 for five. It always looked too good for Gloucestershire who eventually replied with 155 for nine. The first of the rivals heading for defeat was Sussex, eventually beaten by Warwickshire. It was a different story at Cardiff. The Kent

players were off the field and watching anxiously the
television screen as Somerset and Glamorgan fought out a
desperate finish with the Welshmen winning a last ball
thriller by one run. So the helicopter landed and the trophy
belonged to Kent for the third time in five seasons. For the
second time in that spell Denness had led the side to a
double—in each case the Benson & Hedges Cup and the John
Player League.

Unfortunately the Championship form, the annual report
asserted, was 'distinctly disappointing'. The side finished
14th, the lowest position since 1957. There were Test calls
and injuries and for one game David Sayer, their former fast
bowler, had to be called out of retirement to play. Brian
Luckhurst, who retired from first-class cricket at the end of
the season, missed the final three months of the season
because of a broken knuckle in his right hand. Norman
Graham was another casualty and he was severely restricted
by injury.

The final match of the season was against Sussex at
Canterbury. Knott, who earlier in the season had beaten the
Test wicket-keeping record for dismissals by Godfrey
Evans—appropriately his 220th victim was off Derek
Underwood—hit the fastest century of the season in
Championship cricket. His 100 in 70 minutes won him the
Lawrence Trophy. Unfortunately the buzz around the St
Lawrence Ground concerned the future of Denness as Kent
captain was the major topic of the day.

On the last day of the match, and indeed of the season,
Denness gave rise to more speculation by not leading out
Kent for the final session after tea. Instead Knott took over
while Denness attended a meeting with Club officials. There
was no immediate confirmation of the captain's future and
the annual report for 1976 merely said:

> At the end of the season Mike Denness, after discussing the
> question with the Cricket Manager, resigned the cap-
> taincy and the committee appointed Asif Iqbal captain for
> 1977 with Graham Johnson as vice captain.

It was far from being that simple. Denness confirmed that
there had been rumblings in the dressing room about his
captaincy during the 1975 season. There had been a special
team meeting at Swansea during the game with Glamorgan,
when players had the chance to clear the air. Since Denness
had taken the job in 1972 certain players, he felt, had not been

A characteristic leg-glance from Bob Woolmer, an automatic choice for England from 1975 until he joined the Packer organisation (Courtesy of Patrick Eagar).

pleased with his appointment and that there were probably people on the committee who were not for him.

So on 11 July 1976, during Kent's game at The Oval, he suggested informally to Mr Page, the cricket manager, that the time might be right for him to step down and allow a younger player to take over and Denness specified Graham Johnson. The next Denness heard about the matter was when he was invited to go to the home of the cricket club committee chairman, John Pocock, when Page was also present. This meeting took place just before the sub-committee's meeting on 20 August, when Pocock said that captaincy was one of the items on the agenda and that one or two people on the committee were keen to have a change. Pocock denied a suggestion by Denness that the matter had already been decided and the decision confirmed. Denness said that when the question of the timing of his resignation was raised he assumed his views—that Johnson should succeed him—had been accepted. With no further news forthcoming after the meeting on 20 August that view seemed to be confirmed.

How wrong Denness was, because he later discovered that at that meeting it had been agreed there should be a change in captaincy. It was not until 6 October, the day before the general committee met to discuss the recommendations of the cricket sub-committee, that Denness resigned. It mattered very little because at their meeting on 30 September the sub-committee had agreed that Asif should be captain in 1979, with Johnson as vice-captain. Later Denness learned from Pocock that some of the senior players had been canvassed about the captaincy before a decision had been taken. Certainly Knott had not been canvassed and he tried—at 12.40 am one morning—to persuade Denness not to resign. In his book *It's Knott Cricket* he said:

> It was an amazing decision. Kent should have stuck with him because he had improved so much as captain. I was against his going because he had done such a good job—six trophies won in five years.

So why was Denness sacked—because that is what it amounted to? No-one really seemed to know and certainly the fans were not enlightened. Denness was, though, at a meeting he had with the Club Chairman Walter Brice on 22 November. He was told that at the cricket sub-committee meeting on 20 August only one person out of eleven had voted in his favour. When asked for reasons the Chairman said that basically it was because Denness was aloof, stand-offish, non-communicative and not good with the young players. In addition the County was concerned about Kent's low position in the County Championship. Certainly, judging from the annual reports in recent years, that had been upsetting the Kent committee, who seemed to pay almost more attention to the failures in that department than to the very rewarding successes in the limited-overs competitions.

That meeting with the Chairman probably decided the future of Denness. In his book *I Declare* he wrote:

> Having heard the Chairman list my faults I did wonder whether he wanted someone like that in his dressing room any more! . . . I did not like what the Chairman told me at that meeting, but I just wish someone had come out and said it much earlier.

By the start of the 1977 season, Denness had 'transferred' to the other side of the Thames, joining Essex. He said in his book:

> I am absolutely sure that I made the right decision, however regrettable it was. I also did not feel it was right to accept the token of appreciation which had been offered by the County to mark my five years as captain. When it was first discussed the Chairman had made it clear that it was being offered irrespective of whether I remained at Kent or not. I appreciated these sentiments but did not want to accept something that would have reminded me of the sad finale to my Kent career rather than the happy memories which I had enjoyed during my long association with the County.

Certainly he had been the most successful Kent captain ever—six trophies in five years. Were some people jealous? It was a record which most other counties would have been delighted with, irrespective of lack of form in the Championship. Whatever else, it proved that Denness was one of the best captains ever in the limited-overs game. Before Mike Denness departs from this history, it should be recorded that he played for England 28 times in his career, and was captain on 19 of those occasions, between 1973 and 1975.

His departure and the retirement of Luckhurst, who remained with the County as second-eleven captain, finally brought to an end one of the most established opening partnerships on the county circuit. It had, of course, ended when Denness dropped down the order after his appointment as captain, but it was a partnership which had provided much entertainment, not least in the uncanny understanding the pair established in their running between the wickets.

Scarcely had the Denness saga been completed with his move to Essex and the new season opened, when Kent were plunged into further controversy, with the new captain quite firmly involved.

CHAPTER THIRTEEN

CHAMPIONSHIPS AND PACKER PROBLEMS

A DATE THAT WAS TO HAVE significance for cricket throughout the world was 9 May 1977, the day the news broke concerning Kerry Packer's World Series Cricket.

The Kent players immediately involved were the Pakistani Test star Asif Iqbal, in his first year as County captain, the England regulars Alan Knott and Derek Underwood and the West Indian all-rounder Bernard Julien. They were members of a squad of cricketers from England who would be joined in Australia, during the English winter, by teams from other cricketing countries to play five-day and limited-overs games between Australia, England, West Indies and the Rest of the World, in opposition to regular 'establishment' cricket.

As the arguments were advanced—for and against the Packer plan— the Kent players met with their Chairman Mr Walter Brice at Lord's during the game against Middlesex. They were told that provided their involvement with WSC did not interfere with their commitment to Kent then the County was not worried. Unfortunately for all concerned—Club, players and indirectly the supporters—it was not to be that simple.

Meanwhile the club pursued the new season with very much a change in personnel at the top. Graham Johnson who, of course, had been Denness's choice to succeed him as captain, was vice-captain to Asif. Back stage Mr Oliver Grace had retired as Honorary Treasurer, a post now filled by Mr Tony Levick, and there was a new secretary, Maurice Fenner, who had retired from the RAF having played some first-class cricket both for Combined Services and for Kent. His father, G. D. Fenner, had also played for the County. Maurice Fenner took over from Mr Eric Attenborough, who, after three years in the post, had decided to return to his career as a Probation Officer.

Asif was a popular captain whose team selection was influenced considerably by Test calls on Knott, Underwood and Woolmer, who was later to become another Kent WSC recruit.

The new captain and Alan Ealham were the only batsmen

to pass the 1,000-run mark for Kent in a season which saw maiden Championship centuries for three promising young batsmen: Chris Tavaré, Chris Cowdrey and Charles Rowe.

Another young player to make his debut for the County was Paul Downton, then restricted in first-team appearances because he was reading law at Exeter University. He was, however, proudly earmarked as a worthy successor to Alan Knott and after only seven Championship games he was selected for the winter tour of Pakistan and New Zealand.

Interest in the first half of the season mainly concerned the run which took the County through to the final of the Benson & Hedges Cup, with one of the most memorable games being the quarter-final at Canterbury against Sussex. Chasing a victory target of 265, Kent won by six wickets with 17 balls to spare. A first Gold Award went to Christopher Cowdrey, who celebrated his first innings in the competition with a century. His 114 was then the highest score by a Kent player in the competition but it was a characteristic innings by Ealham, full of aggression, which really swung the game Kent's way. He hit an unbeaten 94 and his fourth-wicket stand with Cowdrey realised 146 in 20 overs.

An equally thrilling finish at Northampton saw Kent through to Lord's with a five-run victory, but in the final there was disappointment for Cowdrey, who was left out of the side. The left-handed Grahame Clinton was preferred as Woolmer's opening partner in the hope that he might help to blunt the Gloucestershire pace attack, spearheaded by Mike Procter. Unfortunately Clinton was dismissed for a duck and Kent never recovered from a dreadful start in which they lost half their side for 64. Woolmer and Shepherd, who both hit half-centuries, performed some sort of a face-saving act, but the result was rarely in doubt and Gloucestershire sailed home by a 64-run margin.

So it was all to play for in the Championship, and after the disappointments of Lord's, the side made the best possible recovery by winning both games of Folkestone Week. Mike Denness, re-appearing on a Kent ground for the first time since his move, obliged his many Kent fans with a half-century for his new county Essex, but Kent won the match in a thrilling finish by one wicket. The second match of the week resulted in a slightly more comfortable win—by six wickets over Yorkshire, after Underwood had destroyed the opposition in their second innings, although Boycott had resisted him in determined and polished style—a fascinating duel between batsman and bowler.

Chris Cowdrey's first Championship century—against Glamorgan at Swansea—not only helped towards a six-wicket victory but also allowed him to achieve something his father had never done—a century against the Welsh county.

The final lap of the season was a disaster with seven successive days completely lost through rain. Only six bonus points were achieved in three matches, one of which, against Essex at Colchester, was abandoned without a ball being bowled. There was slightly more time for play in the penultimate match of the season against Sussex at Hove, but rain, which had interfered on the first day, washed out play completely on the third.

So to Edgbaston and the final game against Warwickshire. Kent and Middlesex were level on points, four behind the leaders Gloucestershire. When it came to the final day Kent, after fluctuating fortunes, were on top, but Middlesex were first to clinch victory, beating Lancashire at Blackpool by 3.30 pm. Kent had to wait until the seventh ball after the tea interval to record their 27-run victory, while Gloucestershire, having set Hampshire 271 to win in $3\frac{1}{4}$ hours, were beaten by six wickets—with 80 minutes to spare!

So the title was shared, for the first time since 1950.

However, many Kent fans were riled (and indeed some of the older players still talked about it ten years later) with the decision which allowed Middlesex to postpone a Championship match to accommodate a rained-off Gillette Cup semi-final. During the three days when Middlesex were trying to finish the cup game—it was finally settled only on the last day—Kent's Championship match was being rained off completely. Middlesex transferred their postponed Championship match to Chelmsford a week later and picked up seven priceless bonus points in a drawn game.

Kent nearly achieved a double because the second eleven, now under the leadership of Luckhurst, were unbeaten and finished second to Yorkshire.

For some players the season of 1977 had been disappointing. Johnson, having been officially appointed vice-captain, had to undergo a cartilage operation and missed a third of the season, while Julien, one of the Packer recruits, was not retained. That was a pity, for he was a player with tremendous all-round talent—an exciting batsman and bowler, the type of cricketer that fans could appreciate. His left-arm pace had given the Kent attack an important extra variation and he was one of the finest swing bowlers in the game. As a batsman he could be electrifying, and one of the reasons why he never displayed the consistency for his county was probably that he never command a high enough place in the order. He was not alone in that respect, for these were the days of all-round strength in a Kent side that provided a constant headache for the captain who had to decide the batting order.

For Norman Graham, 1977 was a fabulous year. It was his well deserved benefit year. 'Big Norm's' 6ft 7in figure had helped him become known and then acquire one of the necessary assets of a beneficiary: popularity. When the County annual prophesied that: 'His great personality is sure to reap a bumper benefit', it was not taking any chances. Graham's declared figure of £58,000 was, in 1977, a huge return.

The report of the Kent President on the 1977 season, contained in the 1978 annual, touched on World Series Cricket in just the one paragraph:

> At the time of writing this report the matter is still *sub judice* and comment would not therefore be appropriate. I can, however, assure our members that we shall, of course, abide by the decisions of the Test and County Cricket Board, of which the club is a constitutional member.

The report had obviously been written very quickly after the end of the season when, indeed, the matter was *sub judice* with the High Court action beginning before Mr Justice Slade on 27 September.

That action had been the culmination of the dramatic events of the summer following the announcement of Packer's plans. Tony Greig lost his job as England's captain for the 1977 series against Australia, but he and other Packer recruits, including the Kent men, played in the Tests.

A decision of the International Cricket Council at the end of July led to the action in the High Court. For the Council had decided to ban WSC players from Test cricket, and strongly recommended each member county to pursue at first-class level the implementation of their ruling applicable to Tests. On 10 August the TCCB decided, subject to the High Court ruling, to ban from English county cricket the players who had signed for Packer.

The High Court action lasted for seven weeks and when judgment was delivered on 25 November it was in favour of the three Packer players who had taken the action.

By the time preparations were beginning for the start of the 1978 season the Kent general committee, after much discussion and a great deal of expense in taking legal advice, had decided that they would offer one-year contracts only to their four Packer players—Asif Iqbal, Derek Underwood, Knott and Woolmer—and these would not then be renewed. Asif, like Greig with England, was removed from the position of captain and replaced by Alan Ealham.

Knott, in fact, did not play in the 1978 season. He has always contended that he was told the Kent committee would prefer him not to play. Much was expected of Downton, who had been on the 1977–78 tour to New Zealand and Pakistan. Discussions between the County and Knott were resolved by the following statement:

> The Kent County Cricket Club recently announced that it would be offering one-year contracts only to each of the four Kent players who are contracted to play World Series Cricket. The Committee subsequently announced that those contracts would not be renewed after the 1978 season. It is against that background and the fact that the club naturally wishes to give every opportunity to its younger players and in particular to Paul Downton that the club and Alan Knott have discussed his future. It was mutually agreed that it would be in the interests of Kent cricket that Alan Knott should not play for the County during the 1978 season. The club and player are parting on extremely amicable terms and Alan Knott has agreed that his registration shall remain with Kent for the 1978 season.

To succeed Asif and lead Kent in what looked like being a very difficult year, with three of the senior players virtually under notice—Asif himself, Underwood and Woolmer— the Kent committee chose Alan Ealham.

It was an inspired choice, for Ealham, although without experience of the role at first-class level, had been a popular figure in the dressing room for some years. He had known the ups and downs of a cricketer's life and had remained ever cheerful, while his batting was always positive and entertaining and his fielding both aggressive and spectacular.

He had built a reputation as a match-winning fielder ever since he had appeared as the Kent substitute years earlier and had sprinted round the boundary at Canterbury to take that running, jumping catch which the striker, Trueman, could scarcely believe. Not only did his catches, many of them reserved for television, hit the headlines—so did his marvellous eye when it came to running batsmen out with a direct hit on the wicket. He was to be feared, particularly from mid-off and mid-on.

Naturally during his three years of captaincy his outfielding was restricted, but his main job was to wield together members of a Kent side whose views differed on the cricketing subjects of the day. There was never any problem, however, at dressing-room level and Ealham set the scene for a successful season for himself and the County by steering the side to a four-wicket win over Hampshire at Canterbury after hitting a century in the first innings. That was the second match of the season and it was followed by a 66-run victory at Bath. After the hiccup of an innings defeat by Essex at Ilford, eight of the next ten Championship matches were won. One of the victories was against Middlesex at Lord's, marking the debut of Graham Dilley, whose promise as a pace bowler had been identified in the second eleven. To make your debut at Lord's must be exciting, but much more so when you take five for 32 in 13.5 overs and enjoy a match analysis of seven for 46.

While the fans dreamed of an outright Championship win with the season only at the halfway stage, there was more important business in hand, the Benson & Hedges Cup. Ealham took the Gold Award in the opening zonal game and repeated that feat in the quarter-final at Canterbury against Nottinghamshire, who had inflicted on Kent their only defeat in the qualifying matches. The semi-final was won at Taunton, convincingly enough, and the final against Derbyshire at Lord's was a very comfortable six-wicket win. So the new captain, a member of the side defeated in the previous season's final, had his hands on a trophy and the promise of even better things to come. Not in the Gillette Cup though—Somerset had revenge in the quarter final—not in the John Player Sunday League. But in the Championship there was no holding Ealham's men. Two ten-wicket victories, at Worcester and against Gloucestershire at Folkestone, set up peak crowd interest for the second game of the Festival Week at the seaside against Essex. The rivals from across the Thames had to win to continue their say in the title race, but Kent defied them and hung on to draw.

County champions and Benson and Hedges Cup Winners, 1978. Standing: C. Lewis (scorer), B. W. Luckhurst, N. Kemp, C. Rowe, R. Hills, K. B. S. Jarvis, C. J. Tavaré, P. R. Downton, G. Clinton, J. C.T. Page (manager). Seated: R. A. Woolmer, D. Nicholls, D. L. Underwood, A. G. E. Ealham, G. W. Johnson, J. N. Shepherd, Asif Iqbal.

Moving to the South Coast for the victory that would clinch the title, Kent were beaten by Hampshire, who scored 313 for three in their second innings, but it was all over three days later as Essex failed to beat Derbyshire. So Kent were already Champions when they continued along the coast to play Sussex at Hove, where they ended their season on a losing note by 45 runs.

Two more catches in that final match had taken Chris Tavaré's total for the season to 48. Most of them were in the slips and it was the first time that a Kent player making more than 20 catches in a season had averaged two per match.

For the new captain 1978 was a double success and the universal view was that it could not have happened to a nicer person. He and his side, accompanied by cricket manager Colin Page and officials of the club, were invited to Buckingham Palace where Ealham, as captain of the team winning the Schweppes County Championship, was presented with the Lord's Taverners Trophy by the Duke of Edinburgh. It was the second royal event of the year for the Club's Patron, the Duke of Kent, had visited the St Lawrence Ground during Canterbury Week.

What a proud season it must have been for Claude Lewis, celebrating 50 years of service with the County, as he kept the scores through his testimonial season. He had joined the staff in 1928 and made his first team debut in 1933 when his slow left-arm bowling claimed Patsy Hendren as his first victim. He played for the County until the outbreak of the Second World War and then coached for 20 years where, among the youngsters who passed through his talented hands, were Knott, Underwood and Luckhurst. From coaching he moved to the position of scorer. Whatever role he undertook he was ever popular.

Midway through the season the Packer players' future had been resolved. In the week leading up to the Benson & Hedges final at Lord's, Kent had reversed their decision and announced that the players would be offered contracts in 1979. It was a decision which had unfortunate repercussions for David Clark, a former captain and Chairman of the Club, and President of the MCC, who found himself obliged to resign from the Club's general committee, on which he served as one of the Trustees. As President of the MCC, he was also Chairman of the International Cricket Council, which was meeting the following week. From Clark's viewpoint the timing of the Kent statement was unfortunate.

Whatever his opinion of the Kent decision, he needed to show that he was apart from it, which accounted for his resignation from a committee of which he had always been a most valued member.

For 1979 Kent agreed with Knott that he would play for just the first half of the season. Downton, having had a full summer in 1978, had decided to go back to Exeter University to continue reading for a law degree and would not be available until the term ended.

As the year 1978 closed with Kent double winners again for the third time in the 1970s little did anyone realise it was all over, the days of winning trophies would have to be memories for at least nine seasons.

THE AFTERMATH OF SUCCESS

THE 1970S, WHICH HAD BEGUN so well with that first Championship title since 1913, ended with the cupboard bare. Ealham, who had led the side to win the Championship title in 1978, had to be content with fifth place in 1979 but he very nearly picked up another trophy, for had Kent won their last Sunday game against Middlesex at Canterbury instead of losing by 55 runs, the title would have theirs. It was a disappointing performance because lapses in the field let them down, and when asked to score 187 to win they rarely looked like doing so.

Still, as the annual report for 1979 pointed out, a rise from 11th in the John Player Sunday League the previous season to runners-up, was a noteworthy achievement by any standards.

Derek Underwood took over 100 wickets yet again, and Bob Woolmer and Chris Tavaré topped the batting averages, the only two players to score over 1,000 runs in the season. Sadly the all-round ability of John Shepherd was missing for much of his benefit season because he was hampered by injury and ill health.

The County were still trying to solve the wicket-keeping situation because with Paul Downton still at university—he received his county cap later in the summer—Alan Knott came back and kept wicket during the first half of the season. That was by arrangement with the County, who then asked Knott if he would carry on for the rest of the summer. He declined because he had made other arrangements for his business and holidays. At that stage other counties had been expressing interest in his future because there had been talk about his going to Australia on England's winter tour of 1979–80, and he was feeling that he might want to play again on a more permanent basis.

He did see the Chairman of one county, and there were approaches of a more tentative nature by two county captains who had often talked to him about his future if he decided to leave Kent. One county interested was Nottinghamshire, but the problem was that Knott had also contracted to play again for Kent in the first half of the 1980 season.

It was interesting to note that in the second eleven which,

under Brian Luckhurst, enjoyed a greatly improved season, there seemed to be immense depths of talent among the younger players, in particular Richard Ellison, Neil Taylor, Simon Hinks and Mark Benson.

There were two important events at the St Lawrence ground at Canterbury. History was made there in the middle of June when the women's Test Match was played between England and the West Indies and appropriately the England captain, Sue Goatman, was a Kent girl who lived at Hastingleigh, near Ashford. They had to be educated in the local 'rules' surrounding the famous lime tree which sometimes stands inside the boundary. On those occasions, if the ball touches any part of the tree it is four, even if it goes through the branches, touching them on the way, and over the boundary rope.

Then, during Canterbury Week, 27 former Kent 'capped' players had a reunion in one of the tents. It was the first such venture and was an outstanding success, so that plans were made immediately to hold similar gatherings in the future.

In the winter of 1979–80 the wicket-keeping situation was finally resolved. Both Knott and Downton were offered four-year contracts. Knott accepted and Downton, not surprisingly, decided that he would move elsewhere and joined Middlesex.

The 1980s started disastrously. In the Championship the County's performance sagged so dismally that they dropped to 16th place in the table. They fell at the first hurdle to Yorkshire at Headingley in the second round of the Gillette Cup, failed to qualify for the quarter-finals of the Benson & Hedges Cup, winning only one game, and that by one run, and dropped to 12th in the John Player Sunday League.

Knott was back in the England side, and so too were Derek Underwood and Bob Woolmer. They were joined by Graham Dilley and Chris Tavaré, so quite obviously Test calls were going to cause serious problems for the County side.

Only Tavaré, omitted from the England side after two Tests against the West Indies, topped 1,000 runs for the season, when again injuries were a constant problem. Players were still coming through in promising style in the second eleven, with Derek Aslett and Eldine Baptiste in their first seasons showing encouraging form, while Stuart Waterton promised much as a wicket-keeper-batsman, deputising competently for Knott when he was on Test duty.

The 1980 season was the last for a player who had given unstinting and loyal service to the County for 20 years, David Nicholls, and he was rewarded with a benefit. A left-handed batsman, with an innings of 211 to his credit in 1963 against Derbyshire at Folkestone, he had been content to play second fiddle in the Kent camp, his first team appearances mainly made while Knott was away on Test duty, when he deputised capably behind the stumps. He would have gained a regular place in most county sides and could have done so had he wished, but he preferred to stay loyal to Kent, for whom he scored over 7,000 runs and claimed over 300 wicket-keeping victims. In 1974, against Nottinghamshire at Trent Bridge, he had claimed six victims in an innings, writing his name into the County's record book alongside other wicket-keeping colleagues, for none has ever done better.

Such a season, of course, meant that there would almost certainly be a change at the helm. Alan Ealham was duly sacked. Although it is argued there is no room for sentiment in cricket, it seemed an appalling situation when for the first match of the 1982 season Ealham, in his benefit year, was only 12th man.

Asif was re-appointed to the captaincy and many people felt tremendous sympathy with Ealham, who had never wanted particularly to be captain in the first place. He hadn't asked to do the job but the committee, in a dilemma about who should lead the side, had turned to him. He had done them and the County proud in that first season. One of the 'nice guys' of cricket, Ealham, a tremendously popular figure, did not feel the matter had been handled very satisfactorily and there were many in and outside the County who agreed.

Obviously there was a feeling within the Kent committee that two years of captaincy by Asif would provide the breathing space needed for the two young contenders for the role—Chris Tavaré and Chris Cowdrey—to show what they were worth. Yet again the 1981 season failed to see Kent winning a trophy. The glorious 1970s had whetted the appetite of their fans who expected a continuation along similar lines. The side, however, was still in what the annual report called 'a somewhat delicate stage of transition'.

The nearest Kent came to winning anything was in the Benson & Hedges Cup when they reached the semi-final. There was an improvement in the Championship (there

could hardly fail to be) as the side rose from 16th to ninth. Tavaré was by far the most successful batsman, topping the first-class averages with 1,590 runs and winning an England recall against Australia. Asif also enjoyed a successful season with 1,252, while Mark Benson reached 1,000 runs in his first full season. Kevin Jarvis was the leading wicket-taker with 81 wickets in a fine season. Rowe dropped out of the side mid-way through the season, Ealham played only twice and Dilley, with international calls and a minor injury, took part in only ten Championship matches out of 22. But Richard Ellison, when he came down from university, looked a very useful all-rounder, while Aslett, who finally got his chance, took it in fine style by making 146 not out at Bournemouth in his first-class debut.

On the eve of the new season Colin Page, the cricket manager, was taken ill and his assistant manager, Brian Luckhurst, took over his duties. When Page returned in mid-season the committee decided to make him director of youth coaching, while Luckhurst remained cricket manager.

Asif was re-appointed captain for 1982 but had told the committee it would be his last season, which gave them an

Chris Tavaré, an unlucky cricketer who lost his England place to more dashing batsmen and, like Denness and Ealham, was relieved of the Kent captaincy in summary fashion.

opportunity to say that in his absence either Tavaré or Chris Cowdrey would lead the side. There were those who felt that the committee had a third alternative for captain—Bob Woolmer. He led the side on three occasions, winning two of the Championship matches and almost a third, and was a player who was respected by senior and junior members of the side alike. He would have loved the job, but that was to be the extent of his captaincy with Kent.

In 1982, because of new regulations concerning overseas players, Asif and Baptiste would not be able to play in the same side. The team would also be without Shepherd, who had given such tremendous all-round service to Kent since he arrived from Barbados in 1966. There was sadness about the committee's decision not to retain him. He left the County and joined Gloucestershire.

Before the 1982 season began there was another important and dramatic development in world cricket which was to have an effect in Kent. In the spring a party of England players went on tour to South Africa, among them Knott and Underwood, while Woolmer, who was in South Africa playing and coaching as was his practice during the winters, later joined the party. The tour had gone ahead despite requests from the Test and County Cricket Board for the players to reconsider their decision. The result was that those who played in South Africa during that tour were banned from Test cricket for three years. When the Kent players returned to England they were called to a meeting of the Kent committee. According to the players, the committee made it clear that they were quite prepared for the trio not to play, but were not going to sack them because it would cost too much money. The chairman, Mr John Pocock, added that he, personally, wanted all three to play. They were given a week off to think about it and all decided to play. As with Packer, it was obviously another subject that had caused problems on the committee and, indeed, it caused a difference of opinion among members, as was reflected at the County's annual general meeting.

Tavaré, again, was the most consistent batsman in 1982. Just as the left-handed Benson had emerged during the previous season, so Neil Taylor established himself this summer as an opening batsman. He had scored a century against Sri Lanka on his first-class debut at Canterbury in 1979 and now his devastating form brought him five centuries for the County in all competitions before the middle of June. He walked off with the Gold Award in three of his first four Benson & Hedges Cup games and was awarded his county cap during Canterbury Week.

Aslett played in 15 first-class matches with an average of 31.69 and there was tremendous encouragement in the form of Laurie Potter, a young Englishman who had spent most of his life in Australia, and had come back to England to try to secure a first-class cricket future. He scored 96 and 118 against India at Canterbury and then went on to captain the Young England side against the West Indies. Knott had a tremendous season. Apart from keeping wicket in brilliant style, he only just failed to reach 1,000 runs in first-class matches, but Woolmer, after a brilliant innings of 203 against Sussex at Tunbridge Wells, was out of the game for six weeks with a fractured cheekbone.

The attack, without Shepherd, did not possess a recognised third seam bowler apart from Woolmer, and Penn was pressed into service in that role. A left-handed batsman and right-arm fast-medium bowler from Dover, he did well enough when he got his chance to earn Young England honours. Ellison, in the second half of the season when his university term was over, again showed all-round promise, while Dilley, gradually recovering in confidence, ended the season well.

The season, however, yielded no success in the acquisition of trophies for a side entrenched in a period of transition: 13th in the Championship, an exit in the first round of the NatWest Trophy (previously the Gillette Cup), a quarter-final defeat in the Benson & Hedges Cup, with the slight consolation being fourth place in the John Player Sunday League, albeit 22 points adrift of the winners.

Alan Ealham, who took a well-deserved benefit, left the staff at the end of the season, which he had loyally spent captaining the second eleven, and Asif stood down for the last six matches. The idea was to give younger players a chance, which Eldine Baptiste, an all-rounder from Antigua, was particularly pleased to accept. It also provided the Club with an opportunity to evaluate the capabilities of Chris Cowdrey and Chris Tavaré, the two main contenders for the captaincy.

Asif had two spells of leading the Kent side to set the seal on a brilliant career with the County. Whatever he did, with bat or ball, or in the field, was exciting and entertaining. He was a crowd pleaser—a category of cricketer becoming rarer over the years, particularly at county level, and Kent could look back with a deep satisfaction of his contribution over many years. Asif bowed out of the county scene at Lord's in four days of cricket against Middlesex, where he led the side to a thrilling one-run victory in the Sunday game—just the way he would have chosen to go.

The captaincy issue was resolved by the appointment of Tavaré to lead the side, with Cowdrey to skipper the team when he was absent. Cowdrey spent some time considering his future and there was speculation that he might leave to join another county as captain. In the event he decided to stay—a decision which was to prove rewarding in a comparatively short time.

Taveré's first season as captain coincided with a definite improvement in playing affairs. The team, a young one, came very close to winning all three of the one-day competitions and moved up six places in the Championship to finish seventh.

In the NatWest Trophy the side reached Lord's but were beaten in the final by Somerset in a low-scoring match dominated by bowlers. Kent finally went under by 24 runs as they batted in the gathering darkness. In the John Player Sunday League they were in contention right up to the penultimate game when they were beaten by Somerset at Taunton, and had to be content with third place. The Benson & Hedges Cup provided another good run before they lost badly by nine wickets to Essex in the semi-final at Canterbury.

It was a much improved season and promised better things to come. Support of members was renewed and certainly it seemed the protracted period of transition could be ending. Tavaré was, as so often, a paragon of consistency, and as captain his tactical skills and calmness under pressure were major factors in Kent winning some vital matches by narrow margins. He was out of the side during World Cup and Test matches but Chris Cowdrey, who led the team in Tavaré's absence, had a magnificent season. He averaged 54.60 in the Championship, scoring 1,256 runs, and finishing seventh in the national averages (57.27). It was the first time for ten years that there had been a Cowdrey in the top ten.

Bob Woolmer scored four centuries before being plagued by injuries later in the season and both Benson and Taylor enhanced their reputations. Much of the success was due to the emergence and development of Derek Aslett, Eldine Baptiste and Richard Ellison. All were awarded their county

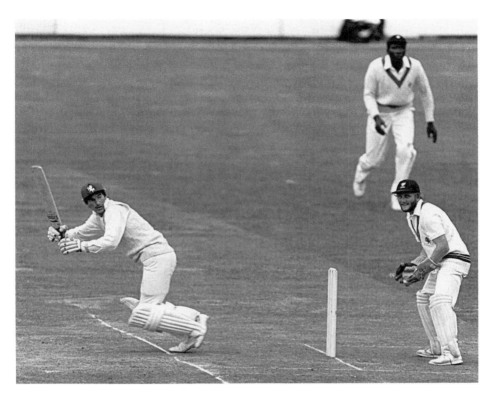

Alan Knott clips a ball off his legs during the 1983 NatWest final against Somerset.

caps with Aslett scoring nearly 1,437 runs in the championship. Baptiste was selected to represent the West Indies on the winter tour to India and Australia and Ellison bowled consistently throughout the season in all competitions. Twice in a Benson & Hedges and then a NatWest game he took three wickets in the last over to win the game, including a hat-trick against Essex at Chelmsford. He batted well on a number of occasions, but going in low down the order meant that opportunities for him to build an innings were limited. Underwood was again the mainstay of the attack, taking 106 wickets at under 20 apiece in the Championship. He was second in the country to reach 100 wickets. He bowled 919 overs in Championship cricket, over 300 more than any other Kent bowler. Dilley started the season well but was then lost to World Cup and Test Match commitments, before he suffered from sore shins and a bruised heel. He returned to bowl at great pace in the NatWest final, which earned him selection for the winter tour. It was a successful season for Johnson in his benefit year and Knott, performing

SUSSEX *v* KENT

Played at Hastings, 30 June and 2, 3 July 1984

MATCH TIED

KENT	FIRST INNINGS		SECOND INNINGS	
L. Potter	c Greig b Le Roux	2	c Greig b Le Roux	14
N. R. Taylor	c Parker b Greig	50	c Smith b Le Roux	7
C. J. Tavaré	c Smith b Greig	2	c Barclay b Wells C.	1
D. G. Aslett	run out	12	c Waller b Greig	0
C. S. Cowdrey	b Wells C.	8	c Green b Wells C.	5
G. W. Johnson	lbw b Wells C.	0	c Reeve b Wells C.	0
R. M. Ellison	b Wells C.	0	c and b Le Roux	18
A. P. E. Knott	b Wells C.	0	c Wells A. b Greig	21
D. L. Underwood	c Smith b Wells C.	6	lbw b Reeve	111
T. M. Alderman	b Le Roux	3	not out	52
K. B. S. Jarvis	not out	0	b Reeve	1
Extras	lb 5, nb 4	9	b 1, lb 3, w 2, nb 7	13
Total		92		243

1st inns: 1-10, 2-18, 3-33, 4-47, 5-52, 6-58, 7-59, 8-77, 9-87, 10-92
2nd inns: 1-22, 2-23, 3-67, 4-68, 5-86, 6-86, 7-110, 8-155, 9-208, 10-243

BOWLING	O	M	R	W	O	M	R	W
Le Roux	15	5	30	2	25	7	69	3
Reeve	10	5	13	0	18.5	6	28	2
Greig	8.3	1	15	2	23	4	87	2
Wells C.	13	4	25	5	16	4	35	3
Waller					3	0	11	0

SUSSEX	FIRST INNINGS		SECOND INNINGS	
G. D. Mendis	c Knott b Jarvis	1	lbw b Alderman	16
A. M. Green	c Knott b Alderman	29	c Alderman b Underwood	25
J. R. T. Barclay	c Alderman b Jarvis	0	c Tavaré b Alderman	10
P. W. G. Parker	c Knott b Alderman	14	c Knott b Jarvis	16
C. M. Wells	c Tavaré b Jarvis	51	c Taylor b Alderman	81
A. P. Wells	c Cowdrey b Alderman	8	c Underwood b Jarvis	6
D. A. Reeve	c Knott b Ellison	0	c Ellison b Alderman	3
I. A. Greig	lbw b Jarvis	15	c Potter b Ellison	27
G. S. Le Roux	c Alderman b Ellison	18	c Tavaré b Ellison	0
D. J. Smith	c Johnson b Alderman	2	c Tavaré b Alderman	1
C. E. Waller	not out	0	not out	1
Extras	lb 1, nb 4	5	lb 1, w 1, nb 4	6
Total		143		192

1st inns: 1-1, 2-2, 3-40, 4-67, 5-79, 6-84, 7-105, 8-125, 9-143, 10-143
2nd inns: 1-39, 2-45, 3-58, 4-58, 5-89, 6-113, 7-186, 8-190, 10-192

BOWLING	O	M	R	W		O	M	R	W
Alderman	16	7	46	4		23.1	7	60	5
Jarvis	16	7	34	4		11	2	33	2
Ellison	14.4	4	29	2		17	5	29	2
Cowdrey	6	1	15	0		4	0	21	0
Underwood	2	0	14	0		13	3	43	1

Umpires: A. G. T. Whitehead and H. D. Bird.

The first tied match in the Championship for ten years. Kent had not been involved in a tied game since 1950, yet only a fortnight later, at Northampton, they were to be concerned in another tie! The match at Hastings was also significant because it provided Derek Underwood, whose favourite ground it had always been as a bowler, with his only century in first-class cricket after he had come in as night watchman.

brilliantly again behind the stumps, scored 848 runs in the Championship. For Potter it was a disappointing season. He was selected for MCC against the Champion County in May but the match was washed out by rain and he was not picked for the County side at the beginning of the season, thereafter being unable to establish himself on a regular basis. In contrast, Simon Hinks, a forceful left-handed batsman, promised well when he got into the County side. All in all, it was felt that if Kent could have more penetrative power in their bowling they could scale the heights in the Championship in 1984 and be an even harder side to beat in the one-day competitions.

During the season, thanks to the generosity of Mrs Nina Pearce, who wished to commemorate her husband, the late Mr T. A. Pearce, a former President, the curators displayed a collection of beautifully framed photographs of all capped players from 1900 to the present day in the pavilion. A plaque to mark this was unveiled by Mrs Pearce at a reception held during Canterbury Week when the County's oldest living capped player, Jack Bryan, was present.

Not surprisingly, the 1984 season started with real hopes of winning one of the one-day competitions, but these, alas, proved ill-founded. It had been clear that in the previous season the bowling often lacked penetration; in 1984 this threatened to be an even more serious problem, with Graham Dilley absent for the whole season. He had returned from the tour of Pakistan early because of trouble with a side injury, and examinations revealed that he needed to have a very delicate neck operation. In fact a piece of bone was cut out of his hip and grafted into his neck. At one stage there were fears that he might have some serious illness but mercifully he recovered from the operation. However, his appearances on Kent grounds were purely in the role of spectator, with doubts about his future as a player. Yet despite his absence the County moved up to fifth place in the Championship table, having been in contention for third place right up to the final matches of the season. The bowling was strengthened by the acquisition of the former Australian Test bowler Terry Alderman, who took 76 wickets and provided the side with a very competitive edge. Ellison again did well and made a successful England debut, while Underwood was still the best left-arm bowler in the country. Those three and Jarvis all figured high in the averages. In fact, Kent had four bowlers in the top 25 in the national bowling averages.

Unfortunately the batting did not live up to its potential—there was no Kent representative in the first 25 in the national batting averages. The County finished bottom of the striking-rate league and if batting points had been merely average—they collected only 45—they would have achieved third place in the Championship.

Tavaré had a disappointing season, and Cowdrey did not have the same impressive figures as the previous year; but he suffered from injury and did enough to gain selection for the England tour of India, his cause being helped by a hard-hit half century in the NatWest final. He again deputised for Tavaré in a season when Bob Woolmer's career ended prematurely because of back trouble and Mark Benson was also sidelined by a pre-season cartilage operation. Underwood was again the most successful bowler, reaping an unexpected reward on one of his most happy hunting grounds—Hastings. Having taken six for 12 on the Sunday against Sussex, becoming the second bowler to reach 300 wickets in that competition, he hit his maiden first-class century the following day amid scenes of great jubilation. That game, in fact, was tied as was the match against Northampton a few weeks later—two in a season must be some sort of record. Indeed, not since 1934 had Kent been involved in a tied match.

The side dropped down in the John Player Sunday League, but again went to a Lord's final, in the NatWest Trophy, when they took part in what was regarded as one of the cricketing classics. Although Middlesex won the trophy, it was argued there was no winner and no loser in such a game. The advantage constantly changed from one side to the other and the result finally rested on the last ball of the last over, which John Emburey hit to the square leg boundary off Richard Ellison. It was then nearly 7.45 and the lights of the scoreboard and neighbouring residences shone brightly through the gloom.

At the end of the season it was announced that Tavaré, after two years as captain, had been sacked. He was replaced by Christopher Cowdrey, the man whom he had narrowly outpointed when the committee met to decide Asif's successor two years earlier. People suggested that the decision to sack Tavaré had been prompted by that Lord's final defeat in general and in particular because of his decision to remove Underwood from the attack after he had taken one for 12 in nine of his meanest overs. That, however, was not the case. The decision, surprisingly enough, had been taken some weeks earlier. So the Kent captaincy changed hands for the sixth time since 1972 when Colin Cowdrey, after a serene reign of 15 years, had been succeeded by Denness.

NATIONAL WESTMINSTER BANK TROPHY FINAL
KENT *v* MIDDLESEX

Played at Lord's, 1 September 1984

MIDDLESEX WON BY 4 WICKETS

KENT

N. R. Taylor	b Slack	49
M. R. Benson	st Downton b Emburey	37
C. J. Tavaré	c Downton b Daniel	28
D. G. Aslett	run out	11
C. S. Cowdrey	c Radley b Daniel	58
R. M. Ellison	not out	23
G. W. Johnson	run out	0
S. N. V. Waterton	not out	4
D. L. Underwood		
T. M. Alderman		
K. B. S. Jarvis		
Extras	b 10, lb 8, w 3, nb 1	22
Total		232

Fall: 1-96, 2-98, 3-135, 4-163, 5-217

BOWLING	O	M	R	W
Cowans	9	2	24	0
Daniel	12	1	41	2
Hughes	10	0	52	0
Edmonds	5	0	33	0
Slack	12	2	33	1
Emburey	12	1	27	1

MIDDLESEX

G. D. Barlow	c Waterton b Jarvis	25
W. N. Slack	b Ellison	20
M. W. Gatting	c Tavaré b Jarvis	37
R. O. Butcher	b Underwood	15
C. T. Radley	c Tavaré b Ellison	67
P. R. Downton	c Cowdrey b Jarvis	40
J. E. Emburey	not out	17
P. H. Edmonds	not out	5
S. P. Hughes, N. G. Cowans,		
W. W. Daniel did not bat		
Extras	lb 7, w 1, nb 2	10
Total		236

Fall: 1-39, 2-60, 3-88, 4-124, 5-211, 6-217

BOWLING

	O	M	R	W
Alderman	12	0	53	0
Jarvis	12	1	47	3
Ellison	12	2	53	2
Cowdrey	12	1	48	0
Underwood	12	2	25	1

Umpires: H. D. Bird and B. J. Meyer.

Bidding to win their first cricket trophy since 1978, Kent were beaten off the last ball of an exciting match when John Emburey, with the scores level and the clock showing nearly 7.45 pm, hit Richard Ellison to the square leg boundary. Had he not scored off that final delivery Kent would have won because, with scores and wickets level, their score at the end of the first 30 overs was higher.

EXIT KNOTT AND UNDERWOOD

KENT'S NEW CAPTAIN, CHRIS COWDREY, had benefited most from that 1984 final at Lord's because his innings of 58 in 57 minutes probably clinched his place in the England party to tour India, when he played in all five Tests, performing usefully without really asserting himself. Back in England in 1985 the challenge of captaining Kent proved to be a frustrating experience for the new skipper and for the County generally. On paper the squad was one of the strongest in the country. Expectations were high, certainly from those who backed the new captain, and the stage was set for the success which had proved so elusive since 1978.

The Club had launched its Project Appeal, designed to raise the funds for a new multi-purpose stand on the St Lawrence ground, so from all points of view good weather and success in the middle were the main ingredients very much needed for the season. They were not forthcoming in either direction. The weather was continually depressing and a handicap to playing success, while the side, troubled further by injuries to key players, lacked consistency.

Cowdrey started the season superbly: in the second Championship match, against Surrey at Canterbury, he scored 159 in the first innings and 95 in the second. Unfortunately he could not maintain that form, but neither he nor Tavaré were probably prepared to agree that batting struggles had anything to do with the cares of captaincy. Batting failure generally was the hallmark of Kent's early-season performance in the Championship. There was a run of six successive Championship innings when the side reached 200 only in the sixth—200 exactly—and that was not enough to save them from the second defeat in a disastrous Week at Tunbridge Wells. It was the batting again which let the side down so dismally when they reached the semi-final of the Benson & Hedges Cup against Leicestershire.

The John Player Sunday League title looked well within their grasp as they led the table with only one defeat in eight games. Then a crushing defeat at Maidstone by Northamptonshire saw them conclude the season without another Sunday victory. Three Championship wins in four games

The club's reigning captain, Chris Cowdrey. An enthusiastic all-rounder, his task is to get Kent back to winning ways in the late 1980s and 1990s.

provided some hope, but that was soon dashed as injuries and inconsistency caused changes in the side.

The left-handed Hinks, from Gravesend, a powerful stroke maker, scored over 1,400 runs in his first full season in the Championship, as did his partner Benson. But Aslett lost his place halfway through the season to Taylor and by the end of the summer Graham Cowdrey, the youngest of Colin Cowdrey's three sons, had forced his way into the first team on the strength of some prolific scoring in the second eleven. Baptiste, back from a season on tour with the West Indies and the only overseas player on the books that summer, enjoyed a successful time with bat and ball. But Jarvis, Ellison and Dilley were all, in varying degrees, afflicted by injuries.

By the end of August the wind of change was really blowing at Canterbury. It was announced that three players would not be re-engaged—Johnson, who was in his 21st year with the County, and two second-eleven players, Lindsay Wood, a slow left-arm bowler, and paceman Kevin Masters.

Johnson's contract was cancelled forthwith, disciplinary action taken on account of his refusal to play against the Australians at Canterbury. About that incident there were weighty arguments on both sides, each being very aggrieved, and it was most unfortunate that a player who had given such very good service over a long period saw his career ended in such a manner. Whatever the rights and wrongs of the affair, the decision inevitably had an unsettling effect in the dressing room. Suffice it to say it was hardly a satisfactory arrangement for the strength and balance of the side because Johnson was a very capable all-round batsman in a wide variety of places in the order in both the one and three-day games. Moreover, his role of off-spinner had still to be filled. The position was further complicated when Potter, who was being groomed as a left-arm spin bowler, having switched from slow-medium pace, announced that he would be leaving the County and subsequently joined Leicestershire, one of several counties who had been quick to bid for his services. Although that summer he had been given more chances in the first eleven, it was more for the hope that he could develop into a spin partner for Underwood, and perhaps in due course a successor, than for his obvious batting talent which, after his brilliant beginning, was emerging only fitfully.

If all that were not enough to cast a shadow over the County's future prospects, the penultimate afternoon of the season yielded the decision of Knott to retire from first-class cricket. Although he had been having little chance to prove his batting ability at the highest level, he had kept wicket so consistently well that he was close to an England recall to add to the 95 caps already earned. Towards the end of the season he had suffered from a recurrence of an ankle injury and that, he said, prompted his retirement. The club acknowledged his 'outstanding services to the County and to English cricket', adding that 'his ability and professionalism have ranked him among the truly great players in the history of the game.' Not only that. He was, of course, one of the real characters. His professional approach dictated that he could not possibly play on if there was the slightest doubt about his fitness. Whether keeping wicket or batting, he always provided superb entertainment in a modest, very likeable manner which endeared him to fans and fellow players alike wherever he went. The sun-hat, the handkerchief protruding from a pocket, the sleeves rolled down, the pieces of sticking plaster adhering to pads and clothing were his own trademarks. They irritated some people, as did the continual exercises which he did in the middle, but it never worried him—he had devised them all for a purpose. He will not be remembered for these trademarks, but for the brilliant diving catches, the superb stumpings which made wicket-keeping look so easy and for the strokes, textbook and otherwise, which left opposing bowlers scratching their heads in wonderment—and one suspects with admiration. So the little man who had been told over 20 years earlier by one of the previous great Kent wicket-keepers, Les Ames, that he might do better to concentrate on his off-spin bowling because Kent were well off for wicket-keepers, had played his last game. There was no time for a farewell match—and that is probably the way he wanted it. For the record his last Championship match was at Worcester, where he was out for just a single and his last victim, caught off Baptiste, was Damian D'Oliveira, son of the legendary Basil with whom Knott had played at international level and admired so much as a great all-round player. When Knott was out for a duck in his last appearance for the County in a Sunday game against Derbyshire, it was at Folkestone, where it had all begun for this very brilliant wicket-keeper-batsman way back in 1964, with his first-class debut against Cambridge University.

Knott's departure meant that the County had to decide once and for all on the merits of their two reserve wicket-keepers, Steven Marsh and Stuart Waterton, who had been given equal opportunities in the first eleven during his absence through injury. It must have been a close run contest but Marsh got the verdict. Waterton decided to try his luck elsewhere and was signed by Northamptonshire. That completed the change of personnel, but had Dilley had his way he would have joined the exodus. Right at the end of the season he asked to have his contract terminated but, as other counties gathered to begin the chase for his services, Kent ruled that he would have to stay because his contract still had another year to run.

So there was a certain amount of shaking down to be done when the 1986 season started. But when it had ended Kent were still left looking for something to put in that trophy cupboard which had been empty for eight years. They had come desperately close to remedying that situation in another Lord's final. Having battled their way through away ties in the quarter-final and semi-final of the Benson & Hedges Cup,

229

they fell at the final hurdle, going under by two runs to Middlesex in a match which they were tantalisingly close to winning. It was that or nothing, because they had been soundly beaten by Nottinghamshire at Trent Bridge three days earlier in the NatWest Trophy. That followed a comfortable passage through the first round at Edinburgh when they played their first competitive match against Scotland.

The Sunday form was too much of a repetition of the previous season to provide ultimate success. A brilliant start could not be maintained, although there was some encouragement to be derived from the move up the table to sixth—four places higher than in the previous summer. In the Championship, Kent finished eighth, one place up, and once more it was inconsistency, particularly in the batting, which proved their downfall.

Throughout the previous winter the pace bowling department of the side had been closely examined by the committee. They were, it seemed, united on the need for an import and it was just a question of who fitted the bill best. Unnamed West Indians and South Africans were considered, and Australia's new pace-bowling hope, Craig McDermott, was approached but declined. Finally Terry Alderman, who had been so successful with the County two years earlier, was welcomed back.

Alderman had spent the winter in South Africa with the Australian touring party but that, quite rightly, was not held against him. Times and opinions had changed since the reaction to Knott, Underwood and Woolmer for their excursion to the same country with an England side four years earlier.

So Kent had to deal with the problems obviously created by having two overseas players on their staff—West Indian Baptiste was the other—and being able to play only one of them. It was resolved by playing Alderman in the three-day game, and Baptiste in the limited-overs cricket, and from the performance viewpoint it could not have worked better.

Alderman, fresh from becoming a father, did not fly in until the third Championship game in which he immediately made an impact—his match haul of nine for 105 helping Kent to a 25-run victory over Essex at Chelmsford. From then on the captain could hardly stop him bowling, and probably did not want to, because he took wickets with monotonous but very agreeable regularity. Only a shoulder injury which sidelined him for the last two matches and prevented him from bowling in the second innings of the previous game stopped him reaching 100 wickets. He finished two short and was bitterly disappointed. But such was the character of the man that, desperately as he wanted to play, he would not risk his side's fortunes by doing so unless fully fit. Alderman was, and is, a top-quality fast-medium bowler who could move the ball appreciably off the wicket and through the air and could bowl much faster at times than batsmen expected. His competitiveness could never be faulted. He had a determination to do well which rubbed off on his colleagues, and was always ready to help and advise other players. The Kent annual report on the 1986 season said:

> Our thanks to Terry Alderman for his invaluable and unstinted service to Kent cricket both on and off the field. His 98 wickets in Championship matches, in spite of persistent injuries throughout the season, reflected great courage and devotion to his adopted county.

The presence of Alderman at the other end brought the best out of Dilley and they dominated the County's pace and

Graham Dilley lets fly. Despite being injury-prone, Dilley had become the leading English fast bowler by the time he left Kent to join Worcestershire for the 1987 season.

seam attack, although Dilley was missing for nearly half the summer because he was on England duty. However, he had the satisfaction of recording his second hat-trick for the County in successive seasons when he achieved the feat against Essex at Chelmsford, having to wait over an hour and 20 minutes to complete it. At The Oval the previous season against Surrey, it had been a straightforward treble but at Chelmsford it was somewhat unusual. He had taken a wicket with his last ball before lunch, which was extended to 84 minutes because of rain. Then he took two wickets with his first two deliveries after lunch to register a hat-trick which escaped the immediate notice of some of the fans. It was recorded in the Kent scorebook by Lewis, who had gone through a very similar experience when he took his only hat-trick—at Trent Bridge against Nottinghamshire way back in 1939. He had taken two wickets with the last two deliveries before lunch, which was of the normal duration, before getting the third with his first ball after the interval. Unfortunately Richard Ellison had a disappointing summer, but the County were encouraged by the form shown by young paceman Alan Igglesden, until a side muscle injury ended his season earlier than expected. The 1986 season was important for Steven Marsh who had taken over an onerous responsibility, replacing Knott behind the wicket. What an act to try and follow—and Marsh was not unappreciative of the enormity of his task. He was determined that it would not worry him and on the face of it no-one could say it did. He had won the right to succeed Knott in a straight fight over the previous few seasons with Waterton, whom many would have argued had the edge as a batsman. Whether Marsh agreed or not he ensured during the winter of 1985–86 that he would concentrate on this aspect of his game. He did, under the watchful and very helpful eye of former Kent and England batsman Bob Woolmer, back in Cape Town working and coaching at the Avendale Club. Woolmer was pleased with the progress of Marsh and so were the Kent officials and fans when he returned. He scored important runs right from the start of the season, which brought him a tally of 857 at an average of 30.60.

The six months between the end of the 1986 season and the start of the 1987 campaign influenced very considerably the fate of Kent in the immediate future. Dilley, who had sought to be released from his contract at the end of the 1985 season without success, became a free agent when his contract expired at the end of 1986. It became obvious that he would move, for many of the other first-class counties were interested in the man who, during that winter in Australia, emerged as England's leading paceman. The battle for his services was joined, with Kent doing their best to retain him and using captain Chris Cowdrey, who journeyed on holiday to Sydney to negotiate on the spot. He was not alone—other counties had sent their representatives to provide serious opposition. Meanwhile Kent had learned that Alderman, who had enjoyed two very successful seasons in English cricket, would not be returning. That was a severe blow, and when eventually Dilley followed his England colleague Ian Botham to Worcestershire the County was suddenly shorn of the services of its two main strike bowlers, both of international calibre. Yet another dark cloud was looming for Richard Ellison, another Test bowler and a player whose all-round strength was so vital to the side, had returned from a winter playing in Tasmania suffering from back trouble. It was admitted that he would be a doubtful starter for the new season. Indeed he was—and what was even more catastrophic, he did not play any first-class cricket during the summer of 1987.

Before the start of the new season Kent had announced the appointment of a county coach for the first time since the late 1950s—and the man they chose was Woolmer, on a one-year contract. Woolmer had been living and working in South Africa since his playing career ended, and had steadily over the years built up a reputation as a top-class coach. He had been a member of that all-conquering Kent side in the 1970s and had great experience of the game at county and international level. His medium-pace bowling in the one-day game, where he quickly assessed the need to bowl a good length and to bowl straight, had been invaluable, and his batting, once he was given the opportunity to go in higher up the order, was of the highest class. He had ended his playing days with Kent as an opener, and those who had seen his double-century on his home ground at Tunbridge Wells were treated to a fine display of batting. So the Kent pattern had changed with the return of a coach instead of a manager, for Luckhurst, at the end of the 1985 season, had switched from the role of cricket manager to that of cricket administrator.

So Kent began the season knowing that they had to rely on youthful but obviously inexperienced bowlers, with Jarvis suddenly finding himself, in his benefit season, much more in demand by the first team than he had probably expected. In the first half of the season the side seemed to be getting through what was basically a crisis in the bowling department. Youngsters like Igglesden, the fastest bowler available, and Penn, gratefully accepting the chance to play more regularly than before, picked up early wickets, and Jarvis responded to the challenge. When Igglesden was injured, Kelleher, nephew of the former Surrey and Northants cricketer H. R. Kelleher, came into the side and was soon among the wickets with his medium pace. Unfortunately more injuries disrupted the side and the cruellest blow of all was when Baptiste sustained groin and side muscle injuries during the Benson & Hedges semi-final and could not finish what had been an excellent start to his 11-over spell.

Kent lost the game to Northamptonshire on the Wednesday, and by the Saturday had signed a new overseas player, R. F. Pienaar, a South African, who made his debut at Ilford. An all-rounder, who had played for Northern Transvaal, Pienaar had started the season with Worcestershire, who agreed to release him. Kent needed him basically for his medium-pace bowling and he played his emergency role well.

Things continued to go against Kent. They lost in the final over to Derbyshire in the NatWest Trophy, and their Sunday form began to lack consistency. More injuries followed—Jarvis was out of the side for six weeks, wicket-keeper Marsh sustained a bad eye injury, which allowed Farbrace to show encouraging form behind the stumps—and with the bat. The weather was a problem too, mainly because it resulted in slow wickets on home grounds, and almost all the leading batsmen made the majority of their runs on opposition soil. Benson, who had his best season so far with 1,725 runs in first-class cricket, did not score one of his five centuries in Kent. The result was that the side's performance in the Championship, the competition by which the committee had always set so much store, was disappointing to say the least. They lost four matches in succession at the end of the season, a run they halted in the final rain-affected game against Leicestershire at Canterbury, which was drawn. The final position was 14th. Only two wins had been gained, the lowest since 1980, and only the second time so few had been won since 20 or more matches had been played in the Championship from 1898. During the closing weeks there was much speculation about changes on the playing staff, and they were resolved three days after the season ended, when Aslett, Jarvis, Baptiste and Goldsmith were not retained. Jarvis had been troubled by injury in his benefit year, which he had well deserved for his years of loyal service. Baptiste had been the leading wicket-taker with 56, and his all-round ability had won him back his place in the West Indies squad for the World Cup. Aslett, after two seasons when he was in and out of the side, had played regularly, scoring 969 first-class runs for an average of 30.28.

There was another departure too—one tinged with great emotion over the final three days of that game against Leicestershire, because Derek Underwood, after 25 years of first-class cricket, had announced his retirement. He was clapped all the way every time he went to the middle, and even more warmly applauded when he returned—particularly on the final afternoon when he completed his last session in the field. That final spell was 27-6-40-0—26 of those overs unchanged—and it was 2.42 pm on Tuesday 15 September when he bowled his final delivery. He did not know that then, but he did when Leicestershire skipper Peter Willey declared at the end of the next over and immediately went to shake Underwood's hand. He led the Kent team off the field and disappeared up the steps to the players' dressing room for

The 1987 Kent squad. Back row: P. Farbrace, S. Goldsmith, R. Davis, C. Penn, T. Ward, D. Sabine. Centre row: G. Popplewell, G. R. Cowdrey, A. Igglesden, D. Kelleher, S. Hinks, C. Lewis (scorer). Front row: M. R. Benson, N. Taylor, S. Marsh, C. J. Tavaré, C. S. Cowdrey, K. B. S. Jarvis, R. Ellison, D. Aslett, R. A. Woolmer (coach).

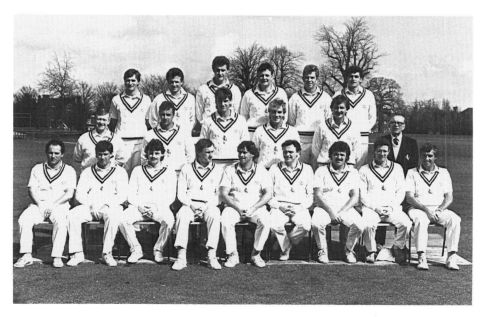

the very last time—with a total of 2,465 wickets in first-class cricket and a worldwide reputation as one of the game's 'greats'. It was not just the end of a season—it was the end of an era. One could almost sense Underwood echoing those words of Woolley over 50 years earlier when he wrote: 'I cannot now imagine what an English summer can be like without playing for Kent.'

The retirement of players like Knott and Underwood may mark the end of an era but they provide the opportunity for a new age to dawn and Kent and their fans will be hoping it can herald success again. Unfortunately, when sides enjoy the sort of success Kent had in the 1970s their members and supporters come almost to expect it, and a cupboard bare of trophies since 1978 is not an easy situation for them to accept. Lack of success can lead not only to a lessening of interest and therefore a decrease in financial receipts through the gate but also to a falling off in sponsorship—so vital these days to the running of a county cricket club. In 1987 Kent did not have a single representative in the England side and, although Test calls have their disadvantages, the presence of England players in the team can influence the targets of the marketing men.

West Indian pace bowler Hartley Alleyne was the new overseas signing for 1988, but Kent will also be looking towards their own young talent to emerge and become the Knotts and Underwoods of the future. Wicket-keepers and spin bowlers have played such a prominent part in Kent's history that all eyes will be on the young men following in those particular footsteps. Can Steve Marsh or Paul Farbrace display the sort of brilliance behind the stumps that enabled Knott to follow so successfully a long line of wicket-keeping greats? Can Richard Davis, whose slow left-arm spin has been progressively introduced into Kent attacks in the last couple of seasons, start picking up wickets with Underwood-like regularity—and economy—in his first full season?

These are, of course, huge responsibilities with which to cope, but they are not alone. The whole side very quickly now has to provide satisfactory answers for the fans. Much in the immediate future will depend on the fitness of Richard Ellison whose all-round strength was sadly missed through-out the 1987 campaign. Here is a player, when fully fit, who cannot only provide Kent with effective all-round support but also feature effectively, as he has done in the past, on the

England scene. With Jarvis, who had been such a stalwart, not re-engaged, the onus will be firmly on the young bowlers like Igglesden and Kelleher to prove themselves. Igglesden is the home-bred pace bowling hope. He has already proved effective in Championship and limited-overs cricket and the County will be hoping that he can steer clear of injury and prove to be a worthy successor to Dilley. Kelleher, of more medium pace, was undeterred when he was thrown in at the deep end in the summer of 1987 and much will depend for the County fortunes on his performances and those of Penn, who was awarded his county cap during the last match of the season. A right-arm medium-pace bowler and a more than useful left-handed bat, Penn enjoyed his best ever season in 1987 when he benefited from the opportunity to play more regular first-class cricket.

With Aslett, a capped player and established batsman, departed, Graham Cowdrey will get his chance to prove himself, probably on a more regular basis in the County side than hitherto. Like his older brother he has shown himself to be well suited to the demands of limited-overs cricket and he and Kent will be keen to see that prowess spread into the three-day game. With Goldsmith released and moving to Derbyshire, Ward, a right-handed batsman, with plenty of success in second-eleven cricket, will have the first chance of the younger players to show he is worth a place in the County side. He has been widely acclaimed as an opening batsman of much promise and impressed on his debut in 1986 against a Hampshire attack spearheaded by Malcolm Marshall. Now his backers will be looking to see him develop into a county-class batsman.

Among the established players like Benson, Taylor, Tavaré, Chris Cowdrey and Hinks there will be a need to sustain, even improve, their form. Certainly, while there is still a question mark over the bowling department, the onus will be on the batsmen to ensure that they produce the flow of runs to win matches in both the Championship and one-day cricket.

Chris Cowdrey himself is under no illusions about the way ahead. He said:

> In recent years we have lost some top-quality players and in Knott and Underwood two great cricketers. Now we have to see our good players developing into very good players. If only we had won one of the three finals in

which we were engaged in four years in the 1980s it would have made a tremendous difference. It would have provided the team with a wonderful confidence booster because we need to become accustomed to winning again.

His sentiments will be echoed everywhere by the loyal Kent supporters.

STATISTICAL SECTION

BIOGRAPHICAL DETAILS OF KENT PLAYERS

NAME AND EXTENT OF CAREER	BIRTH-PLACE	DATE OF BIRTH	DATE OF DEATH
Charles Gordon Aboyne, Sixth Earl of *1836*	Orton, Hunts	4. 1.1792	18. 9.1863
Charles Alfred Absolom *1868–1879*	Blackheath	7. 6.1846	30. 7.1889
Thomas Miles Adams *1836–1858*	Gravesend	2. 5.1813	20. 1.1894
John Edward Aitchison *1949–1950*	Gillingham	27.12.1928	
Ian Stanley Akers-Douglas *1929–1938*	Kensington	16.11.1909	16.12.1952
Terence Michael Alderman *1984–1986*	Subiaco, Australia	12. 6.1956	
Charles Dallas Alexander *1864*	Calcutta	25.12.1839	22. 1.1917
Charles Robert Alexander *1867–1869*	Westminster	8.11.1847	17. 2.1902
James Moffat Allan *1954–1957*	Leeds, Yorks	2. 4.1932	
Cyril George Prat Alliston *1922*	W Kensington	1.11.1891	21. 7.1973
Leslie Ethelbert George Ames *1926–1951*	Elham	3.12.1905	
Henry Wyche Andrews *1852–1863*	Eling, Hants	4.10.1821	13.12.1865
Geoffrey Frank Anson *1947*	Sevenoaks	8.10.1922	4.12.1977
Reginald James Hugh Arbuthnot *1881–1890*	Brighton	2. 6.1853	19. 9.1917
Robert George Chadwick Armstrong *1859–1861*	Gravesend	12. 8.1836	9. 6.1863
William Henry Ashdown *1920–1937*	Bromley, Kent	27.12.1898	15. 9.1979
Arthur Harry Ashwell *1933–1934*	Charing	2. 8.1908	
Asif Iqbal Razvi *1968–1982*	Hyderabad, India	6. 6.1943	
Derek George Aslett *1981–1987*	Dover	12. 2.1958	
Frederick Mark Atkins *1882–1897*	Boxley	28. 3.1864	13. 1.1941
Geoffrey Lewis Austin *1861–1868*	Canterbury	11. 9.1837	29. 5.1902
Ronald Anthony Bailey *1948*	Camberwell	30. 7.1923	
Reginald Sydney Habershon Baiss *1895–1901*	Belvedere	6. 3.1873	2. 5.1955
David William Baker *1961–1963*	Hull	27. 7.1935	
Edward Baker *1875*	Plaxtol	9. 2.1846	30. 6.1913
George Baker *1859–1863*	Cobham, Kent	31. 5.1838	2. 6.1870
Herbert Zouch Baker *1903(USA)–1904*	Beckenham	7. 2.1880	26. 8..1958
Percy Charles Baker *1900–1902*	Bromley, Kent	2. 5.1874	30.12.1939
William Baker *1858*	Cobham, Kent	1832	unknown
William de Chair Baker *1841–1853*	Canterbury	21. 4.1824	20. 2.1888

Name	Place	Born	Died
Edward Richard Rupert George Banks *1842–1846*	Glamorgan	12. 8.1820	7. 1.1910
William John Banks *1846–1848*	Swansea	25. 4.1822	17. 1.1901
Bernard Douglas Bannon *1895–1900*	Goudhurst	7.12.1874	18.12.1938
Eldine Ashworth Elderfield Baptiste *1981–1987*	Liberta, WI	12. 3.1960	
Henry William Barber *1861–1864*	Bloomsbury	5.11.1841	10. 7.1924
Keith Barlow *1910*	Kensington	27. 8.1890	5. 4.1930
Amos Bartholomew *1858–1864*	Sevenoaks	26. 5.1825	4.11.1907
Victor Alexander Barton *1889–1890*	Netley, Hants	6.10.1867	23. 3.1906
Henry John Bass *1871–1875*	Canterbury	14.10.1852	24. 1.1904
John Robert Laurie Emilius Bayley *1842–1844*	Bloomsbury	16. 5.1823	4.12.1917
Lyttelton Holyoake Bayley *1846–1847*	Bloomsbury	6. 5.1827	4. 8.1910
Thomas Hugh Pitt Beeching *1920–1921*	Maidstone	10. 3.1900	31.12.1971
Charles Harris Belton *1847*	Aylesford	1821	1. 1.1891
Ferdinando Wallis Bennet *1874*	Newlyn	13.12.1850	17.10.1929
George Bennett *1853–1873*	Shorne Ridgway	12. 2.1829	16. 8.1886
Robert Bennett *1863–1864*	Tunbridge Wells	1831	5.10.1875
William Anthony Burlton Bennett *1844*	Calcutta	25.11.1807	20. 2.1886
Mark Richard Benson *1980–1987*	Shoreham, Sussex	6. 7.1958	
George Prior Beslee *1925–1930*	Cliffe	27. 3.1904	3.11.1975
William Finlay Best *1890–1892*	Smarden	30. 5.1865	3. 8.1942
George Betts *1835*	Bearsted	1809	7.10.1861
Morton Peto Betts *1872–1881*	Bloomsbury	30. 8.1847	19. 4.1914
John Bickley *1854*	Keyworth, Notts	16. 1.1819	15.11.1866
Arthur Frederic Bickmore *1919–1929*	Tonbridge	19. 5.1899	18. 3.1979
Albert Edgar Birch *1894*	Bethnal Green	11. 8.1868	6.11.1936
Henry Brydges Biron *1857–1864*	Hythe	13. 6.1835	7. 4.1915
Arthur Blackman *1879–1880*	Dartford	13.10.1853	6. 4.1908
George Patrick Maxwell Blackmore *1948*	Gillingham	8.10.1908	29. 1.1984
Everard McLeod Blair *1893–1900*	Bangalore	26. 7.1866	16. 5.1939
Richard Norman Rowsell Blaker *1898–1908*	Bayswater	24.10.1879	11. 9.1950
Edward Vesey Bligh *1849–1864*	Belgravia	28. 2.1829	22. 4.1908
Henry Bligh *1854–1860*	Belgravia	10. 6.1834	4. 3.1905
Ivo Francis Walter Bligh *1877–1883*	Westminster	13. 3.1859	10. 4.1927
Lodovick Edward Bligh *1878–1884*	Dover	24.11.1854	16. 5.1924
John Douglas Jeremy Bluett *1950*	Kensington	29. 5.1930	
Arthur Blunden *1931–1933*	East Malling	5. 9.1906	
Colin Blythe *1899–1914*	Deptford	30. 5.1879	8.11.1917

Maurice Bonham-Carter *1902*	Paddington	11.10.1880	7. 6.1960
Stephen Hovey Botting *1867–1875*	Higham	5.11.1845	23. 1.1927
Herbert Edward Bouch *1892*	Bickley	15. 4.1868	28. 7.1929
Sidney Boucher *1922*	Rochester	17. 9.1899	4. 8.1963
John James Boys *1875–1881*	Titchfield	17. 8.1856	1. 8.1883
Walter Morris Bradley *1895–1903*	Sydenham	2. 1.1875	19. 6.1944
James Bray *1879–1882*	Limehouse	18. 1.1853	30. 8.1898
Henry Mellor Braybrooke *1891–1899*	Kandy,		
	Ceylon	11. 2.1869	28.10.1935
Alan Frederick Brazier *1955–1956*	Paddington	7.12.1924	
Henry Brenchley *1849–1851/1854–1857*		1827	24. 2.1887
Thomas Harman Brenchley *1849–1851*	Milton-next-		
	Gravesend	1822	19. 9.1894
James Broad *1854*	Cobham,		
	Kent	9. 5.1814	27.12.1888
Alan Brown *1957–1970*	Rainworth,		
	Notts	17.10.1935	
Stevens William Brown *1899*	Cliffe	15. 4.1875	21.10.1957
Franklin Doughty Browne *1899–1903*	Tufnell Park	4. 3.1873	12. 8.1946
Godfrey James Bryan *1920–1933*	Beckenham	29.12.1902	
John Lindsay Bryan *1919–1932*	Beckenham	26. 5.1896	
Ronald Thurston Bryan *1920–1937*	Beckenham	30. 7.1898	27. 7.1970
— Bull *1871*			
Charles Harry Bull *1929–1930*	Lewisham	29. 3.1909	28. 5.1939
George Humphrey Burke *1877*	Greenwich	18. 8.1848	21. 7.1920
Cuthbert James Burnup *1896–1907*	Blackheath	21.11.1875	5. 4.1960
John Chambers Burton *1862–1864*	Oare, Kent	7. 5.1837	19. 2.1887
John Edmund Byass *1874–1876*	Upper		
	Clapton	8. 5.1854	6. 6.1936
William Caffyn *1858*	Reigate	2. 2.1828	28. 8.1919
Ian Parry Campbell *1946*	Purley	5. 2.1928	
William Candlett *1880*		1847	20. 6.1904
Charles John Capes *1923–1928*	Forest Hill	5. 1.1898	16. 2.1933
Tom Caplen *1897*	Rusthall	23.11.1879	17. 4.1945
Stephen Capon *1950*	Snodland	25. 4.1927	
Douglas Ward Carr *1909–1914*	Cranbrook	17. 3.1872	23. 3.1950
James Carroll *1865–1869*	Gravesend	18. 3.1843	1. 4.1926
William Carter *1845–1846*	Southfleet	1822	10.10.1847
Sidney Castle *1890–1893*	Westminster	21. 1.1864	5.12.1937
Anthony William Catt *1954–1964*	Edenbridge	2.10.1933	
Peter Victor Ferdinand Cazalet *1927–1932*	Westminster	15. 1.1907	29. 3.1973
Arthur James Ceely *1854*	Aylesbury	14.10.1834	31.12.1866
Frederick Gerald Hudson Chalk *1933–1939*	Sydenham	7. 9.1910	17. 2.1943
George Ernest Champion *1892*	Stockbury	15. 7.1867	30. 8.1933

Arthur Percy Frank Chapman *1924–1938*	Reading	3. 9.1900	16. 9.1961
Thomas Cheesman *1854*	Luddesdown	1816	15. 8.1874
John Clifford Christopherson *1931–1935*	Blackheath	1. 6.1909	
Percy Christopherson *1887*	Blackheath	31. 3.1866	4. 5.1921
Stanley Christopherson *1883–1890*	Blackheath	11.11.1861	6. 4.1949
David Graham Clark *1946–1951*	Barming	27. 1.1919	
William Clarke *1854*	Nottingham	24.12.1798	25. 8.1856
Francis Seath Clifford *1849–1860*	Bearsted	17.12.1826	17.11.1869
William Clifford *1834–1841*	Bearsted	1812	5. 9.1841
Edward Henry Stuart Bligh Clifton, Lord (later Seventh Earl of Darnley)	Cobham, Kent	21. 8.1851	30.10.1900
Grahame Selvey Clinton *1974–1978*	Sidcup	5. 5.1953	
John Collard Cocker *1842*	Thurnham	1815	27. 3.1885
Colin Gibson Cole *1935–1938*	Sittingbourne	7. 7.1916	
Eric Stuart Cole *1938*	Malta	10. 2.1906	
George Edward Coles *1873*	Bombay	11. 2.1851	21. 6.1903
Benjamin Collins *1856*	Cuxton	1820	26. 8.1903
Christopher Collins *1881–1885*	Cobham, Kent	14.10.1859	11. 8.1919
George Collins *1874–1882*	Cobham, Kent	29.10.1851	11. 3.1905
George Christopher Collins *1911–1928*	Gravesend	21. 9.1889	23. 1.1949
William Thomas Constable *1876*	Poplar	21. 3.1851	31. 1.1894
David John Constant *1961–1963*	Bradford-on-Avon	9.11.1941	
Geoffrey William Cook *1957*	Beckenham	9. 2.1936	
Bransby Beauchamp Cooper *1868–1869*	Dacca, India	15. 3.1844	7. 8.1914
Charles Osborn Cooper *1894–1896*	Plaistow	5. 8.1868	23.11.1943
Sidney Alfred Cope *1924*	Hastings	12. 8.1904	
Charles Coppinger *1870*	Bexleyheath	10. 4.1851	1. 8.1877
Edward Thomas Coppinger *1873*	Bexley	25.11.1846	26. 2.1927
William Coppinger *1868–1873*	Bexley	3. 6.1849	unknown
Wykeham Stanley Cornwallis *1919–1926*	Linton	14. 3.1892	4. 1.1892
William Thomas Court *1867*	Sydney, NSW	1842	31. 5.1910
Christopher Stuart Cowdrey *1977–1987*	Farnborough, Kent	20.10.1957	
Graham Robert Cowdrey *1984–1987*	Farnborough	27. 6.1964	
Michael Colin Cowdrey *1950–1976*	Ootacamund	24.12.1932	
Frank Fairbairn Crawford *1870–1879*	Hastings	17. 6.1850	16. 1.1900
John Charles Crawford *1872–1877*	Hastings	29. 5.1849	21. 2.1935
Thomas Alan Crawford *1930–1951*	Hoo	18. 2.1910	5.12.1979
Aidan Merivale Crawley *1927–1947*	Benenden	14. 4.1908	
Sydney James Croft *1902*	Gravesend	14. 1.1883	16. 7.1965

William Crowhurst *1877*	Chislehurst	24.10.1849	4. 7.1915
Henry Croxford *1869–1877*	Hadlow	14. 6.1845	15.12.1892
Edmund Crush *1946–1949*	Dover	25. 4.1917	
Barry Stephenson Cumberlege *1923–1924*	Newcastle-on-Tyne	5. 6.1891	22. 9.1970
Charles Morley Cunliffe *1877–1880*	Leyton	2. 9.1858	15.10.1884
Edward Witherden Curteis *1877*	Warminster	17. 4.1853	25. 2.1902
Arthur Daffen *1890–1891*	East Retford	30.12.1861	9. 7.1938
Christopher Stephen Dale *1986*	Canterbury	15.12.1961	
John Ronald Dale *1958*	Cleethorpes	24.10.1930	
Bruce Stanley Darvell *1952*	Chipperfield, Herts	29. 4.1931	
Jack Gale Wilmot Davies *1934–1951*	Broadclyst, Devon	10. 9.1911	
Percy Vere Davis *1946*	Forest Hill	4. 4.1922	
Richard Peter Davis *1986–1987*	Westbrook, Kent	18. 3.1966	
John Jennings Davison *1860–1963*	Alkham	20. 7.1828	10. 5.1871
Charles Vinicombe Butler Davy *1892*	Mercara, India	24.10.1869	10. 9.1931
Arthur Percival Day *1905–1925*	Blackheath	10. 4.1885	22. 1.1969
Sydney Ernest Day *1922–1925*	Blackheath	9. 2.1884	7. 7.1970
Samuel Hulme Day *1897–1919*	Peckham Rye	29.12.1878	21. 2.1950
Alexander Frederick Henry Debnam *1948–1949*	Belvedere	12.10.1922	
John Arthur Deed *1924–1930*	Sevenoaks	12. 9.1901	19.10.1980
Robert Augustus De Lasaux *1858*	Canterbury	24.11.1834	7.12.1914
Lambert Henry Denne *1860–1863*	Thames Ditton	21. 1.1831	13.12.1898
Michael Henry Denness *1962–1976*	Bellshill, Scotland	1.12.1940	
John Dicker *1840*	Cudham	30. 3.1815	30. 3.1895
George Caldwell Dickins *1849–1864*	Elmham, Norfolk	17.11.1821	5.12.1903
Graham Roy Dilley *1977–1986*	Dartford	18. 5.1959	
Edward Wentworth Dillon *1900–1923*	Penge	15. 2.1881	20. 4.1941
Hugh Pochin Dinwiddy *1933–1934*	Kensington	16.10.1912	
Brian Elvin Disbury *1954–1957*	Bedford	30. 9.1929	
Alan Leonard Dixon *1950–1970*	Dartford	27.11.1933	
Alban Dorrinton *1836*	West Malling	24.12.1800	28.11.1872
William Dorrinton *1836–1848*	West Malling	29. 4.1809	8.11.1848
Raymond Randall Dovey *1938–1954*	Chislehurst	18. 7.1920	27.12.1974
George Charles Downton *1948*	Bexley	1.11.1928	
Paul Rupert Downton *1977–1979*	Farnborough, Kent	4. 4.1957	

Name	Place	Born	Died
William Draper *1874–1880*	Penshurst	12.11.1849	13. 3.1919
Clive Frederick Dring *1955*	Shooter's Hill	30. 6.1934	
Eliot Albert Cross Druce *1898–1900*	Weybridge	20. 6.1876	24.10.1934
Arthur Houssemayne du Boulay *1899*	Chatham	18. 6.1880	25.10.1918
John Noble Dudlow *1841*	West Malling	28. 7.1796	11. 8.1879
John Duke *1855*	Penshurst	24. 8.1830	7.11.1890
Frank Dutnall *1919–1920*	Canterbury	30. 3.1896	24.10.1971
William Dutnall *1923*	Canterbury	29. 8.1888	18. 3.1960
John Cooper James Dye *1962–1971*	Gillingham	24. 7.1942	
Alan George Ernest Ealham *1966–1982*	Willesborough	30. 8.1944	
Joseph William Easby *1894–1899*	Appleton-upon-Wiske	12. 8.1867	7. 2.1915
Brian Robert Edrich *1947–1953*	Cantley, Norfolk	18. 8.1922	
William Edwards *1884*	Bloomsbury	27. 6.1859	21. 8.1947
Alfred Elcome *1862*	Ash-next-Ridley	1833	25. 3.1889
George Frederick Elliott *1874*	Farnham, Surrey	1. 5.1850	23. 4.1913
Richard Mark Ellison *1981–1987*	Ashford, Kent	21. 9.1959	
Richard Burtenshaw Elms *1970–1976*	Sutton, Surrey	5. 4.1949	
Alfred John Evans *1921–1928*	Newtown, Hants	1. 5.1889	18. 9.1960
Thomas Godfrey Evans *1939–1967*	Finchley	18. 8.1920	
Arthur Edward Fagg *1932–1957*	Chartham	18. 6.1915	13. 9.1977
John Frederick Fagge *1834–1851*	Chartham	5.10.1814	30. 3.1884
Colin Fairservice *1929–1933*	Hadlow	6. 8.1909	
William John Fairservice *1902–1921*	Nunhead	16. 5.1881	26. 6.1971
Paul Farbrace *1987*	Ash	7. 7.1967	
Charles Leslie Dinsdale Fawcus *1924*	Bromley, Kent	8.12.1898	8.12.1967
Nicholas Felix (Wanostrocht) *1834–1852*	Camberwell	5.10.1804	3. 9.1876
James Fellowes *1873–1881*	Cape of Good Hope	25. 8.1841	3. 5.1916
George David Fenner *1925–1927*	Linton, Kent	15.11.1896	14. 9.1971
Maurice David Fenner *1951–1954*	Linton, Kent	16. 2.1929	
George Hanbury Field *1856–1859*	Clapham	1. 3.1834	24. 1.1901
Arthur Fielder *1900–1914*	Plaxtol	19. 7.1877	30. 8.1949
Edward William Joseph Fillary *1963–1966*	Heathfield	14. 4.1944	
Frederick Francis Finch *1862*	East Grinstead	1930	5. 5.1892
Ian Douglas Keith Fleming *1934*	Georgetown, BG	21. 8.1908	
William Foord-Kelcey *1874–1883*	Smeeth	21. 4.1854	3. 1.1922
Geoffrey Norman Foster *1921–1922*	Malvern	16.10.1884	11. 8.1971

James Bryan Foster *1880–1881*	Ramsgate	9. 3.1854	22.11.1914
Jack Heygate Nedham Foster *1930*	Chatham	8. 9.1905	16.11.1976
Peter Geoffrey Foster *1939–1946*	Beckenham	19.10.1916	
Charles John Macdonald Fox *1888–1893*	Dum Dum, India	5.12.1858	1. 4.1901
Frederick George Foy *1937–1938*	Maidstone	11. 4.1915	
Alfred Percy Freeman *1914–1936*	Lewisham	17. 5.1888	28. 1.1965
Douglas Percy Freeman *1937*	Sherborne, Dorset	21. 7.1914	
Lovick Bransby Friend *1886–1887*	Halfway Street	25. 4.1856	19.11.1944
William Henry Fryer *1852–1872*	Greenwich	29. 3.1829	19. 1.1919
Arthur William Fulcher *1878–1887*	Pau, France	7. 1.1855	17. 5.1932
Eric Jesser Fulcher *1919*	Bearsted	12. 3.1890	14. 2.1923
Frederick Gale *1845*	Woodborough, Wilts	16. 7.1823	24. 4.1904
Walter George *1875*	Selling	20. 9.1847	2.11.1938
Arthur Cracroft Gibson *1883–1884*	Sittingbourne	7.11.1863	8.12.1895
Alfred Gillow *1860*	St Nicholas at Wade	2. 5.1835	12. 8.1897
George Goldsmith *1875*	Brighton	7. 8.1850	5. 4.1916
Steven Clive Goldsmith *1987*	Ashford, Kent	19.12.1964	
William Goodhew *1854–1866*	Chislehurst	24. 5.1828	1. 5.1897
John Frederick Gosling *1858*	North Cray	19. 2.1833	16.10.1882
William Gilbert Grace *1877*	Downend, Bristol	18. 7.1848	23.10.1915
John Norman Graham *1964–1977*	Hexham	8. 5.1943	
James Martin Hilary Graham-Brown *1974–1976*	Thetford	11. 7.1951	
William Green *1841–1842*	Sevenoaks	1817	25.11.1870
William James Green *1856–1861*	Gravesend	1834	11. 1.1876
Edward Greenwood *1873*	St Johns Wood	19. 1.1845	25. 1.1899
James William Travis Grimshaw *1934*	Darlington	17. 2.1912	26. 9.1944
Brian George Herbert Gunn *1946*	Gravesend	19. 9.1921	
John Bernard Guy *1938*	Ramsgate	16. 5.1916	
David John Halfyard *1956–1964*	Winchmore Hill	3. 4.1931	
Cyril Penn Hamilton *1935*	Adelaide, Austr	12. 8.1909	10. 2.1941
Leonard Alison Hall Hamilton *1892–1892*	Mt Abu, India	23.12.1862	14. 3.1957
William Hammond *1857*	Maidstone		unknown
Edward Hoare Hardcastle *1883–1884*	Manchester	6. 3.1862	20. 5.1945
Norman Walter Harding *1937–1947*	Woolstan, Hants	19. 3.1916	25. 9.1947

Name	Place	Born	Died
Edmund Stracey Hardinge *1861*	Bidborough	27. 3.1833	8. 4.1924
Harold Thomas William Hardinge *1902–1933*	Greenwich	25. 2.1886	8. 5.1965
Archibald Richard Harenc *1840*	Foots Cray	20. 9.1821	5. 8.1884
Charles Joseph Harenc *1834–1848*	Foots Cray	3. 8.1811	14.12.1877
William Henry Hargreaves *1893*		1873	19. 4.1948
Herbert Henry Harington *1897*	Chichester	14. 8.1868	1. 1.1948
George Robert Canning Harris (4th Baron) *1870–1911*	St Anne's, WI	3. 2.1851	24. 3.1932
Thomas Harris *1864*	Bellary, India	9. 5.1845	28. 3.1918
William Philip Harrison *1904–1905*	Barnet, Herts	13.11.1885	7. 9.1964
Frederick Hassan *1879*		1860	15. 4.1940
Thomas Hassell *1847*	Eynsford	1819	unknown
Charles Eric Hatfield *1910–1914*	Hartsdown	11. 3.1887	21. 9.1918
Henry Thomas Hayman *1873*	West Malling	20.11.1853	8. 2.1941
Robert John Haywood *1878*	Eltham	3. 3.1858	9. 5.1922
Peter Hearn *1947–1956*	Tunbridge Wells	18.11.1925	
Sidney George Hearn *1922–1926*	Harbledown	28. 7.1899	23. 8.1963
Alec Hearne *1884–1906*	Ealing	22. 7.1863	16. 5.1952
Frank Hearne *1879–1889*	Ealing	23.11.1858	14. 7.1949
George Gibbons Hearne *1875–1895*	Ealing	7. 7.1856	13. 2.1932
Herbert Hearne *1884–1886*	Chalfont St Giles	15. 3.1862	13. 6.1906
Walter Hearne *1887–1896*	Chalfont St Giles	15. 1.1864	2. 4.1925
Lionel Paget Hedges *1919–1924*	Streatham	13. 7.1900	12. 1.1933
Walter Coote Hedley *1888*	Sidbrook, Som	12.12.1865	27.12.1937
Leon Hellmuth *1951–1952*	Blackheath	14. 8.1934	
Edward Henty *1865–1881*	Hawkhurst	11. 8.1839	20. 1.1900
Allen William Henry Herbert *1874*	Hythe	20.10.1852	14. 9.1897
Harold Lawrence Hever *1921–1925*	Southborough	23. 6.1895	18. 7.1958
John Arthur Hibbard *1893*	Chatham	7. 9.1863	17.10.1905
Edward Hickmott *1875–1888*	Maidstone	20. 3.1850	7. 1.1934
William Edward Hickmott *1914–1921*	Boxley	10. 4.1893	16. 1.1968
Alan Lake Hilder *1924–1929*	Beckenham	8.10.1901	2. 5.1970
Robert Hills *1836–1838*	Ash-next-Ridley	9.1813	25. 7.1884
Richard William Hills *1973–1980*	Borough Green	8. 1.1951	
Thomas Hills *1840*	Stansted, Kent	17.11.1796	19. 4.1866
Charles Hillyer *1868*	Biddenden	4. 8.1845	4.10.1872
William Richard Hillyer *1835–1853*	Leybourne	5. 3.1813	8. 1.1861

Philip Hilton *1865–1873*	Selling	10. 3.1840	26. 5.1906
Trevitt Reginald Hine-Haycock *1885–1886*	Old Charlton	3.12.1861	2.11.1953
Edmund Hinkly *1846–1858*	Benenden	12. 1.1817	8.12.1880
Simon Graham Hinks *1982–1987*	Northfleet	12.10.1960	
Arthur Hoare *1869–1873*	Withyham,		
	Sussex	16. 9.1840	26.12.1896
Charles Arthur Richard Hoare *1872*	Blackfriars	18. 5.1847	22. 5.1908
Richard Greaves Hodgson *1871–1874*	Manchester	9. 3.1845	1.11.1931
Frederick Hollands *1849–1859*	Leeds, Kent	7.10.1822	30. 6.1898
Lewis Hollingworth *1845–1846*	Boxley	23. 2.1826	unknown
William Hollis *1841*	Lewisham	1816	unknown
Charles Victor Lisle Hooman *1910*	Ditton	3.10.1887	21.11.1969
Andrew James Mendez Hooper *1966–1969*	Denmark Hill	17. 9.1945	
William Hopkinson *1861–1863*	Staveley,		
	Derbys	29. 4.1835	25.11.1913
Alfred Hoppe *1854*	Aldgate	6. 6.1830	15. 4.1919
Thomas Hopper *1856*	Gravesend	1828	13. 7.1877
Gerald de Lisle Hough *1919–1920*	Kensington	14. 5.1894	29. 9.1959
Charles William Howard *1844*	Bridge	1823	10. 9.1908
James Alan Howgego *1977*	Folkestone	3. 8.1948	
Christopher Burfield Howland *1965*	Whitstable	6. 2.1936	
Bernard Howlett *1922–1928*	Stoke		
	Newington	18.12.1898	29.11.1943
George Cairns Hubbard *1895*	Benares, India	23.11.1867	18.12.1931
Harold John Hubble *1929–1931*	Headcorn	3.10.1904	
John Charlton Hubble *1904–1929*	Wateringbury	10. 2.1881	26. 2.1965
Francis Edward Huish *1895*	Clapham	9.12.1867	1955
Frederick Henry Huish *1895–1914*	Clapham	15.11.1869	16. 3.1957
Edward Humphreys *1899–1920*	W Hoathley	24. 8.1881	6.11.1949
Frederick Hunt Hunt *1897–1898*	Aldworth,		
	Berks	13. 9.1875	31. 3.1967
Charles Herbert Hunter *1895*	Lee, Kent	18. 4.1867	2. 4.1955
Christopher Salkeld Hurst *1908–1927*	Beckenham	20. 7.1886	18.12.1963
Frederick Vaughan Hutchings *1901–1905*	Southborough	3. 6.1880	6. 8.1934
Kenneth Lotherington Hutchings *1902–1912*	Southborough	7.12.1882	3. 9.1916
William Edward Colebrooke Hutchings *1899*	Southborough	31. 5.1879	8. 3.1948
Alan Paul Igglesden *1986–1987*	Farnborough,		
	Kent	8.10.1964	
Alfred Markham Inglis *1887*	Rugby	24. 9.1857	17. 6.1919
John Frederic Inglis *1883*	Peshawar	16. 7.1853	27. 2.1923
Isaac Ingram *1878–1879*	Leigh, Kent	14. 5.1855	19.11.1947
Frederick Schomberg Ireland *1878–1887*	Port Louis	6. 4.1860	16. 3.1937
Leonard George Irvine *1927*	Bombay	11. 1.1906	27. 4.1973

John Jackson *1858*	Bungay	21. 5.1833	4.11.1901
William James *1881*			
Kevin Bertram Sidney Jarvis *1975–1987*	Dartford	23. 4.1953	
Herbert Jenner Fust *1828–1836*	Mayfair	23. 2.1806	30. 7.1904
David William Jennings *1909–1914*	Kentish Town	4. 6.1889	6. 8.1918
Graham William Johnson *1965–1985*	Beckenham	8.11.1946	
Conrad Powell Johnstone *1919–1933*	Sydenham	19. 8.1895	23. 6.1974
Alfred Jones *1847*			
Peter Henry Jones *1953–1967*	Woolwich	19. 6.1935	
Richard Stoakes Jones *1877–1886*	Dymchurch	14. 3.1857	9. 5.1935
Anthony Douglas Jose *1951–1952*	Adelaide	17. 2.1929	3. 2.1972
Bernard Denis Julien *1970–1977*	Carenage Village, WI	13. 3.1950	
George Keeble *1876*	Southfleet	26. 9.1849	26. 5.1923
Harry Walter Keeling *1893*	Cliftonville, Sussex	8.11.1873	19. 2.1898
Daniel John Michael Kelleher *1987*	Southwark	5. 5.1966	
George Mortimer Kelson *1859–1873*	Sevenoaks	8.12.1835	29. 3.1920
Arthur Fitch Kemp *1884*	Foxbush, Kent	1. 8.1863	14. 2.1940
Charles William Middleton Kemp *1878*	Forest Hill	26. 4.1856	15. 5.1933
Manley Colchester Kemp *1880–1895*	Sydenham	7. 9.1861	30. 6.1951
Nicholas John Kemp *1977–1981*	Bromley	16.12.1956	
George Herbert Kibble *1889*	Greenwich	9.10.1865	4. 1.1923
Percy Marmaduke Kidd *1874*	Blackheath	13. 2.1851	21. 1.1942
Simon Edward Anthony Kimmins *1950–1951*	Belgravia	26. 5.1930	
Frederick King *1871*	Harbledown	12.11.1850	16. 6.1893
John King *1881*	Tonbridge	1861	unknown
Henry Bloomfield Kingscote *1867*	Kingscote, Glos	28. 2.1843	1. 8.1915
Henry Edward Knatchbull *1834–1848*	Mersham Hatch	20. 8.1808	31. 8.1876
Cecil Marcus Knatchbull-Hugessen *1884*	Chelsea	27.11.1863	15. 2.1933
William Western Knatchbull-Hugessen *1859*	Mersham Hatch	23. 5.1837	6. 9.1864
Brook John Knight *1844*	Godmersham	9.1808	10. 1.1878
Wyndham William Knight *1862*	Chawton, Hants	5.12.1828	17. 9.1918
Alan Philip Eric Knott *1964–1984*	Belvedere	9. 4.1946	
Charles Harold Knott *1921–1939*	Tunbridge Wells	20. 3.1901	
Frederick Hammett Knott *1910–1914*	Tunbridge Wells	30.10.1891	10. 2.1972

William Lancelot Knowles *1892–1903*	Twineham	27.11.1871	1.12.1943
David Geffrey Lacy-Scott *1946*	Calcutta	18. 8.1920	
John Gordon Larking *1946*	Maidstone	4.11.1921	
Hervey Major Lawrence *1899*	Hadlow	24. 3.1881	17. 9.1975
David Allen Laycock *1969–1973*	Woolwich	2. 9.1947	
Alfred Richard Layman *1893*	Norwood	24. 4.1858	8.11.1940
Edwin Leaney *1892*	Woolwich	3. 6.1860	1. 9.1904
Stuart Edward Leary *1951–1971*	Cape Town	30. 4.1933	
Frederick Marshall Lee *1895*	Kensington	8. 1.1871	18.11.1914
John Lefeaver *1841–1854*	Stile Bridge	25.12.1817	20.12.1879
John le Fleming *1889–1899*	Tonbridge	23.10.1865	9.10.1942
Lawrence Julius le Fleming *1897–1899*	Tonbridge	3. 6.1879	21. 3.1918
William Murray Leggatt *1926*	Crail, Fife	2. 9.1900	11. 8.1946
Geoffrey Bevington Legge *1924–1931*	Bromley, Kent	26. 1.1903	21.11.1940
Frederick Barcham Leney *1905*	Maidstone	29.11.1876	25. 7.1921
Herbert Leney *1873–1877*	Wateringbury	8. 9.1850	18.11.1915
William Howard Vincent Levett *1930–1947*	Goudhurst	25. 1.1908	
Claude Lewis *1933–1953*	Sittingbourne	27. 7.1908	
William O'Brien Lindsay *1931*	Canterbury	8.10.1909	20.10.1975
Frank Lipscomb *1882–1884*	East Peckham	13. 3.1863	25. 9.1951
Robert Lipscomb *1862–1873*	Penshurst	28. 2.1837	8. 1.1895
Charles William Little *1893*	Tonbridge	22. 5.1870	20. 5.1922
Robert O'Hara Livesay *1895–1904*	Old Brompton, Kent	27. 6.1876	23. 3.1946
Bernard Henry Lock *1952*	Exeter	8. 6.1915	
Thomas Cuthbert Longfield *1927–1939*	High Halstow	12. 5.1906	21.12.1981
Richard Geoffrey Harvey Lowe *1926*	Wimbledon	11. 6.1904	
Alfred Lubbock *1863–1875*	London	31.10.1845	17. 7.1916
Edgar Lubbock *1871*	London	22. 2.1847	9. 9.1907
Nevile Lubbock *1860*	Pimlico	31. 3.1839	12. 9.1914
Frederick Charles Lucas *1954*	Slade Green	29. 9.1933	
Brian William Luckhurst *1958–1985*	Sittingbourne	5. 2.1939	
Kenneth McAlpine *1885–1886*	Leamington	11. 4.1858	10. 2.1923
George McCanlis *1873–1878*	Landguard Ft	3.12.1847	18.10.1937
William McCanlis *1862–1877*	Woolwich	30.10.1840	19.11.1925
Frederick Finch Mackenzie *1880*	Kensington	14. 7.1849	17. 7.1934
Francis Alexander Mackinnon *1875–1885*	Kensington	9. 4.1848	27. 2.1947
Charles Arthur Blake McVittie *1929*	Rugeley, Staffs	30. 7.1908	4. 9.1973
Ernest Malden *1893*	Sheldwich	10.10.1870	13. 9.1955
Eustace Malden *1892–1893*	Brighton	19. 8.1863	3.12.1947
Anthony William Haward Mallet *1946–1953*	Dulwich	29. 8.1924	

Eric William Mann *1902–1903*	Sidcup	4. 3.1882	15. 2.1954
Francis Marchant *1883–1905*	Matfield	22. 5.1864	13. 4.1946
Charles Stowell Marriott *1924–1937*	Heaton Moor	14. 9.1895	13.10.1966
Steven Andrew Marsh *1982–1987*	Westminster	27. 1.1961	
Anthony Granville Marshall *1950–1954*	Isleworth	10. 9.1932	
Algernon James Bullock Marsham *1946–1947*	Chart Sutton	14. 8.1919	
Cloudesley Henry Bullock Marsham *1900–1922*	Stoke Lyne, Oxon	10. 2.1879	19. 7.1928
George Marsham *1876–1877*	Allington	10. 4.1849	2.12.1927
John Marsham *1873*	Boxley	25. 7.1842	16. 9.1926
William George Marten *1865–1871*	Tunbridge Wells	5. 9.1845	25.11.1907
Edward Martin *1845–1851*	Brenchley	24.11.1814	31.10.1869
Frederick Martin *1885–1899*	Dartford	12.10.1861	13.12.1921
George Martin *1856–1863*	Penshurst	11.10.1833	21. 9.1876
John William Martin *1939–1953*	Catford	16. 2.1917	
William Martingell *1841–1852*	Nutfield, Surrey	20. 8.1818	29. 9.1897
James Ernest Mason *1900*	Blackheath	29.10.1876	8. 2.1938
John Richard Mason *1893–1914*	Blackheath	26. 3.1874	15.10.1958
Kevin David Masters *1983–1984*	Chatham	19. 5.1961	
William May *1834*	Linton, Kent	1808	5. 8.1888
Richard Mayes *1947–1953*	Littlebourne	7.10.1922	
Henry Blair Mayne *1835–1844*	Limpsfield	23. 8.1813	17. 1.1892
William Simons Meers *1866*	Stoke, Kent	27. 3.1844	12. 7.1902
Francis Hamilton Mellor *1877–1878*	Bloomsbury	13. 5.1854	27. 4.1925
James Edward Melville *1962–1963*	Streatham	3. 3.1936	
James Mewett *1860*		1833	2.11.1904
Frederic Meyrick Meyrick-Jones *1893–1896*	Blackheath	14. 1.1867	25.10.1950
Henry Augustus Milles *1888–1897*	Lees Court, Kent	24.11.1867	30. 7.1937
Charles Mills *1840*		1816	unknown
Richard Mills *1834–1843*	Benenden	16. 2.1798	25. 1.1882
Robert Ernest Frederick Minns *1959–1963*	Penang	18.11.1940	
Clement Mitchell *1890–1892*	Cambridge	20. 2.1862	6.10.1937
Thomas Frank Mitchell *1928–1934*	Johannesburg	22.10.1907	20. 5.1960
Walter Baptist Money *1867*	Sternfield, Suffolk	27. 7.1848	1. 3.1924
Eustace Charles Mordaunt *1896–1897*	Wellesbourne	6. 9.1870	21. 6.1938
Gerald John Mordaunt *1895–1897*	Wellesbourne	20. 1.1873	5. 3.1959
Percival Ernest Morfee *1910–1912*	Ashford	2. 5.1886	1954
Norman Morris *1870–1872*	Peckham	1849	20. 1.1874

Robert John Morris *1950*	Swansea	27.11.1926	
William Morris *1896*	Lee, Kent	23.11.1873	6. 5.1945
Arthur Edward Munds *1896*	Lydd	20. 1.1870	19. 7.1940
Raymond Munds *1902–1908*	Lydd	28.12.1882	29. 7.1962
William Murray-Wood *1936–1953*	Dartford	30. 6.1917	21.12.1968
Harry Robert Murrell *1899–1905*	Hounslow	19.11.1879	15. 8.1952
Alfred Mynn *1834–1859*	Goudhurst	19. 1.1807	1.11.1861
Walter Parker Mynn *1835–1848*	Goudhurst	24.11.1805	17.10.1878
Arthur Rex Beale Neame *1956–1957*	Faversham	14. 6.1936	
Peter John Mytton Nelson *1946*	Finchley	16. 5.1918	
David Nicholls *1960–1977*	East Dereham	8.12.1943	
Frederick Norley *1864–1865*	Canterbury	23. 2.1846	unknown
James Norley *1870–1871*	Canterbury	5. 1.1847	24.12.1900
Charles Lloyd Norman *1853*	Bromley Common	10. 3.1833	17. 2.1889
Frederick Henry Norman *1858–1864*	Bromley	23. 1.1839	6.10.1916
George Warde Norman *1834–1836*	Bromley	20. 9.1793	4. 9.1882
Henry Norman *1834–1835*	Bromley	12.12.1801	28.12.1867
Percy Northcote *1889–1895*	Islington	18. 9.1866	3. 3.1934
Bradbury Norton *1858–1866*	West Malling	23. 8.1834	21. 2.1917
Selby Norton *1863*	West Malling	13. 9.1836	11.11.1906
William Owens John Norton *1853–1859*	Aylesford	1820	25. 4.1873
William South Norton *1849–1870*	West Malling	8. 6.1831	19. 3.1916
Henry Nuttall *1889–1894*	Erith	6. 2.1855	8.10.1945
Sydney O'Linn *1951–1954*	Cape Town	5. 5.1927	
Mike Francis Olton *1962*	San Fernando, WI	20. 6.1938	
Cyril Winnington Onslow *1841*	Newington, Surrey	17.12.1815	24. 7.1866
Edward O'Shaughnessy *1879–1885*	Canterbury	16.11.1860	6. 8.1885
Cuthbert John Ottaway *1869–1870*	Dover	20. 7.1850	2. 4.1878
John Colin Theodore Page *1950–1963*	Mereworth	20. 5.1930	
Richard Palmer *1873–1882*	Hadlow	13. 9.1848	2. 3.1939
William Thomas Palmer *1867–1870*	Canterbury	5. 1.1847	2. 9.1906
Elliot Anderson Parke *1874*	Belgravia	19. 7.1850	22. 6.1923
Henry Parker *1841*	Ongar	3. 8.1819	20.10.1901
George Parr *1854–1858*	Radcliffe-on-Trent	22. 5.1826	23. 6.1891
John Irwin Patterson *1881–1882*	Sandhurst, Berks	11. 3.1860	22. 9.1943
William Henry Patterson *1880–1900*	Sandhurst, Berks	11. 5.1859	3. 5.1946
Walter Badeley Pattisson *1876–1887*	Witham, Essex	27. 8.1854	6.11.1913

Name	Place	Born	Died
Tom Edward Pawley 1880–1887	Farningham	21. 1.1859	3. 8.1923
Henry Anthony Pawson 1946–1953	Chertsey	22. 8.1921	
Charles Payne 1863–1870	East Grinstead	12. 5.1832	18. 2.1909
Joseph Spencer Payne 1864	East Grinstead	29. 4.1829	12. 4.1880
Charles William Peach 1930–1931	Calehill	3. 1.1900	27. 2.1977
Thomas Alexander Pearce 1930–1946	Hong Kong	18.12.1910	11. 8.1982
William Pearce 1878	Poplar	18. 3.1853	24. 8.1932
Herbert Richard Peel 1851–1852	Canterbury	8. 2.1831	2. 6.1885
Alfred Penn 1875–1884	Lewisham	6. 1.1855	18.10.1889
Christopher Penn 1982–1987	Dover	19. 6.1963	
Frank Penn 1875–1881	Lewisham	7. 3.1851	26.12.1916
Frank Penn Jun 1904–1905	Owsden, Sffk	18. 8.1884	23. 4.1961
William Penn 1870–1878	Lewisham	29. 8.1849	15. 8.1921
John Pentecost 1882–1890	Brighton	15.10.1857	23. 2.1902
John Alfred Pepys 1859–1869	Marylebone	16. 4.1838	22. 3.1924
Thomas Tosswill Norwood Perkins 1893–1900	Strood	19.12.1870	20. 7.1946
John Pettiford 1954–1959	Freshwater, NSW	29.11.1919	11.10.1964
Arthur Henry Phebey 1946–1961	Catford	1.10.1924	
John Brydon Mills Phillips 1955	Canterbury	19.11.1933	
Walter Phillips 1903	West Malling	1. 4.1881	21. 6.1948
Roy Francis Pienaar 1987	Johannesburg	17. 7.1961	
Fuller Pilch 1836–1854	Horningtoft	17. 3.1804	1. 5.1870
William Pilch 1840–1854	Brinton	18. 6.1820	11. 1.1882
Howard John Pocock 1947–1949	Maidstone	8. 4.1921	
Ian Caesar Potter 1959–1961	Woking	2. 9.1938	
Joseph Potter 1871	Northampton	13. 1.1839	2. 6.1906
Laurie Potter 1981–1985	Bexleyheath	7.11.1962	
Arthur Povey 1921–1922	West Bromwich	16. 5.1886	13. 2.1946
William Allan Powell 1912–1921	Blundellsands	19. 1.1885	1. 1.1954
Harold Edward Westray Prest 1909–1922	Beckenham	9. 1.1890	5. 1.1955
Henry John Berridge Preston 1907–1913	Bareilly, India	25.10.1883	23. 4.1964
John Frederick Pretlove 1955–1959	Camberwell	23.11.1932	
Roger Malcolm Prideaux 1960–1961	Chelsea	13. 7.1939	
Thomas Leslie Pritchard 1956	Kaupokanui, NZ	10. 3.1917	
John Michael Prodger 1956–1967	Forest Hill	1. 9.1935	
Barry James Keith Pryer 1947–1949	Plumstead	1. 2.1925	
Douglas Charles Gordon Raikes 1948	Bristol	26. 1.1910	
William Rashleigh 1885–1901	Farningham	7. 3.1867	13. 2.1937
Herbert Edward Rawson 1873	Port Louis	3. 9.1852	18.10.1924
Lionel Walther Recordon 1927–1929	Anerley	25. 2.1907	

George Henry Remnant *1868–1878*	Rochester	20.11.1846	24. 2.1941
Henry Waugh Renny-Tailyour *1873–1883*	Missouri,		
	India	9.10.1849	15. 6.1920
James Francis Reynolds *1890–1897*	Tonbridge	2. 5.1866	6. 9.1950
Henry Adair Richardson *1866–1868*	Bayswater	31. 7.1846	17. 9.1921
Peter Edward Richardson *1959–1965*	Hereford	4. 7.1931	
Frederick Ridgway *1946–1961*	Stockport	10. 8.1923	
Arthur William Ridley *1877*	Newbury	11. 9.1852	10. 8.1916
Giles Nicholas Spencer Ridley *1965*	Bulawayo	27.11.1944	
John Pickersgill Rodger *1870*	Marylebone	12. 2.1851	19. 9.1910
William Wallace Rodger *1867–1873*	Marylebone	13. 1.1847	23.10.1888
Batchelor Roper *1835*	Bredgar	1799	10. 1.1876
Charles James Castell Rowe *1974–1981*	Hong Kong	27.11.1951	
Robert Edwin Rumsey *1875*	Greenwich	17. 2.1844	12. 6.1884
David John Sabine *1987*	Papakura, NZ	2. 6.1966	
Philip Menzies Sankey *1852*	Brompton	17. 4.1830	9. 3.1909
William Godfrey Molyneux Sarel			
1912–1914	Dover	15.12.1875	5. 4.1950
David Michael Sayer *1955–1976*	Romford	19. 9.1936	
Thomas Selby *1839–1841*	Gillingham	4.11.1791	7. 5.1874
Robert Page Sewell *1884*	Maldon, Essex	3. 9.1866	7. 2.1901
Thomas Sewell *1852*	Mitcham,		
	Surrey	5. 5.1806	1.11.1888
Thomas Sewell *1856–1866*	Mitcham,		
	Surrey	15. 3.1830	13. 6.1871
James Seymour *1902–1926*	West Hoathly,		
	Sussex	25.10.1879	30. 9.1930
George Shaw *1872*	Sutton-in-		
	Ashfield	20. 5.1839	17. 8.1905
John Monson Shaw *1865–1866*	Rochester	1.10.1832	4. 9.1912
Vero Kemball Shaw *1875–1878*	Belgaum,		
	India	14. 1.1854	18.12.1905
Edward James Sheffield *1933*	New Eltham	20. 6.1908	28. 4.1971
Peter Anthony Shenton *1960*	Redcar	5. 5.1936	
John Neil Shepherd *1966–1981*	Belleplaine,		
	WI	9.11.1943	
Eustace Beverley Shine *1896–1899*	Port of Spain	9. 7.1873	11.11.1952
Alexander Campbell Shirreff *1950–1956*	Ealing	12. 2.1919	
John Shuter *1874*	Thornton		
	Heath	9. 2.1855	5. 7.1920
Ernest Herbert Simpson *1896*	Clapton	17.12.1875	2.10.1917
Gerard Amyatt Simpson *1929–1931*	Edinburgh	29. 3.1886	22. 2.1957
Kanwar Shumshere Singh *1901–1902*	Bahraich,		
	India	21. 6.1879	12. 5.1975

Name	Place	Born	Died
Geoffrey Smith *1951–1958*	Huddersfield	30.11.1925	
Stephen Smith *1855–1856*	Blackheath	1822	20. 2.1890
William Smith *1849–1857*	Gravesend	1819	6. 2.1883
William Allan Smith-Masters *1875*	Humber, Herefords	13. 3.1850	27. 8.1937
Benjamin Smyth *1858*	Calcutta	20. 6.1838	5.10.1906
Arthur Owen Snowden *1911*	Ramsgate	7. 5.1885	22. 5.1964
Edward Philip Solbe *1921–1924*	Bromley	10. 5.1902	28.12.1961
Frank de Lisle Solbe *1891–1892*	Chefoo, China	1. 6.1871	12. 1.1933
John George Spanswick *1955–1956*	Folkestone	30. 9.1933	
Guy Dennis Spelman *1980–1982*	Westminster	18.10.1958	
Thomas William Spencer *1935–1946*	Deptford	22. 3.1914	
William Hugh Spottiswoode *1890*	Belgravia	12. 7.1864	20. 8.1915
Alfred Staines *1863–1864*	Charlton	22. 5.1838	13. 6.1910
Edward Stanhope *1861*	Belgravia	24. 9.1840	21.12.1893
William Stearman *1836–1840*	Aldborough	1813	11. 4.1846
Haldane Campbell Stewart *1892–1903*	Notting Hill	28. 2.1868	16. 6.1942
Frederic Stokes *1871–1875*	Inhurst, Berks	12. 7.1850	7. 1.1929
Graham Stokes *1880–1881*	Greenwich	22. 3.1858	19.12.1921
Leonard Stokes *1877–1880*	Greenwich	12. 2.1856	3. 5.1933
Lord Strathavon (see Aboyne, Sixth Earl of)			
Richard John Streatfeild *1856*	Chiddingstone	7.11.1833	22. 3.1877
Alexander McNeill Streatfeild-Moore *1885–1888*	Charts Edge	17.10.1863	30.12.1940
Francis Edward Street *1875–1877*	Hampstead	16. 2.1851	4. 6.1928
Peter Regan Sunnucks *1934–1946*	Boughton-Monchelsea	22. 6.1916	
Henry Boyd Sutherland *1871*	Croydon	4.12.1844	27. 8.1915
John Swaffer *1873*	Ruckinge	10.11.1852	26. 7.1936
Edward Gibbon Swann *1844–1845*	Coppet, Geneva	13. 8.1823	20.12.1900
Thomas Francis Swinford *1874*	Margate	9. 5.1839	23. 1.1915
Anton Hugh Syree *1879*	Port Corrie, SA	21.10.1959	9. 1.1924
Edward Taswell *1860–1861*	Canterbury	21. 6.1826	1. 6.1889
Christopher James Tavaré *1974–1987*	Orpington	27.10.1954	
Robert Frederick Tayler *1865*	Hastings	17. 3.1836	1. 1.1888
Howard Taylor *1937*	Woolwich	5. 4.1908	
Horace James Taylor *1922–1925*	Sevenoaks	26.12.1895	13.10.1961
Neil Royston Taylor *1979–1987*	Farnborough	21. 7.1959	
Edward William Taylor-Jones *1894*	Sydenham	28. 5.1866	15. 9.1956
Robert Jenkin Terry *1860*	Lydd	1.1830	23. 2.1908

Frederick George Theobald *1862*	New Brompton, Kent	1. 2.1839	5. 1.1888
Richard Thomas *1835*	Chatham	1792	30. 5.1881
Henry Shepherd Thomson *1876*	Ramsgate	4. 6.1854	unknown
Albert James Thornton *1884–1891*	Folkestone	17. 1.1856	14. 6.1931
Charles Inglis Thornton *1867–1872*	Llanwarne	20. 3.1850	10.12.1929
Richard Thornton Thornton *1881–1888*	Folkestone	28. 3.1853	30. 5.1928
Ronald Stanley Thresher *1957*	Tonbridge	31.12.1930	
George Edward Milles Throwley, Viscount *1882–1884*	Lees Court	11. 5.1861	1.10.1907
Thomas Tidy *1868*	Hurstpierpoint	6.10.1847	11. 9.1918
Henry Charles Lenox Tindall *1893–1895*	Margate	4. 2.1863	10. 6.1940
Leslie John Todd *1927–1950*	Catford	19. 6.1907	20. 8.1967
William Fox Tomson *1861*	Ramsgate	18. 5.1842	12. 6.1882
John Norton Tonge *1884–1897*	Otford	9. 7.1865	8. 7.1903
Edward Tootell *1872*	Maidstone	22.11.1851	20. 3.1878
Peter Alan Topley *1972–1975*	Canterbury	29. 8.1950	
William Matt Torrens *1890*	Hayes, Kent	19.10.1869	18. 2.1931
William Frederick Traill *1860–1866*	Lewisham	7. 1.1838	3.10.1905
Lionel Holmes Wood Troughton *1907–1923*	Seaford	17. 5.1879	31. 8.1933
Medhurst Albert Troughton *1864–1873*	Milton-next-Gravesend	25.12.1839	1. 1.1912
Carleton Fowell Tufnell *1878–1879*	Northfleet	20. 2.1856	26. 5.1940
John Sackville Richard Tufton, Hon *1897–1898*	Hothfield	8.11.1873	21.12.1952
James Richard Tylden *1923*	Milsted	26. 4.1889	24. 2.1949
Edward Ferdinando Sutton Tylecote *1875–1883*	Marston Moretaine	23. 6.1849	15. 3.1938
Derek Gilbert Ufton *1949–1962*	Crayford	31. 5.1928	
Derek Leslie Underwood *1963–1987*	Bromley	8. 6.1945	
William Usmar *1841*	West Malling	14.10.1813	12. 5.1879
Bryan Herbert Valentine *1927–1948*	Blackheath	17. 1.1908	2. 2.1983
Alan Otto Charles Verrinder *1977*	Henley-on-Thames	28. 7.1955	
Jack Walker *1949*	Cobham, Kent	2. 3.1914	29. 5.1968
Conrad Adolphus Wallroth *1872*	Lee, Kent	17. 5..1851	22. 2.1926
James Walton *1875*	Greenwich	1857	unknown
Nicholas Wanostrocht (see N. Felix)			
Geoffrey Hubert Ward *1949*	Rainham	22.11.1926	
Trevor Robert Ward *1986–1987*	Faringham	18. 1.1968	
Frederick Warde *1871–1877*	West Farleigh	18. 3.1852	14. 5.1899

Name	Place	Birth	Death
Stuart Nicholas Varney Waterton *1980–1985*	Dartford	6.12.1960	
Arthur Cave Wathen *1863–1864*	Streatham	27. 3.1841	14. 3.1937
William Hulbert Wathen *1863*	Streatham	5. 5.1836	29. 3.1913
George Sutton Watson *1928–1929*	Milton Regis	10. 4.1907	1. 4.1974
Alan Edward Watt *1929–1939*	Limpsfield Chart	19. 6.1907	3. 2.1974
James Watts *1859–1869*	Hythe	15.12.1835	15.12.1919
George Webb *1892*	Tonbridge	1859	unknown
George William Webb *1880*	Barham	23.10.1859	26.12.1931
Robert Webb *1864*			
Gerald John Villiers Weigall *1891–1903*	Wimbledon	19.10.1870	17. 5.1944
James Turner Welldon *1867–1869*	Felsted	3. 8.1847	6. 2.1927
Joseph Wells *1862–1863*	Penshurst	14. 7.1828	14.10.1910
Edward Gower Wenman *1834–1854*	Benenden	18. 8.1803	28.12.1879
George Wenman *1834*	Benenden	27.10.1805	19. 1.1837
John Gude Wenman *1836–1837*	Benenden	11. 8.1803	25.11.1877
William Wenman *1862–1864*	Benenden	22. 5.1832	23.11.1921
Thomas Brand Whitby *1837*	Eynsford	2.11.1813	7.12.1881
Edward Albert White *(1867–1875*	Yalding	16. 3.1844	3. 5.1922
Lionel Algernon White *1869*	Wateringbury	9.11.1850	25. 6.1917
George William Edendale Whitehead *1914*	Bromley	27. 8.1895	17.10.1918
Peter Michael William Whitehouse *1937–1938*	Birchington	27. 4.1917	19.11.1943
Charles Gustavus Whittaker *1839–1847*	Barming	8. 9.1819	8.11.1886
George Wigzell *1852–1860*	Sevenoaks	6. 5.1818	unknown
Robert William Wilkinson *1959–1963*	Rotherhithe	23.12.1939	
Edmund Henry Lacon Willes *1852–1853*	Hythe, Hants	7. 7.1832	9. 9.1896
Alfred Edward Augustus Williams *1865*	Ashford, Kent	20.11.1844	7. 1.1914
Charles Francis Willis *1850*	Hawkhurst	15. 4.1827	19.11.1895
Thomas Wentworth Spencer Wills *1855–1856*	Molomgolo Plains, NSW	19. 8.1835	2. 5.1880
Edgar Willsher *1850–1875*	Little Halden	22.11.1828	7.10.1885
William Willsher *1847*	Little Halden	1814	30.11.1861
Erasmus Albert Willson *1898*	Sittingbourne	13.10.1878	17. 4.1948
Cecil Wilson *1882–1890*	Canonbury	9. 9.1860	20. 1.1941
Leslie Wilson *1883–1897*	Canonbury	16. 3.1859	15. 4.1944
Robert Colin Wilson *1952–1967*	Bapchild	18. 2.1928	
John Wisden *1854*	Brighton	5. 9.1826	5. 4.1884
Edwin George Witherden *1951–1955*	Goudhurst	1. 5.1922	
George Edward Charles Wood *1919–1927*	Blackheath	22. 8.1893	18. 3.1971
Henry Wood *1876–1882*	Dartford	14.12.1853	30. 4.1919
Lindsay Jonathan Wood *1981–1982*	Ruislip	12. 5.1961	

Anthony Frank Woollett *1950–1954*	Lambeth	20. 9.1927	
Frank Edward Woolley *1906–1938*	Tonbridge	27. 5.1887	18.10.1978
Robert Andrew Woolmer *1968–1984*	Kanpur, India	14. 5.1948	
James Wootton *1880–1890*	Sutton-at-Hone	9. 3.1860	21. 2.1941
Edward Wormald *1870*	Islington	4.12.1848	16.10.1928
Charles Robert Worthington *1898*	Surbiton	28. 2.1877	7.12.1950
Albert Charles Wright *1921–1931*	Borstal	4. 4.1895	26. 5.1959
Douglas Vivian Parson Wright *1932–1957*	Sidcup	21. 8.1914	
Edward Campbell Wright *1902*	South Shields	23. 4.1874	28. 7.1947
Walter Wright *1888–1899*	Hucknall Torkard	29. 2.1856	22. 3.1940
William Yardley *1868–1878*	Bombay, India	10. 6.1849	28.10.1900
Alfred Joseph Karney Young *1890*	Victoria, BC	1. 8.1865	5. 1.1942

CAREER RECORDS OF KENT CRICKETERS 1834–1987

The career records are for first-class matches for Kent only. The first-class matches are those as listed in the Association of Cricket Statisticians 'Guides' to first-class cricket.

Name	Inns	NO	Runs	HS	Avge	100s	Runs	Wkts	Avge	Best	5wI
Aboyne, Sixth Earl of	I	0	II	II	11.00						
Absolom, C. A.	106	7	1644	70	16.60	0	2245	89	25.22	6/52	5
Adams, T. M.	187	5	2291	78	12.58	0	379	25(64)	15.16	6/39	2
Aitchison, J. E.	3	0	6	4	2.00	0	88	3	29.33	3/33	—
Akers-Douglas, I. S.	67	3	1520	123	23.75	2	61	3	20.33	2/20	—
Alexander, C. D.	2	0	II	8	5.50	0					
Alexander, C. R.	6	0	61	41	10.16	0					
Allan, J. M.	67	4	1329	121★	21.09	3	2116	88	24.04	5/31	3
Alliston, C. G. P.	I	0	0	0	0.00	0					
Ames, L. E. G.	717	64	28951	295	44.33	78	697	22	31.68	3/23	—
Andrews, H. M.	30	2	422	58	15.07	0					
Alderman, T. M.	48	21	322	52★	11.92	0	3607	174	20.73	8/46	15
Anson, G. F.	13	0	231	51	17.76	0					
Arbuthnot, R. J. H.	4	0	8	5	2.00	0					
Armstrong, R. G. C.	13	2	76	10★	6.90	0	18	0			
Ashdown, W. H.	804	76	22309	332	30.64	38	19290	595	32.42	6/23	12
Ashwell, A. H.	5	2	42	21★	14.00	0	139	0			
Asif Iqbal	399	42	13231	171	37.06	26	2096	73	28.71	4/11	—
Aslett, D. G.	199	20	6128	221★	34.23	12	1253	17	73.70	4/119	—
Atkins, F. M.	46	2	425	52	9.65	0					
Austin, G. L.	4	0	51	23	12.75	0					
Bailey, R. A.	5	I	0	0★	0.00	0	250	2	125.00	1/76	—
Baiss, R. S. H.	13	2	230	38	20.90	0					
Baker, D. W.	28	9	85	15	4.47	0	2419	68	35.57	5/47	3
Baker, E.	2	0	0	0	0.00	0	19	I	19.00	1/19	—
Baker, G.	38	8	165	21	5.50	0	667	45(3)	14.82	7/52	2
Baker, H. Z.	17	0	211	82	12.41	0	40	3	13.33	1/2	—
Baker, P. C.	67	2	1600	130	24.61	2					
Baker, W.	2	0	3	3	1.50	0					
Baker, W. de C.	26	2	119	20	4.95	0					
Banks, E. R. R. G.	17	3	115	24	8.21	0					
Banks, W. J.	8	0	36	32	4.50	0					
Bannon, B. D.	40	I	755	78	19.35	0					
Baptiste, E. A. E.	127	20	3195	136★	29.86	3	6209	218	28.48	8/76	8
Barber, H. W.	18	5	124	45	9.53	0	4	0			
Barlow, K.	3	0	II	6	3.66	0					
Bartholomew, A.	4	0	9	5	2.25	0	II	2	5.50	2/11	—
Barton, V. A.	18	2	161	32	10.06	0	215	II	19.54	3/28	—
Bass, H. J.	5	0	II	8	2.20	0					
Bayley, J. R. L. E.	16	4	165	33	3.25	0					
Bayley, L. H.	7	3	52	18	13.00	0					
Beeching, T. H. P.	13	0	217	38	16.69	0					
Belton, C. H.	4	0	41	23	10.25	0					
Bennet, F. W.	I	0	0	0	0.00	0					

Name	Inns	NO	Runs	HS	Avge	100s	Runs	Wkts	Avge	Best	5wI
Bennett, G.	234	22	3143	82	14.82	0	7700	449(12)	17.14	9/113	30
Bennett, R.	12	0	32	12	2.66	0					
Bennett, W. A. B.	2	2	1	1*	—	0					
Benson, M. R.	261	20	9476	162	39.31	24	273	3	91.00	2/55	0
Beslee, G. P.	86	25	439	24	7.19	0	4199	133	31.57	4/27	—
Best, W. F.	8	0	103	26	12.87	0	69	5	13.80	3/29	—
Betts, G.	2	0	0	0	0.00	0		(1)		1/?	—
Betts, M. P.	3	1	44	39*	22.00	0					
Bickley, J.	2	0	11	8	5.50	0	54	2	27.00	2/49	
Bickmore, A. F.	74	6	1589	120	23.36	2	98	0			
Birch, A. E.	2	0	3	3	1.50	0					
Biron, H. B.	23	2	208	30	9.50	0	31	1	31.00	1/31	—
Blackman, A.	6	0	78	36	13.00	0					
Blackmore, G. P. M.	2	0	4	4	2.00	0	64	2	32.00	1/14	—
Blair, E. McL.	10	0	190	61	19.00	0					
Blaker, R. N. R.	188	18	4060	122	23.88	2	92	1	92.00	1/25	—
Bligh, E. V.	41	6	392	53	11.20	0	128	6(2)	21.33	1/4	—
Bligh, H.	8	1	40	23	5.71	0					
Bligh, I. F. W.	82	3	1493	105	18.89	1					
Bligh, L. E.	18	4	107	20	7.64	0	157	5	31.40	2/36	—
Bluett, J. D. J.	2	0	16	10	8.00	0					
Blunden, A.	12	4	33	9*	4.12	0	586	18	32.55	4/31	—
Blythe, C.	506	111	3964	82*	10.03	0	36859	2210	16.67	10/30	195
Bonham-Carter, M.	2	0	17	16	8.50	0	9	0			
Botting, S. H.	4	0	27	20	6.75	0					
Bouch, H. E.	2	0	7	7	3.50	0	52	1	52.00	1/52	—
Boucher, S.	1	0	0	0	0.00	0	45	0			
Boys, J. J.	5	0	34	21	6.80	0					
Bradley, W. M.	185	50	795	67*	5.88	0	11886	536	22.17	9/87	39
Bray, J.	37	10	74	9	2.74	0	1464	87	16.82	8/103	6
Braybrooke, H. M.	37	2	607	53	17.34	0	21	0			
Brazier, A. F.	34	3	357	51*	11.51	0	151	4	37.75	2/45	—
Brenchley, H.	5	1	17	9	4.25	0					
Brenchley, T. H.	9	3	40	18	6.66	0					
Broad, J.	2	1	12	12*	12.00	0	62	4	15.50	4/62	—
Brown, A.	301	81	2120	81	9.63	0	17534	707	24.80	8/47	25
Brown, S. W.	6	1	3	1*	0.60	0	217	5	43.40	2/36	—
Browne, F. D.	17	3	262	53*	18.71	0					
Bryan, G. J.	83	7	1904	179	25.03	3	1543	29	53.20	5/148	1
Bryan, J. L.	187	17	6174	236	36.31	12	239	5	47.80	1/12	—
Bryan, R. T.	60	9	1154	89*	22.62	0	22	1	22.00	1/9	—
Bull, –	2	1	10	8*	10.00	0	22	0			
Bull, C. H.	6	0	33	23	5.50	0	64	0			
Burke, G. H.	1	0	9	9	9.00	0	51	4	12.75	3/16	—
Burnup, C. J.	271	17	9668	200	38.06	20	1795	41	43.78	5/44	1
Burton, J. C.	24	2	162	40	7.36	0					
Byass, J. E.	6	0	31	17	5.16	0					
Caffyn, W.	4	0	47	18	11.75	0	119	3	39.66	1/28	—
Campbell, I. P.	1	1	0	0*	—	0					
Candlett, W.	2	1	3	3	3.00	0	29	0			
Capes, C. J.	41	8	534	65*	16.18	0	1381	55	25.10	7/20	2
Caplen, T.	2	1	6	5*	6.00	0	74	2(0)	37.00	2/74	—

Name	Inns	NO	Runs	HS	Avge	100s	Runs	Wkts	Avge	Best	5wI
Capon, S.	1	0	4	4	4.00	0	98	0			
Carr, D. W.	54	13	398	48	9.70	0	4529	290	15.61	8/36	27
Carroll, J.	56	6	610	48	12.20	0	257	8	32.12	2/21	—
Carter, W.	6	1	6	3	1.20	0	13	0(1)	1/?	—	
Castle, S.	6	0	25	6	4.16	0					
Catt, A. W.	199	35	2862	162	17.45	1	2	0			
Cazalet, P. V. F.	6	1	203	150	40.60	1					
Ceely, A. J.	2	0	23	15	11.50	0					
Chalk, F. G. H.	169	12	4436	198	28.25	5	137	2	68.50	2/25	—
Champion, G. E.	2	0	0	0	0.00	0					
Chapman, A. P. F.	269	21	6681	260	26.93	8	151	3	50.33	2/24	—
Cheesman, T.	2	0	14	14	7.00	0					
Christopherson, J. C.	4	0	29	14	7.25	0					
Christopherson, P.	1	0	27	27	27.00	0					
Christopherson, S.	83	5	720	47	9.23	0	4090	179	22.84	8/41	13
Clark, D. G.	133	9	1959	78	15.79	0	44	1	44.00	1/19	—
Clarke, W.	2	1	3	3*	3.00	0	94	2	47.00	2/81	—
Clifford, F. S.	80	6	800	60*	10.81	0					
Clifford, W.	30	6	273	46	11.37	0					
Clifton, Lord	12	2	121	52	12.10	0	9	0			
Clinton, G. S.	50	2	1142	88	24.29	0	9	2	4.50	2/8	—
Cocker, J. C.	2	0	16	11	8.00	0					
Cole, C. G.	43	14	228	23*	7.86	0	2110	61	34.59	6/62	2
Cole, E. S.	5	0	43	14	8.60	0	309	7	44.14	4/78	—
Coles, G. E.	4	0	39	19	9.75	0	98	11	8.90	6/23	1
Collins, B.	2	0	0	0	0.00	0					
Collins, C.	13	2	97	41	8.81	0	305	16	19.06	4/9	—
Collins, G.	21	3	182	36	10.11	0	68	3	22.66	2/15	—
Collins, G. C.	316	37	6237	110	22.35	4	8964	378	23.71	10/65	24
Constable, W. T.	2	0	1	1	0.50	0					
Constant, D. J.	14	2	132	49*	11.00	0					
Cook, G. W.	5	1	89	51*	22.25	0	36	0			
Cooper, B. B.	16	2	328	83	23.42	0					
Cooper, C. O.	19	1	237	44	13.16	0					
Cope, S. A.	1	0	0	0	0.00	0	27	1	27.00	1/27	—
Coppinger, C.	2	1	13	11*	13.00	0					
Coppinger, E. T.	4	0	17	10	4.25	0	29	5	5.80	5/29	1
Coppinger, W.	14	3	52	16	4.72	0	98	2	49.00	2/49	—
Cornwallis, W. S.	128	47	953	91	10.76	0	3785	117	32.35	6/37	5
Court, W. T.	2	0	11	11	5.50	0					
Cowdrey, C. S.	325	48	8987	159	32.47	15	5160	126	40.94	5/69	1
Cowdrey, G. R.	44	4	893	75	22.32	0	92	2	46.00	1/17	0
Cowdrey, M. C.	651	85	23779	250	42.01	58	1285	27	47.59	4/22	—
Crawford, F. F.	29	1	335	29	11.96	0					
Crawford, J. C.	20	1	191	35	10.05	0	174	6	29.00	3/5	—
Crawford, T. A.	16	1	150	32	10.00	0	13	0			
Crawley, A. M.	52	3	1560	175	31.83	2	84	1	84.00	1/11	—
Croft, S. J.	4	0	18	13	4.50	0					
Crowhurst, W.	2	0	1	1	0.50	0	46	1	46.00	1/26	—
Croxford, H.	51	11	472	53	11.80	0	677	31	21.83	6/45	2
Crush, E.	72	5	1078	78	16.08	0	3163	83	38.10	6/50	2
Cumberlege, B. S.	11	2	365	76	40.55	0	1	0			

Name	Inns	NO	Runs	HS	Avge	100s	Runs	Wkts	Avge	Best	5wI
Cunliffe, C. M.	41	4	365	47	9.86	0	1242	84	14.78	7/25	10
Curteis, E. W.	2	0	9	8	4.50	0					
Daffen, A.	27	3	399	72★	16.62	0	144	7	20.57	4/5	—
Dale, C. S.	3	1	18	16	9.00	0	142	0			
Dale, J. R.	1	0	0	0	0.00	0	31	1	31.00	1/31	—
Darvell, B. S.	1	0	5	5	5.00	0	2	0			
Davies, J. G. W.	167	7	4059	168	25.36	3	5874	197	29.81	7/20	4
Davis, P. V.	10	0	74	33	7.40	0					
Davis, R. P.	10	5	43	21★	8.60	0	594	16	29.56	3/38	—
Davison, J. J.	8	1	83	25★	11.85	0					
Davy, C. V. B.	2	0	35	32	17.50	0	41	1	41.00	1/6	—
Day, A. P.	217	22	6532	184★	33.49	13	3236	129	25.08	8/49	4
Day, S. E.	17	4	245	45★	18.84	0					
Day, S. H.	206	18	5893	152★	31.34	5	201	7	28.71	3/46	—
Debnam, A. F. H.	15	3	88	21	7.33	0	669	16	41.81	5/87	1
Deed, J. A.	99	17	1863	133	22.71	2					
De Lasaux, R. A.	2	0	0	0	0.00	0					
Denne, L. H.	6	1	98	35	19.60	0					
Denness, M. H.	562	44	17047	178	32.90	21	55	2	27.50	1/7	—
Dicker, J.	4	0	4	2	2.00	0					
Dickins, G. C.	4	2	53	34★	26.50	0					
Dilley, G. R.	116	39	993	81	12.89	0	7146	257	27.80	6/57	10
Dillon, E. W.	348	22	9415	141	28.88	12	1321	27	48.92	3/20	—
Dinwiddy, H. P.	14	3	188	45	17.09	0	35	0			
Disbury, B. E.	21	3	288	74★	16.00	0	204	5	40.80	2/76	—
Dixon, A. L.	576	71	9561	125★	18.93	3	23869	929	25.69	8/61	46
Dorrinton, A.	2	0	4	4	2.00	0					
Dorrinton, W.	100	10	674	40★	7.48	0		(1)		1/?	
Dovey, R. R.	391	72	3768	65★	11.81	0	20489	751	27.28	8/23	25
Downton, G. C.	11	5	37	16	6.16	0					
Downton, P. R.	45	10	396	31★	11.31	0					
Draper, W.	17	2	108	28	7.71	0	290	20	14.50	5/51	1
Dring, C. F.	2	0	8	8	4.00	0					
Druce, E. A. C.	2	0	22	22	11.00	0	36	0			
Du Boulay, A. H.	8	2	250	58	41.66	0	137	2	68.50	1/33	—
Dudlow, J. N.					selected for one match: did not play						
Duke, J.	2	0	0	0	0.00	0	26	3	8.66	3/23	—
Dutnall, F.	5	0	26	16	5.20	0	9	0			
Dutnall, W.	2	0	3	3	1.50	0					
Dye, J. C. J.	127	66	320	27★	5.24	0	9318	371	25.11	7/118	12
Ealham, A. G. E.	466	68	10996	153	27.62	7	189	3	63.00	1/1	—
Easby, J. W.	110	9	1851	73	18.32	0	424	13	32.61	2/8	—
Edrich, B. R.	220	17	4275	193★	21.05	4	4534	137	33.09	7/41	4
Edwards, W.	4	1	44	25	14.66	0	27	3	9.00	3/16	—
Elcome, A.	2	0	9	8	4.50	0					
Elliott, G. F.	4	2	35	17★	17.50	0	13	0			
Ellison, R. M.	43	16	759	63	28.11	0	2068	71	29.12	5/73	1
Elms, R. B.	57	19	362	31★	9.52	0	3591	89	40.34	5/38	4
Evans, A. J.	53	1	1303	143	25.05	4	605	19	31.84	3/64	—
Evans, T. G.	451	15	9325	144	21.38	4	215	2	107.50	2/50	—
Fagg, A. E.	767	44	26072	269★	36.06	55	47	0			
Fagge, J. F.	26	0	112	23	4.30	0		(1)		1/?	—

Name	Inns	NO	Runs	HS	Avge	100s	Runs	Wkts	Avge	Best	5wI
Fairservice, C.	85	11	1338	110	18.08	1	651	18	36.16	3/49	—
Fairservice, W. J.	417	96	4922	61*	15.33	0	19272	853	22.59	7/44	38
Farbrace, P.	7	3	134	75*	33.50	0					
Fawcus, C. L. D.	2	0	5	5	2.50	0					
Felix, N.	94	3	1528	113	16.79	1		(2)		2/?	
Fellowes, J.	15	1	179	32	12.78	0	690	47	14.68	7/24	4
Fenner, G. D.	3	1	13	10*	6.50	0	10	0			
Fenner, M. D.	21	1	264	55	13.20	0					
Field, G. H.	8	1	37	11	5.28	0					
Fielder, A.	329	154	2000	112*	11.42	1	24014	1150	20.88	9/108	88
Fillary, E. W. J.	24	4	387	46	19.35	0	556	15	37.06	5/52	1
Finch, F. F.	2	0	2	1	1.00	0					
Fleming, I. D. K.	4	1	60	42*	20.00	0					
Foord-Kelcey, W.	112	3	1613	105	14.79	1	3909	202	19.35	8/49	12
Foster, G. N.	15	0	250	71	16.66	0					
Foster, J. B.	3	0	10	6	3.33	0					
Foster, J. H. N.	2	0	1	1	0.50	0					
Foster, P. G.	41	2	755	107	19.35	1	7	0			
Fox, C. J. M.	124	10	2084	103	18.28	1	818	46	17.78	5/21	3
Foy, F. G.	17	1	153	25	9.56	0	18	0			
Freeman, A. P.	630	170	4257	66	9.25	0	58944	3340	17.64	10/53	348
Freeman, D. P.	2	0	10	6	5.00	0					
Friend, L. B.	6	0	70	22	11.66	0					
Fryer, W. H.	138	6	1425	65	10.79	0	928	49	18.93	8/40	1
Fulcher, A. W.	12	1	156	44*	14.18	0					
Fulcher, E. J.	6	1	61	32	12.20	0	41	0			
Gale, F.	1	0	0	0	0.00	0					
George, W.	8	5	4	2*	1.33	0	315	22	14.31	7/86	2
Gibson, A. C.	8	2	35	17*	5.83	0	50	0			
Gillow, A.	3	0	4	3	1.33	0					
Goldsmith, G.	2	1	3	2*	3.00	0					
Goldsmith, S. C.	4	0	49	25	12.25	0	37	1	37.00	1/37	—
Goodhew, W.	129	14	1354	70	11.77	0	350	17	20.58	3/19	—
Gosling, J. F.	2	0	2	2	1.00	0					
Grace, W. G.	2	0	108	58	54.00	0	74	3	24.66	2/58	—
Graham, J. N.	175	71	404	23	3.88	0	13462	600	22.43	8/20	25
Graham-Brown, J. M. H.	15	5	149	29*	14.90	0	239	3	79.66	1/4	—
Green, W.	3	1	18	16	9.00	0					
Green, W. J.	6	1	17	12	3.40	0					
Greenwood, E.	2	0	13	13	6.50	0					
Grimshaw, J. W. T.	2	0	30	17	15.00	0	80	4	20.00	3/29	—
Gunn, B. G. H.	7	0	105	39	15.00	0					
Guy, J. B.	2	0	0	0	0.00	0					
Halfyard, D. J.	274	31	2538	79	10.44	0	18822	769	24.47	9/39	49
Hamilton, C. P.	2	0	2	1	1.00	0	13	0			
Hamilton, L. A. H.	36	2	628	117*	18.47	1	50	2	25.00	2/24	—
Hammond, W.	2	0	20	17	10.00	0					
Hardcastle, E. H.	2	0	12	7	6.00	0	64	3	21.33	3/29	—
Harding, N. W.	123	22	966	71	9.56	0	6481	229	28.30	5/31	9
Hardinge, E. S.	2	1	7	6	7.00	0					
Hardinge, H. T. W.	990	98	32549	263*	36.48	73	9773	370	26.41	7/64	8

Name	Inns	NO	Runs	HS	Avge	100s	Runs	Wkts	Avge	Best	5wI
Harenc, A. R.	3	0	15	12	5.00	0		(2)		2/?	
Harenc, C. J.	25	5	154	28	7.70	0	19	0			
Hargreaves, W. H.	2	0	10	10	5.00	0					
Harington, H. H.	4	0	49	34	12.25	0					
Harris, Fourth Baron	278	17	7842	176	30.04	10	1523	64	23.79	5/57	1
Harris, T.	2	0	3	3	1.50	0	35	1	35.00	1/35	—
Harrison, W. P.	10	2	162	37	20.25	0					
Hassan, F.	2	0	0	0	0.00	0	12	1	12.00	1/5	
Hassell, T.	2	1	10	9*	10.00	0					
Hatfeild, C. E.	64	4	999	74	16.65	0	283	5	56.60	1/11	—
Hayman, H. T.	4	0	37	29	9.25	0					
Haywood, R. J.	2	1	0	0*	0.00	0	15	0			
Hearn, P.	344	31	7892	172	25.21	6	1093	19	57.52	3/34	—
Hearn, S. G.	43	7	414	54*	11.50	0	355	20	17.75	3/15	—
Hearne, A.	687	63	13598	162*	21.79	11	20323	1018	19.96	8/15	46
Hearne, F.	222	17	3338	144	16.28	2	1020	41	24.87	5/45	1
Hearne, G. G.	444	44	7148	126	17.87	4	9393	569	16.50	8/21	35
Hearne, H.	36	9	252	36	9.33	0	1415	57	24.82	5/27	3
Hearne, W.	92	19	553	34*	7.57	0	4349	273	15.93	8/40	28
Hedges, L. P.	80	3	1887	130	24.50	2	24	0			
Hedley, W. C.	5	0	61	31	12.20	0	157	17	9.23	8/31	2
Hellmuth, L.	13	1	34	11	2.83	0	383	8	47.87	2/11	—
Henty, E.	204	62	1135	72	7.99	0	10	1	10.00	1/3	—
Herbert, A. W. H.	1	0	4	4	4.00	0					
Hever, H. L.	10	5	20	11*	4.00	0	266	9	29.55	2/39	—
Hibbard, J. A.	7	3	19	7	4.75	0					
Hickmott, E.	15	2	85	44	6.53	0					
Hickmott, W. E.	5	2	29	13*	9.66	0	318	10	31.80	4/94	—
Hilder, A. L.	23	2	299	103*	14.24	1	93	3	31.00	2/14	—
Hills, R.	14	5	51	14*	5.66	0	66	6	11.0	3/32	—
Hills, R. W.	95	25	995	45	14.21	0	4494	161	27.91	6/64	2
Hills, T.	2	0	6	6	3.00	0					
Hillyer, C.	2	0	6	6	3.00	0	34	1	34.00	1/6	—
Hillyer, W. R.	145	27	688	29	5.83	0	1262	109(383)	11.57	8/?	49
Hilton, P.	45	0	537	74	11.93	0					
Hine-Haycock, T. R.	11	1	156	42	15.60	0	4	0			
Hinkly, E.	62	22	268	24	6.70	0	1001	62(77)	16.14	10/?	14
Hinks, S. G.	147	8	3914	131	28.15	5	261	4	65.25	1/10	0
Hoare, A.	2	0	49	39	24.50	0					
Hoare, C. A. R.	2	0	18	14	9.00	0					
Hodgson, R. G.	6	0	77	47	12.83	0					
Hollands, F.	52	4	306	52	6.37	0	1133	92(24)	12.31	6/15	10
Hollingworth, L.	6	1	6	3	1.20	0					
Hollis, W.	1	1	0	0	0.00	0					
Hooman, C. V. L.	24	2	569	73	25.86	0					
Hooper, A. J. M.	13	4	70	35	7.77	0	493	16	30.81	6/92	1
Hopkinson, W.	20	0	167	40	8.35	0	27	2	13.50	2/3	—
Hoppe, A.	2	0	8	8	4.00	0					
Hopper, T.	2	2	8	8*		0					
Hough, G. de L.	18	3	327	77	21.80	0	21	1	21.00	1/7	—
Howard, C. W.	2	0	15	10	7.50	0					
Howgego, J. A.	2	0	91	52	45.50	0					

Name	Inns	NO	Runs	HS	Avge	100s	Runs	Wkts	Avge	Best	5wI
Howland, C. B.	2	0	21	13	10.50	0					
Howlett, B.	31	13	103	29	5.72	0	1669	39	42.79	3/62	—
Hubbard, G. C.	4	0	61	36	15.25	0	25	1	25.00	1/25	—
Hubble, H. J.	21	3	285	50	15.83	0	33	1	33.00	1/5	—
Hubble, J. C.	496	61	10229	189	23.51	5	1	0			
Huish, F. E.	8	4	32	12	8.00	0	433	11	39.36	5/52	1
Huish, F. H.	686	122	7247	93	12.84	0	87	0			
Humphreys, E.	590	44	15308	208	28.03	19	8122	306	26.54	7/33	5
Hunt, F. H.	10	3	32	8	4.57	0	179	7	25.57	3/40	—
Hunter, C. H.	3	0	13	6	4.33	0					
Hurst, C. S.	31	4	733	124	27.14	3	22	0			
Hutchings, F. V.	4	0	81	31	20.25	0					
Hutchings, K. L.	238	12	7977	176	35.29	19	493	15	32.86	4/73	—
Hutchings, W. E. C.	3	0	31	19	10.33	0					
Igglesden, A. P.	20	6	111	30	7.92	0	1723	63	27.34	5/45	3
Inglis, A. M.	2	0	12	8	6.00	0					
Inglis, J. F.	1	1	0	19	19		19.00	0			
Ingram, I.	20	1	112	25	5.89	0					
Ireland, F. S.	8	1	125	87	17.85	0	44	3	14.66	3/27	—
Irvine, L. G.	1	1	8	8★	0	0	72	2	36.00	2/37	—
Jackson, J.	4	1	31	26★	10.33	0	118	22	5.36	9/27	2
James, W.	2	0	0	0	0.00	0					
Jarvis, K. B. S.	180	79	321	19	3.17	0	18525	631	29.35	8/97	19
Jenner, H.	6	0	79	31	13.61	0		(1)			
Jennings, D. W.	48	4	1064	106	24.18	3	80	1	80.00	1/13	—
Johnson, G. W.	582	73	12549	168	24.65	11	17058	555	30.73	7/76	22
Johnstone, C. P.	56	2	1186	102	21.96	2	204	8	25.50	3/4	—
Jones, A.	4	1	23	12	7.66	0					
Jones, P. H.	230	32	4152	132	20.96	2	6527	231	28.25	6/41	6
Jones, R. S.	86	5	1412	83	17.43	0					
Jose, A. D.	9	1	26	7	3.25	0	346	8	43.25	3/64	—
Julien B. D.	109	15	2057	98	21.88	0	5256	198	26.54	7/66	—
Keeble, G.	2	1	8	6★	8.00	0	37	1	37.00	1/21	—
Keeling, H. W.	3	0	40	24	13.33	0	48	0			
Kelleher, D. J. M.	12	1	81	20	7.36	0	878	34	25.82	6/109	2
Kelson, G. M.	124	6	1810	122	15.33	1	868	41	21.17	6/30	1
Kemp, A. F.	5	0	30	13	6.00	0	44	1	44.00	1/26	1
Kemp, C. W. M.	1	0	17	17	17.00	0					
Kemp, M. C.	141	24	1522	51	13.00	0					
Kemp, N. J.	13	2	89	23	8.09	0	621	12	51.75	6/119	1
Kibble, G. H.	2	0	9	6	4.50	0					
Kidd, P. M.	2	0	0	0	0.00	0	36	0			
Kimmins, S. E. A.	21	1	338	70	16.90	0	641	17	37.70	5/42	1
King, F.	2	0	11	6	5.50	0	15	0			
King, J.	3	1	26	16★	13.00	0	130	5	26.00	3/43	—
Kingscote, H. B.	2	0	14	9	7.00	0					
Knatchbull, H. E.	6	0	45	18	7.50	0					
Knatchbull-Hugessen, C. M.	2	0	6	5	3.00	0					
Knatchbull-Hugessen, W. W.	2	0	16	9	8.00	0					
Knight, B. J.	2	0	2	1	1.00	0					

Name	Inns	NO	Runs	HS	Avge	100s	Runs	Wkts	Avge	Best	5wI
Knight, W. W.	2	1	1	1*	1.00	0					
Knott, A. P. E.	505	94	11339	144	27.58	9	13	1	13.00	1/5	—
Knott, C. H.	157	20	4026	154*	29.38	6	375	10	37.50	4/34	—
Knott, F. H.	17	2	426	114	28.40	1					
Knowles, W. L.	59	2	1322	127	23.19	2					
Lacy-Scott, D. G.	2	0	6	5	3.00	0					
Larking, J. G.	6	1	15	8	3.00	0					
Lawrence, H. M.	8	3	14	4	2.80	0	194	3	64.66	2/57	—
Laycock, D. A.	16	2	266	58	19.00	0					
Layman, A. R.	2	0	1	1	0.50	0					
Leaney, E.	11	3	76	33*	9.50	0					
Leary, S. E.	617	92	16169	158	30.79	18	4714	140	33.67	5/22	2
Lee, F. M.	4	0	12	12	3.00	0	20	0			
Lefeaver, J.	18	0	124	35	6.88	0	32	2	16.00	2/9	—
Le Fleming, J.	65	2	1201	134	19.06	1	120	3	40.00	2/44	—
Le Fleming, L. J.	16	0	205	40	12.81	0					
Leggatt, W. M.	8	0	229	92	28.62	0					
Legge, G. B.	158	5	3282	113	21.45	3	80	2	40.00	1/15	—
Leney, F. B.	2	0	39	30	19.50	0	23	1	23.00	1/0	—
Leney, H.	6	1	58	33	11.60	0	7	0			
Levett, W. H. V.	214	44	2054	76	12.08	0	6	0			
Lewis, C.	187	72	738	27	6.41	0	8198	301	27.23	8/58	14
Lindsay, W. O'B.	2	0	22	22	11.00	0					
Lipscomb, F.	29	4	158	28	6.32	0	1138	48	23.71	5/19	1
Lipscomb, R.	86	16	363	22	4.53	0	3855	206	18.71	9/88	12
Little, C. W.	6	0	50	19	8.33	0					
Livesay, R. O'H.	46	3	986	78	22.93	0	7	0			
Lock, B. H.	2	0	59	57	29.50	0					
Longfield, T. C.	43	6	731	72	19.75	0	1524	23	66.26	4/96	—
Lowe, R. G. H.	2	2	17	9*	—	0	53	3	17.66	2/5	—
Lubbock, A.	8	0	98	29	12.25	0	82	4	20.50	2/62	—
Lubbock, E.	2	0	65	54	32.50	0	23	0			
Lubbock, N.	3	0	24	17	8.00	0					
Lucas, F. C.	4	0	62	38	15.50	0	17	0			
Luckhurst, B. W.	568	65	19096	215	38.00	39	2617	61	42.90	4/32	—
McAlpine, K.	6	0	30	10	5.00	0					
McCanlis, G.	31	2	364	60	12.55	0	117	3	39.00	1/9	—
McCanlis, W.	86	4	1113	67	13.57	0	496	18	27.55	4/67	—
Mackenzie, F. F.	3	0	6	4	2.00	0					
Mackinnon, F. A.	144	11	2184	115	16.42	2					
McVittie, C. A. B.	1	0	30	30	30.00	0					
Malden, Ernest	2	0	22	22	11.00	0	15	0			
Malden, Eustace	19	1	130	27	7.22	0					
Mallett, A. W. H.	46	4	793	97	18.82	0	2658	72	36.91	5/115	2
Mann, E. W.	10	0	73	19	7.30	0	8	0			
Marchant, F.	382	10	7779	176	20.91	7	373	11	33.90	2/17	—
Marriott, C. S.	105	31	356	21	4.81	0	9391	463	20.28	7/52	32
Marsh, S. A.	77	16	1448	80	23.73	0					
Marshall, A. G.	9	1	29	7	3.62	0	308	7	44.00	4/50	—
Marsham, A. J. B.	10	0	75	39	7.50	0	197	5	39.40	3/54	—
Marsham, C. H. B.	224	14	4397	128	20.93	4	162	2	81.00	1/0	—
Marsham, G.	5	2	36	20	12.00	0					

266

Name	Inns	NO	Runs	HS	Avge	100s	Runs	Wkts	Avge	Best	5wI
Marsham, J.	4	0	5	3	1.25	0					
Marten, W. G.	27	7	111	27★	5.55	0	672	21	32.00	4/55	—
Martin, E.	57	3	474	31★	8.77	0	2	0(3)		1/?	—
Martin, F.	362	78	3375	90	11.88	0	17201	947	18.16	8/45	64
Martin, G.	27	4	168	24	7.30	0					
Martin, J. W.	55	12	519	35	12.07	0	2906	129	22.52	7/53	7
Martingell, W.	87	9	873	43	11.19	0	658	64(68)	10.23	7/27	11
Mason, J. E.	1	0	1	1	1.00	0					
Mason, J. R.	491	33	15563	183	33.98	31	16969	769	22.06	8/29	31
Masters, K. D.	7	1	1	1	0.16	0	294	6	49.00	2/26	—
May, W.	2	0	6	3	3.00	0					
Mayes, R.	144	7	2689	134	19.62	4	46	0			
Mayne, H. B.	3	1	21	14	10.50	0					
Meers, W. S.	1	0	11	11	11.0	0					
Mellor, F. H.	8	0	35	20	4.37	0					
Melville, J. E.	8	4	20	6	5.00	0	422	14	30.14	4/78	
Mewett, J.	2	1	1	1★	1.00	0					
Meyrick, Jones, F. M.	10	1	192	62	21.33	0					
Milles, H. A.	2	0	11	11	5.50	0	16	1	16.00	1/16	
Mills, C.	2	0	4	2	2.00	0					
Mills, R.	31	1	298	47	9.67	0	17	0(6)		3/?	—
Minns, R. E. F.	3	0	88	53	29.33	0					
Mitchell, C.	14	1	126	38★	9.69	0					
Mitchell, T. F.	39	3	546	64	15.16	0	67	0			
Money, W. B.	2	1	32	19★	32.00	0	24	0			
Mordaunt, E. C.	10	0	111	21	11.10	0	40	1	40.00	1/24	—
Mordaunt, G. J.	27	1	466	81★	17.92	0					
Morfee, P. E.	17	7	132	32	13.20	0	934	28	33.35	5/47	1
Morris, N.	20	0	211	34	10.55	0	14	0			
Morris, R. J.	3	0	26	16	8.66	0					
Morris, W.	4	0	14	6	3.50	0					
Munds, A. E.	2	0	10	9	5.00	0	6	0			
Munds, R.	11	1	121	29	12.10	0					
Murray-Wood, W.	135	13	1658	107	13.59	1	1913	47	40.70	4/67	—
Murrell, H. R.	46	3	421	68★	9.79	0	69	0			
Mynn, A.	167	12	1971	92	12.71	0	1033	100(312)	10.33	8/?	37
Mynn, W. P.	83	6	701	41	9.10	0		(1)		1/?	—
Neame, A. R. B.	6	0	55	22	9.16	0					
Nelson, P. J. M.	2	0	3	3	1.50	0	9	1	9.00	1/9	—
Nicholls, D.	340	24	7026	211	22.23	2	23	2	11.50	1/0	—
Norley, F.	13	3	61	12	6.10	0	200	9	22.22	5/52	1
Norley, J.	16	3	60	21★	4.61	0	108	3	36.00	1/16	0
Norman, C. L.	2	0	19	18	9.50	0					
Norman, F. H.	18	1	88	27	5.17	0					
Norman, G. W.	4	3	65	37★	65.00	0					
Norman, H.	4	1	9	7★	3.00	0					
Northcote, P.	6	2	71	27★	17.75	0	78	1	78.00	1/47	—
Norton, B.	18	2	181	56	11.31	0					
Norton, S.	1	0	10	10	10.00	0					
Norton, W. O. J.	5	1	44	15	11.00	0					
Norton, W. S.	113	13	1350	120★	13.50	1	404	18(2)	22.44	6/31	1
Nuttall, H.	19	6	39	8	3.00	0					

Name	Inns	NO	Runs	HS	Avge	100s	Runs	Wkts	Avge	Best	5wI
O'Linn, S.	51	10	1275	111*	31.09	1	12	0			
Olton, M. F.	2	1	14	13*	14.00	0	123	2	61.50	2/86	—
Onslow, C. W.	1	1	4	4*	—	0					
O'Shaughnessy, E.	104	9	1070	98	11.26	0	1421	77	18.45	7/16	5
Ottaway, C. J.	4	0	70	51	17.50	0					
Page, J. C. T.	273	124	818	23	5.48	0	14967	521	28.73	8/117	22
Palmer, R.	25	6	104	20	5.47	0	20	0			
Palmer, W. T.	31	1	328	37	10.93	0	14	1	14.00	1/8	—
Parke, E. A.	2	0	56	47	28.00	0	3	0			
Parker, H.	1	0	0	0	0.00	0					
Parr, G.	6	0	73	27	12.16	0	10	0			
Patterson, J. I.	9	2	27	9	3.85	0	166	11	15.09	5/12	—
Patterson, W. H.	264	18	6646	181	27.01	9	865	23	37.60	4/13	—
Pattisson, W. B.	20	0	214	38	10.70	0					
Pawley, T. E.	7	1	23	10	3.83	0	11	3	3.66	3/11	—
Pawson, H. A.	70	7	2100	137	33.33	2	131	4	32.75	2/26	—
Payne, C.	50	6	802	135*	18.22	1	105	2	52.50	1/35	—
Payne, J. S.	2	0	32	32	16.00	0	30	1	30.00	1/10	—
Peach, C. W.	25	10	108	20	7.20	0	830	30	27.66	4/38	—
Pearce, T. A.	77	8	1177	106	17.05	1	22	1	22.00	1/22	—
Pearce, W.	6	0	50	14	8.33	0	88	6	14.66	3/16	—
Peel, H. R.	4	0	9	5	2.25	0					
Penn, A.	70	8	487	66	7.85	0	3019	197	15.32	8/34	18
Penn, C.	56	12	829	115	18.84	1	3276	93	35.22	5/52	3
Penn, F.	109	10	2906	160	29.35	5	311	8	38.87	3/36	—
Penn, F. Jun	9	0	130	43	14.44	0					
Penn, W.	33	1	358	39	11.18	0					
Pentecost, J.	97	25	552	38	7.66	0	20	1	20.00	1/19	—
Pepys, J. A.	21	0	229	44	10.90	0					
Perkins, T. T. N.	40	4	709	109	19.69	1	43	0			
Pettiford, J.	251	37	5103	133	23.84	2	5780	194	29.79	6/134	5
Phebey, A. H.	585	33	14299	157	25.90	12	4	0			
Phillips, J. B. M.	6	0	4	4	0.66	0	374	7	53.42	2/42	—
Phillips, W.	2	0	3	2	1.50	0					
Pienaar, R. F.	8	0	327	153	40.87	1	427	15	28.46	4/66	—
Pilch, F.	156	11	2844	98	19.61	0	72	2(13)	36.00	1/4	—
Pilch, W.	84	9	601	38	8.01	0	32	5(8)	6.40	3/7	—
Pocock, H. J.	11	1	118	34	11.80	0	70	1	70.00	1/53	—
Potter, I. C.	5	5	12	11*	—	0	197	12	16.41	4/36	—
Potter, J.	4	1	13	6	4.33	0	114	2	57.00	1/23	—
Potter, L.	90	8	2413	165*	29.42	4	1531	43	35.60	4/63	—
Povey, A.	8	4	64	21*	16.00	0					
Powell, W. A.	16	1	154	48	10.26	0	316	11	28.72	3/37	—
Prest, H. E. W.	23	2	521	133*	24.80	1	4	1(0)	4.00	1/4	—
Preston, H. J. B.	27	14	84	18	6.46	0	865	43	20.11	5/23	1
Pretlove, J. F.	143	11	3128	112	23.69	4	350	17	20.58	4/59	—
Prideaux, R. M.	64	7	1325	116	23.24	1	4	0			
Pritchard, T. L.	7	1	49	30	8.16	0	435	11	39.54	3/95	—
Prodger, J. M.	259	22	4831	170*	20.38	3	14	1	14.00	1/14	—
Pryer, B. J. K.	3	0	7	7	2.33	0	147	4	36.75	3/44	—
Raikes, D. C. G.	3	1	7	4*	3.50	0					
Rashleigh, W.	165	3	4003	163	24.70	7	29	0			

Name	Inns	NO	Runs	HS	Avge	100s	Runs	Wkts	Avge	Best	5wI
Rawson, H. E.	2	0	0	0	0.00	0					
Recordon, L. W.	16	3	242	64★	18.61	0	86	0			
Remnant, G. H.	79	8	564	62	7.94	0	325	19	17.10	5/24	1
Renny-Tailyour, H. W.	32	3	694	124	23.93	1	66	4	16.50	2/28	—
Reynolds, J. F.	2	0	21	13	10.50	0	63	3	21.00	3/63	—
Richardson, H. A.	20	1	454	92	23.89	0	5	1	5.00	1/5	—
Richardson, P. E.	290	12	9975	172	35.88	18	164	4	41.00	2/32	—
Ridgway, F.	442	100	3812	94	11.14	0	22740	955	23.81	8/39	38
Ridley, A. W.	2	0	40	31	20.00	0	29	0			
Ridley, G. N. S.	1	0	10	10	10.00	0	26	0			
Rodger, J. P.	2	0	7	4	3.50	0					
Rodger, W. W.	33	2	298	32	9.93	0	20	0			
Roper, B.	2	0	5	4	2.50	0					
Rowe, C. J. C.	194	33	4226	147★	26.24	5	2301	59	39.00	6/46	3
Rumsey, R. E.	5	1	20	13	5.00	0	140	7	20.00	5/48	1
Sabine, D. J.											
Sankey, P. M.	2	1	14	12★	14.00	0	10	0			
Sarel, W. G. M.	14	2	213	93	17.75	0	8	1	8.00	1/8	—
Sayer, D. M.	173	64	835	39	7.66	0	10587	441	24.00	7/37	11
Selby, T.	6	0	19	17	3.16	0					
Sewell, R. P.	3	0	12	8	4.00	0					
Sewell, T.	4	1	33	19★	11.00	0					
Sewell, T. Jun	35	2	309	42	9.36	0	713	46(5)	15.50	8/45	2
Seymour, J.	881	60	26818	218★	32.62	53	680	15	45.33	4/62	—
Shaw, G.	4	2	17	13★	8.50	0	178	11	16.18	5/89	1
Shaw, J. M.	6	0	31	13	5.16	0					
Shaw, V. K.	44	5	494	74	12.66	0	501	24	20.87	4/11	0
Sheffield, E. J.	9	0	143	51	15.88	0	379	10	37.90	4/57	—
Shenton, P. A.	6	3	29	10★	9.66	0	402	16	25.12	5/68	1
Shepherd, J. N.	431	74	9401	170	26.33	8	22106	832	26.56	8/83	45
Shine, E. B.	37	6	266	49	8.58	0	2268	93	24.38	7/45	7
Shirreff, A. C.	78	8	1503	87★	21.47	0	3697	121	30.55	8/111	3
Shuter, J.	2	1	4	3	4.00	0					
Simpson, E. H.	14	0	219	94	15.64	0					
Simpson, G. A.	4	1	14	5★	4.66	0					
Singh, K. S.	7	0	140	45	20.00	0					
Smith, G.	71	12	728	60	12.33	0	3766	165	22.82	8/110	10
Smith, S.	4	0	16	11	4.00	0					
Smith, W.	13	1	103	24	8.58	0					
Smith-Masters, W. A.	1	0	7	7	7.00	0					
Smyth, B.	2	0	1	1	0.50	0					
Snowden, A. O.	2	1	12	12	12.00	0	13	0			
Solbe, E. P.	24	2	371	66	18.86	0	6	0			
Solbe, F. de L.	5	0	14	9	2.80	0					
Spanswick, J. G.	22	1	135	24	6.42	0	1175	36	32.63	4/64	—
Spelman, G. D.	7	1	9	4	1.50	0	357	10	35.70	2/27	—
Spencer, T. W.	120	13	2152	96	20.11	0	19	1	19.00	1/19	—
Spottiswoode, W. H.	3	0	51	37	17.00	0					
Staines, A.	10	4	6	2	1.00	0					

Name	Inns	NO	Runs	HS	Avge	100s	Runs	Wkts	Avge	Best	5wI
Stanhope, E.	2	0	33	17	16.50	0					
Stearman, W.	21	2	200	26*	10.52	0					
Stewart, H. C.	124	3	2788	142	23.04	2	87	2	43.50	1/2	—
Stokes, F.	7	1	125	65	20.83	0	206	7	29.42	2/20	—
Stokes, G.	8	0	39	27	4.87	0					
Stokes, L.	6	1	43	17	8.60	0	135	6	22.50	3/56	—
Streatfeild, R. J.	1	0	10	10	10.00	0					
Streatfeild-Moore, A. McN.	14	0	127	36	9.07	0					
Street, F. E.	7	0	21	12	3.00	0					
Sunnucks, P. R.	121	8	2016	162	17.84	1					
Sutherland, H. B.	2	0	7	4	3.50	0	32	2	16.00	2/32	—
Swaffer, J.	2	0	18	18	9.00	0					
Swann, E. G.	12	1	87	30	7.90	0					
Swinford, T. F.	8	0	89	50	11.12	0					
Syree, A. H.	2	0	7	7	3.50	0	10	0			
Taswell, E.	4	1	27	13	9.00	0					
Tavaré, C. J.	389	49	12771	168*	37.55	25	493	5	98.60	1/20	—
Tayler, R. F.	4	0	31	20	7.75	0					
Taylor, H.	6	0	53	29	8.83	0	121	2	60.50	1/34	—
Taylor, H. J.	13	3	181	33	18.10	0					
Taylor, N. R.	262	36	78.59	155*	34.77	18	788	14	56.28	2/20	—
Taylor-Jones, E. W.	4	0	22	11	5.50	0	12	0			
Terry, R. J.	1	1	0	0*	—	0					
Theobald, F. G.	2	0	14	13	7.00	0					
Thomas, R.	1	0	6	6	6.00	0					
Thomson, H. S.	3	0	44	27	14.66	0	86	3	28.66	1/14	—
Thornton, A. J.	37	5	680	137	21.25	1	486	16	30.37	4/20	—
Thornton, C. I.	34	1	959	124	29.06	3	205	8	25.62	2/12	—
Thornton, R. T.	77	9	1447	79	21.27	0	58	1	58.00	1/11	—
Thresher, R. S.	3	0	20	19	6.66	0	232	6	38.66	3/70	—
Throwley, Viscount	8	1	119	82	17.00	0	125	5	25.00	3/29	—
Tidy, T.	2	0	21	16	10.50	0					
Tindall, H. C. L.	3	0	49	32	16.33	0	110	2	55.00	1/17	—
Todd, L. J.	709	93	19407	174	31.50	36	15197	555	27.38	6/26	20
Tomson, W. F.	1	0	2	2	2.00	0					
Tonge, J. N.	65	3	855	60	13.79	0	356	9	39.55	3/14	—
Tootell, E.	6	0	42	24	7.00	0	55	2	27.50	1/27	—
Topley, P. A.	17	3	150	38*	10.71	0	669	14	47.78	2/28	—
Torrens, W. M.	7	1	86	43	14.33	0					
Traill, W. F.	18	2	227	49	14.18	0	325	15	21.66	5/21	2
Troughton, L. H. W.	235	30	3477	104	16.96	1	20	0			
Troughton, M. A.	71	8	981	87	15.57	0	218	10	21.80	5/70	1
Tufnell, C. F.	11	3	101	26	12.62	0	208	12	17.33	3/31	—
Tufton, J. S. R.	11	0	140	25	12.72	0					
Tylden, J. R.	2	0	19	19	9.50	0					
Tylecote, E. F. S.	41	1	949	104	23.72	2	14	0			
Ufton, D. G.	242	48	3915	119*	20.18	1					
Underwood, D. L.	538	154	3793	111	9.87	1	37578	1952	19.25	9/28	41
Usmar, W.	2	1	0	0*	0.00	0					
Valentine, B. H.	491	28	14131	242	30.52	25	648	18	36.00	2/8	—

Name	Inns	NO	Runs	HS	Avge	100s	Runs	Wkts	Avge	Best	5wI
Verrinder, A. O. C.	2	1	24	23	24.00	0	39	0			
Walker, J.	2	1	19	19*	19.00	0					
Wallroth, C. A.	2	0	8	5	4.00	0					
Walton, J.	2	0	13	13	6.50	0	15	1	15.00	1/15	—
Ward, G. H.	4	2	19	6*	9.50	0					
Ward, T. R.	4	1	60	29	20.00	0					
Warde, F.	10	1	65	18	7.22	0	56	3	18.66	2/5	—
Waterton, S. N. V.	28	5	386	50	16.78	0					
Wathen, A. C.	18	1	147	42*	8.64	0					
Wathen, W. H.	2	0	43	38	21.50	0					
Watson, G. S.	13	1	133	52*	11.08	0					
Watt, A. E.	326	37	4018	96	13.90	0	17325	608	28.49	8/100	34
Watts, J.	4	0	10	6	2.50	0					
Webb, G.	2	1	0	0*	0.00	0	45	1	45.00	1/30	—
Webb, G. W.	1	1	5	5*	—	0	30	0			
Webb, R.	2	0	2	1	1.00	0					
Weigall, G. J. V.	209	20	3459	138*	18.30	1	26	0			
Welldon, J. T.	7	1	60	37	10.00	0					
Wells, J.	12	3	46	10	5.11	0	128	14	9.14	6/35	1
Wenman, E. G.	89	5	926	52	11.02	0		(1)		1/?	
Wenman, G.	4	1	9	6	3.00	0					
Wenman, J. G.	6	0	19	8	3.33	0					
Wenman, W.	22	3	179	29	9.42	0					
Whitby, T. B.	2	0	12	11	6.00	0	12	0			
White, E. A.	57	6	805	81	15.78	0					
White, L. A.	8	0	84	34	10.50	0					
Whitehead, G. W. E.	4	0	12	5	3.00	0					
Whitehouse, P. M. W.	15	1	160	30	11.42	0	340	11	30.00	3/46	—
Whittaker, C. G.	65	14	309	24*	6.05	0	12	0(2)		2/?	—
Wigzell, G.	14	6	80	35	10.00	0	419	35	11.97	7/20	2
Wilkinson, R. W.	39	7	635	63	19.84	0	626	10	62.60	2/31	—
Willes, E. H. L.	4	1	22	17	7.33	0					
Williams, A. E. A.	5	2	28	13*	9.33	0	16	3	5.33	3/9	—
Willis, C. F.	1	0	0	0	0.00	0					
Wills, T. W. S.	6	0	40	15	6.66	0	59	2	29.50	2/31	—
Willsher, E.	265	20	3221	89	13.14	0	9480	754(32)	12.57	8/16	64
Willsher, W.	2	0	0	0	0.00	0					
Willson, E. A.	2	0	9	8	4.50	0	46	1	46.00	1/21	—
Wilson, C.	49	6	956	127	22.23	1	199	4	49.75	1/2	—
Wilson, L.	184	9	3459	132	19.76	1	265	6	44.16	2/17	—
Wilson, R. C.	644	38	19458	159*	32.10	30	90	4	22.50	3/38	—
Wisden, J.	2	0	10	6	5.00	0	87	4	21.75	3/36	—
Witherden, E. G.	71	9	1380	125*	22.25	2	371	9	41.22	5/32	1
Wood, G. E. C.	60	6	855	63*	15.83	0	9	0			
Wood, H.	16	2	72	25	5.14	0	13	0			
Wood, L. J.	2	0	5	5	2.50	0	182	4	45.50	4/124	—
Woollett, A. F.	81	4	1445	96	18.76	0					
Woolley, F. E.	1213	67	47868	270	41.77	122	31653	1680	18.84	8/22	115
Woolmer, R. A.	428	68	12634	203	35.09	28	7810	334	23.38	7/47	12
Wootton, J.	187	48	1021	40	7.34	0	10223	596	17.15	8/27	49

Name	Inns	NO	Runs	HS	Avge	100s	Runs	Wkts	Avge	Best	5wI
Wormald, E.	2	0	16	15	8.00	0	11	0			
Worthington, C. R.					1 match: did not bat or bowl						
Wright, A. C.	298	49	3280	81	13.09	0	14463	596	24.26	7/31	24
Wright, D. V. P.	595	188	5074	84★	12.46	0	38774	1709	22.68	9/47	132
Wright, E. C.	3	0	52	29	17.33	0	26	3	8.66	2/5	—
Wright, W.	307	77	2751	70★	11.96	0	13989	696	20.09	9/72	47
Yardley, W.	63	3	1473	126★	24.55	1	126	7	18.00	2/10	—
Young, A. J. K.	2	0	10	6	5.00	0					

TEST CAREER RECORDS OF KENT PLAYERS

Name	Country	Years	M	Runs	Avge	Wkts	Avge
T. M. Alderman	Australia	1981–1984	22	113	6.27	79	32.87
C. A. Absolom	England	1878	1	58	29.00		
L. E. G. Ames	England	1929–1938	47	2434	40.56	(74 *ct* 23 *st*)	
Asif Iqbal	Pakistan	1964–1979	58	3575	38.85	53	28.33
E. A. E. Baptiste	West Indies	1983–1984	9	224	24.88	15	32.40
V. A. Barton	England	1981	1	23	23.00		
M. R. Benson	England	1986	1	51	25.50		
I. F. W. Bligh	England	1882	4	62	10.33		
C. Blythe	England	1901–1909	19	183	9.63	100	18.63
W. M. Bradley	England	1899	2	23	23.00	6	38.83
A. Brown	England	1961	2	3	—	3	50.00
D. W. Carr	England	1909	1	0	0.00	7	40.28
A. P. F. Chapman	England	1924–1930	26	925	28.90		
S. Christopherson	England	1884	1	17	17.00	1	69.00
B. B. Cooper	Australia	1876	1	18	9.00		
C. S. Cowdrey	England	1984	5	96	19.20	4	72.00
M. C. Cowdrey	England	1954–1974	114	7624	44.06		
M. H. Denness	England	1969–1975	28	1667	39.69		
G. R. Dilley	England	1979–1987	30	391	13.48	99	30.02
P. R. Downton	England	1980–1986	27	701	19.47	(61 *ct* 5 *st*)	
R. M. Ellison	England	1984–1986	11	202	13.46	35	29.94
A. J. Evans	England	1921	1	18	9.00		
T. G. Evans	England	1946–1959	91	2439	20.49	(173 *ct* 46 *st*)	
A. E. Fagg	England	1936–1939	5	150	18.75		
A. Fielder	England	1903–1907	6	78	11.14	26	27.34
A. P. Freeman	England	1924–1929	12	154	14.00	66	25.86
W. G. Grace	England	1880–1899	22	1098	32.29	9	26.22
H. T. W. Hardinge	England	1921	2	30	15.00		
Lord Harris	England	1878–1884	4	145	29.00		
A. Hearne	England	1891	1	9	9.00		
F. Hearne	England & South Africa	1888–1895	6	168	16.80	2	20.00
G. G. Hearne	England	1891	1	0	0.00		
K. L. Hutchings	England	1907–1909	7	341	28.41	1	81.00
B. D. Julien	West Indies	1973–1976	24	866	30.92	50	37.36
A. P. E. Knott	England	1967–1981	95	4389	32.75	(250 *ct* 19 *st*)	
G. B. Legge	England	1927–1929	5	299	49.83		
W. H. V. Levett	England	1933	1	7	7.00	(3 *ct*)	
B. W. Luckhurst	England	1970–1974	21	1298	36.05	1	32.00
F. A. Mackinnon	England	1878	1	5	2.50		

C. S. Marriott	England	1933	1	0	0.00	11	8.72
F. Martin	England	1890–1891	2	14	7.00	14	10.07
J. W. Martin	England	1947	1	26	13.00	1	129.00
J. R. Mason	England	1897	5	129	12.90	2	74.50
S. O'Linn	South Africa	1961	7	297	27.00		
R. M. Prideaux	England	1968	3	102	20.40		
P. E. Richardson	England	1956–1963	34	2061	37.47	3	16.00
F. Ridgway	England	1951	5	49	8.16	7	54.14
J. N. Shepherd	West Indies	1969–1970	5	77	9.62	19	25.21
J. Shuter	England	1888	1	28	28.00		
C. J. Tavaré	England	1980–1984	30	1753	33.07		
E. F. S. Tylecote	England	1882–1886	6	152	19.00	(5 ct 5 st)	
D. L. Underwood	England	1966–1981	86	937	11.56	297	25.83
B. H. Valentine	England	1933–1938	7	454	64.85		
G. E. C. Wood	England	1924	3	7	3.50	(5 ct 1 st)	
H. Wood	England	1888–1891	4	204	68.00	(2 ct 1 st)	
F. E. Woolley	England	1909–1934	64	3283	36.07	83	33.91
R. A. Woolmer	England	1975–1981	19	1059	33.09	4	74.75
D. V. P. Wright	England	1938–1950	34	289	11.11	108	39.11

CAPTAINS OF KENT

1859–1870	W. S. Norton
1871–1874	No official appointment
1875–1889	Lord Harris
1890–1893	F. Marchant and W. H. Patterson
1894–1897	F. Marchant
1898–1902	J. R. Mason
1903	C. J. Burnup
1904–1908	C. H. B. Marsham
1909–1913	E. W. Dillon
1914–1923	L. H. W. Troughton
1924–1926	W. S. Cornwallis
1927	A. J. Evans
1928–1930	G. B. Legge
1931–1936	A. P. F. Chapman
1937	R. T. Bryan and B. H. Valentine
1938–1939	F. G. H. Chalk
1946–1948	B. H. Valentine
1949–1951	D. G. Clark
1952–1953	W. Murray-Wood
1954–1956	D. V. P. Wright
1957–1971	M. C. Cowdrey
1972–1976	M. H. Denness

1977	Asif Iqbal
1978–1980	A. G. E. Ealham
1981–1982	Asif Iqbal
1983–1984	C. J. Tavaré
1985–1987	C. S. Cowdrey

RESULTS OF ALL INTER-COUNTY FIRST-CLASS MATCHES

Year	DY	EX	GM	GS	HA	LA	LE	MX	NR	NT	SM	SY	SX	WA	WO	YO	CA	P	W	L	D	T
1836													LL					2	0	2	0	0
1837										W			WW					3	3	0	0	0
1838													WW					2	2	0	0	0
1839													WW					2	2	0	0	0
1840								L										1	0	1	0	0
1841										W			WW					3	3	0	0	0
1842													WW					2	2	0	0	0
1843													WW					2	2	0	0	0
1844													LW					2	1	1	0	0
1845								LW					LL					4	1	3	0	0
1846												DL	WW					4	2	1	1	0
1847												WT	WW					4	3	0	0	1
1848													LD					2	0	1	1	0
1849													WW	W				3	3	0	0	0
1850												L	DW					3	1	1	1	0
1851													LL					2	0	2	0	0
1852												W	LL					3	1	2	0	0
1853												L						1	0	1	0	0
1854													LL					2	0	2	0	0
1855													LW					2	1	1	0	0
1856												L	WL					3	1	2	0	0
1857												L	WW					3	2	1	0	0
1858													LW					2	1	1	0	0
1859						LL							LL					4	0	4	0	0
1860													WW					2	2	0	0	0
1861												WW	WW		L			5	4	1	0	0
1862												LL	LW	WL	L			7	2	5	0	0
1863							LD					LL	WL		W			7	2	4	1	0
1864							LL					LL	LL	L				7	0	7	0	0
1865												LL	D LW		DW			7	2	3	2	0
1866												WL	D DD					5	1	1	3	0
1867			W WD									LD		W LL				8	3	3	2	0
1868								WL				WW	WL		LW			8	5	3	0	0
1869			LL									WD	W WW					7	4	2	1	0
1870										LL		WL	WL		LL			8	2	6	0	0
1871		WL										DW	LL					6	2	3	1	0
1872												LL	LL					4	0	4	0	0
1873				W								WL	WL					5	3	2	0	0
1874	LL			WD														4	1	2	1	0
1875	LL					WW	LL					LL						8	2	6	0	0
1876	WL		LL	WL								WL	WL					10	4	6	0	0
1877	LL					WW	WW			LW		LD	WW					12	7	4	1	0
1878	WW					WW	LL			LD		WD	WL					12	6	4	2	0
1879		DL								LL		LL	LW	WL				10	2	7	1	0
1880	WL			LL								WD	WW	WD				10	5	3	2	0
1881	LW			LL								LL	WW	LL				10	3	7	0	0
1882				LL				L				LL	WD	WL				9	2	6	1	0
1883				WL			LL					DD	WL	LL				10	2	6	2	0
1884	WW			WL	LW		LL				WW	WD	LD	LL				16	7	7	2	0

Year	DY	EX	GM	GS	HA	LA	LE	MX	NR	NT	SM	SY	SX	WA	WO	YO	CA	P	W	L	D	T
1885					WW	L		WL				LD	WW			DW		11	6	3	2	0
1886	WW				WL	DL		LD				LL	LW			WD		14	5	6	3	0
1887			DD		LL	DL		LL				LD	WL			DL		14	1	8	5	0
1888			LL		WW			WW	WD			LL	WW			LD		14	7	5	2	0
1889			DW		LL	W		WL				LL	WW			WW		13	7	5	1	0
1890			WD		LL			WW	DD			DW	WW			DL		14	6	3	5	0
1891			DD		L			WW	DD	LW		LL	DL			WD		15	4	5	6	0
1892			WL		LD			LD	LD	LL		LL	WD			DL		16	2	9	5	0
1893			LD		WW			LW	DD	WD	WD		LL					16	6	4	6	0
1894			WW		WW			WD	LD	LL		WL	LD	DL		L		17	6	7	4	0
1895			LD		LL			LL	WD	WL		LL	LL	WD		LD		18	3	11	4	0
1896			LW		DL			DL	LD	WD		WL	LW	WL		LL		18	5	9	4	0
1897			LL		LD			WL	DD	WL		LL	LD	DD		LL		18	2	10	6	0
1898		WD	DL		DD			LL	DL	WD		DL	DW	WD		WL		20	5	6	9	0
1899		LL	LD		D			WL		DW	WD	DL	LW	WL		WL		19	6	8	5	0
1900		WD	DL	WW	DD			WL		DL	WW	DD	DD		W	LD		21	7	4	10	0
1901		DD	WD	WL	WL			LD	D	WW	WW	LD		LD		LL		21	7	7	7	0
1902		DL		WW	WW	LL		LD		DD	WL	WD	LD		WW	LL		22	8	8	6	0
1903		WL		DL	WW	LW		D		LL	WD	DW	D		WD	DL		20	7	6	7	0
1904		WD		WD	WW	LL		WL		LD	WW	WD	DD		WW	DD		22	10	4	8	0
1905		DW		WW	WW	LL		LD		LW	WW	WT	LL		DD	LW		22	10	7	4	1
1906		WD		WW	WW	WL	WW	DW			WW	WW	WW		WD	LD		22	16	3	4	0
1907	WW	LL		LL	WL	LL	WW	LD	WW		WW	WL	DW		WD	DD		26	12	9	5	0
1908	WW	WD		WW	LW	DW	WW	W	WW		WW	WL	WD		WD	DL		25	17	3	5	0
1909	WW	DD		WW	WW	WW	LW	WD	WW		WD	WD	DW		LW	DW		26	16	2	8	0
1910	WW	WL		WW	WD	WD	WL	WW	DW		WW	DL	WW		WW	WW		26	19	3	4	0
1911	LW			WW	DD	LW	WW	WW	LW	DW	WW	WL	DW		WW	WD		26	17	4	5	0
1912	WW			DW	DD	WL	WW	LD	LL	DW	WW	WW	WD		WW	LD		26	14	5	7	0
1913	WW			WL	WW	WW	WW	WW	WW	LD	WW	WL	WW	WW	DW	DD		28	20	3	5	0
1914	WD			WW	LL	DL	DW	WL	WW	LW	WW	DL	LD	WW	WW	WW		28	16	7	5	0
1919	DD			DW	DW			WD				WL	WW			DD		14	6	1	7	0
1920	WD			WW	WW	LL	WW	LL	WW	DD		WL	LW	WW	WW	WD		26	16	6	4	0
1921	WD			WW	WL	DL	WW	WL	WW	LW		DL	WL	WW	WW	LW		26	16	7	3	0
1922	WD			WW	DW	DD	WD	WD	WL	WD	DW	WL	WW	WW	WW	LL		28	16	3	9	0
1923	WW			WW	WW	LD	WL	LD	WW	LL	WW	LD	WW	LW	WW	LD		28	16	8	4	0
1924	DD			WD	WW	WW	LW	WW	LL	DW	DD	WW	DL	WD	DD			28	12	4	12	0
1925	WW	WD		WW	WL	WL	WW	LD	DL	LW	WD	LD	WW	WW		LD		28	15	7	6	0
1926	DD	WD		WW	WW	WW	WW	WW	DW	DD	DL	WW				DD		28	15	2	11	0
1927	LW	LW		L	WL	DD	DD	WD	WW	WW	WW	DL	DL	DD	WW	D		28	12	6	10	0
1928	DW	WW		WW	WW	LL	DD	WD	WW	LL	WW	DL	WD	WD	WD	DD		30	15	5	10	0
1929	DW	WD		DW	DD	LD	WW	LW	WL	DL	WW	DL	WL	WL		WL		28	12	8	8	0
1930	WL	WW		DL	DW	LL		DW	WW	DL	DW	DD	LD	WW	WD	LW		28	12	7	9	0
1931	DW	WL		DW	DD	WW	WW	WW	WL	WW	LD	LD	LD	DL	LD			28	12	7	9	0
1932	WD	WW	WW	LW	DW	WD	WW	DW	WD			DD	LD	WD	WD	L		27	14	3	10	0
1933	WL	DL		WL	DL	DL	WW	WW	WW	WD	LW	WD	LW	WD	WD	WL		30	15	8	7	0
1934	LD	LW	WW	LW	DD	DW		DL	WW	WL	WD	WD	LD	WW	LD			30	12	7	11	0
1935	DL	WL	WW	WW	LW	LD	WL	WL			DL	LW	LW	LD	DD	D	LL	29	10	12	7	0
1936	WL	WL	DW	WD	DD	LL		DL		LD	WW	LD	DD	DW	LW	WL		28	9	9	10	0
1937	WL	LL	DL	WL	WL	DL	WW	LL		LD	WL	DL	LL		WW	LL		28	8	16	4	0
1938	LD	WD	WL	WL	WW	LW	LW	WL		LL	DL	LL	DL		WD	LD		28	8	14	6	0
1939	WL	WD	DW	WL	LW	WL	WW	L		LW	LD	DW	WW		LW	LL		27	14	9	4	0
1946	WD	D	D	L	WD	W	WL	LW	D	WL	LL	LD	WW	WW	W	LL		26	11	8	7	0
1947	WD	D	L	L	WW	L	WW	DW	W	DL	WD	LL	LW	WL	W	WD		26	12	8	6	0
1948	L	DD	LL	DL	DL	WL	W	LD	DL	D	W	LL	DD	D	WD	L		26	4	11	11	0
1949	W	LD	WL	LL	WW	WL	W	LL	LL	W	L	DL	LD	D	LL	L		26	7	15	4	0
1950	WL	DL	L	DD	DT	LL	WW	WW	LL	LD	L	WL	LD	D	DD	L		28	6	12	9	1
1951	LD	DL	D	WD	DL	LL	WL	LL	LW	DD	L	LD	LD	L	WL	L		28	4	15	9	0
1952	D	LW	DL	D	DL	LL	LL	LL	LL	DW	W	DW	LL	DL	LW	D	LL	28	5	15	8	0
1953	D	DL	DL	L	DL	LD	DL	LL	LW	DW	L	WL	DL	LD	LW	W	DL	28	4	14	10	0
1954	LL	DD	D	DD	DW	DD	LL	DW	LW	WL	L	DD	DD	D	WD	D		28	5	7	16	0
1955	LL	WL	W	DW	LD	DL	LL	WW	WD	DL	L	LW	WL	D	LW	L		28	9	12	7	0
1956	L	LD	WL	L	DD	WD	DD	LL	LL	D	WL	LL	DL	LD	D	DD		28	3	13	12	0
1957	W	DL	LL	W	WD	DL	DD	LW	LD	W	LL	LL	LD	LD	W	LD		28	6	13	9	0
1958	WL	DL	L	DD	LL	W	WW	LW	WL	DW	W	WL	DD	D	DL	L		27	9	10	8	0
1959	LL	DW	W	LL	LW	DL	DD	LL	WL	WW	L	LD	DD	W	WD	L		28	8	12	8	0

Year	DY	EX	GM	GS	HA	LA	LE	MX	NR	NT	SM	SY	SX	WA	WO	YO	CA	P	W	L	D	T
1960	W	LD	DD	DW	DL	WD	L	LD	D	W	DD	DL	WL	DD	WW	LD		28	7	7	14	0
1961	D	DL	DW	LL	DW	DD	L	WD	L	W	LL	DD	DL	LW	DW	WD		28	7	9	12	0
1962	D	DL	WD	DL	DL	WD	W	WD	D	W	DD	DL	LW	WL	DL	LL		28	7	9	12	0
1963	D	DD	DD	L	DD	DL	WD	DW	DD	D	LD	WL	LD	DW	D	LD		28	4	6	18	0
1964	W	WW	DL	D	DD	DD	DW	DW	DD	W	DW	DL	LW	DL	L	LW		28	9	6	13	0
1965	DW	DW	L	WW	DD	DD	DD	WD	DL	DD	W	DD	DL	W	WL	L		28	8	5	15	0
1966	LW	LW	D	WL	DW	LW	WL	DW	DL	DD	W	DD	WW	D	WL	L		28	11	8	9	0
1967	D	WD	WL	D	WD	WD	DL	WD	DD	D	WD	DW	WW	W	W	LD		27	11	3	13	0
1968	D	WD	WW	D	WD	WD	LW	DL	WW	L	WW	LD	DD	WL	W	DD		28	12	5	11	0
1969	L	DW	D	D	LL	DD	DD	WW	DD	D	W	DL	DD	L	L	D		24	4	6	14	0
1970	D	LW	L	W	WD	DD	WW	DL	LD	W	W	WD	DW	L	D	D		24	9	5	10	0
1971	LD	L	L	L	WD	W	D	DW	D	DD	W	WD	DL	L	DD	WW		24	7	6	11	0
1972	D	D	W	L	WD	L	D	W	WD	D	D	DD	WL	L	W	W		20	7	4	9	0
1973	D	W	L	D	DD	L	D	LW	D	W	D	DD	DW	D	D	D		20	4	3	13	0
1974	W	D	W	W	LL	D	D	LD	L	L	L	DW	LW	D	L	D		20	5	8	7	0
1975	W	L	L	D	DD	W	L	LD	W	W	W	DD	WW	D	W	D		20	8	4	8	0
1976	W	D	D	L	LD	D	L	WL	W	D	L	DD	DW	L	W	L		20	5	7	8	0
1977	W	W	W	W	DD	D	WD	WD	L	W	D	DD	DD	W	L	W		21	9	2	10	0
1978	W	DL	W	W	WL	D	WW	WW	D	D	W	WW	WL	D	W	D		22	13	3	6	0
1979	W	DD	W	W	DW	D	LW	DD	D	W	D	LD	DD	L	D	D		22	5	3	13	0
1980	D	LL	L	L	DW	D	DD	DD	D	L	L	DL	DD	W	D	L		22	2	8	12	0
1981	L	LL	D	D	WW	D	DW	LD	D	D	L	DW	WL	L	D	D		22	5	7	10	0
1982	D	DD	D	D	LW	D	WD	LD	D	L	D	DL	WD	D	D	D		22	3	4	15	0
1983	D	DW	DW	D	DL	D	WL	L	D	W	WD	LD	WW	DD	D	D		24	7	4	13	0
1984	WW	WW	D	LD	WW	DD	D	WD	T	D	D	WD	LT	L	D	D		24	8	3	11	2
1985	D	DD	D	L	DD	W	D	D	WD	LD	D	DW	LD	D	LL	WD		24	4	5	15	0
1986	L	LW	DD	L	DW	W	WD	D	D	L	DL	DL	DL	WD	D	D		24	5	7	12	0
1987																						

Notes: CA = Cambridgeshire; T = tied.

RESULTS OF ALL SUNDAY LEAGUE MATCHES

Year	DY	EX	GM	GS	HA	LA	LE	MX	NR	NT	SM	SY	SX	WA	WO	YO	P	W	L	D	T
1969	W	L	W	L	W	L	W	W	W	T	W	L	W	W	L	L	16	9	6	0	1
1970	W	W	L	W	L	W	L	W	W	W	W	W	W	W	W	L	16	12	4	0	0
1971	L	L	L	W	W	L	W	W	W	L	W	L	W	L	L	W	16	8	8	0	0
1972	W	W	W	W	A	L	W	L	W	L	L	W	W	W	W	W	16	11	4	1	0
1973	W	W	W	W	L	L	W	A	W	W	W	W	A	W	W	W	16	12	2	2	0
1974	W	W	W	A	W	W	W	A	L	W	L	W	L	W	W	L	16	10	4	2	0
1975	W	W	W	W	L	W	W	W	L	W	W	W	L	L	W	W	16	12	4	0	0
1976	W	L	W	W	L	W	W	W	L	W	L	L	W	L	W	W	16	10	6	0	0
1977	W	L	A	L	L	A	L	W	A	W	L	W	W	W	W	L	16	7	6	3	0
1978	L	W	L	W	L	W	L	L	A	A	L	W	L	W	W	L	16	6	8	2	0
1979	W	L	W	W	W	W	W	L	W	A	W	W	W	W	L	A	16	11	3	2	0
1980	L	L	W	W	L	L	L	W	W	W	L	L	A	T	L	W	16	6	8	1	1
1981	L	L	A	L	W	T	L	W	L	W	W	W	W	L	L	W	16	7	7	1	1
1982	W	L	W	W	L	W	L	W	L	L	W	W	L	W	W	L	16	9	7	0	0
1983	A	L	W	W	W	W	A	L	A	W	L	W	A	W	W	A	16	8	3	5	0
1984	L	L	L	W	W	W	A	L	W	L	L	A	W	W	L	L	16	6	8	2	0
1985	L	L	W	W	A	L	A	W	L	W	L	W	L	W	A	L	16	6	7	3	0
1986	W	L	W	W	L	L	A	W	L	W	L	T	W	A	W	A	16	7	5	3	1

RESULTS IN GILLETTE CUP/NATWEST TROPHY

1963 *1st Round*: lost to Sussex.

1964 *1st Round*: bye; *2nd Round*: lost to Lancashire.

1965 *1st Round*: bye; *2nd Round*: lost to Hampshire.

1966 *1st Round*: beat Suffolk; *2nd Round*: lost to Hampshire.

1967 *1st Round*: bye; *2nd Round*: beat Essex; *Q/Final*: beat Surrey; *S/Final*: beat Sussex; *Final*: beat Somerset by 32 runs.

1968 *1st Round*: bye; *2nd Round*: lost to Gloucestershire.

1969 *1st Round*: bye; *2nd Round*: lost to Leicestershire.

1970 *1st Round*: bye; *2nd Round*: beat Worcestershire; *Q/Final*: lost to Sussex.

1971 *1st Round*: beat Northamptonshire; *2nd Round*: beat Yorkshire; *Q/Final*: beat Leicestershire; *S/Final*: beat Warwickshire; *Final*: lost to Lancashire by 24 runs.

1972 *1st Round*: bye; *2nd Round*: beat Gloucestershire; *Q/Final*: beat Essex; *S/Final*: lost to Lancashire by 7 runs.

1973 *1st Round*: bye; *2nd Round*: beat Hampshire; *Q/Final*: lost to Sussex.

1974 *1st Round*: beat Buckinghamshire; *2nd Round*: beat Durham; *Q/Final*: beat Leicestershire; *S/Final*: beat Somerset; *Final*: beat Lancashire by 4 wickets.

1975 *1st Round*: bye; *2nd Round*: lost to Nottinghamshire.

1976 *1st Round*: bye; *2nd Round*: lost to Sussex.

1977 *1st Round*: lost to Middlesex.

1978 *1st Round*: bye; *2nd Round*: beat Northamptonshire; *Q/Final*: lost to Somerset.

1979 *1st Round*: beat Glamorgan; *2nd Round*: beat Lancashire; *Q/Final*: lost to Somerset.

1980 *1st Round*: bye; *2nd Round*: lost to Yorkshire.

1981 *1st Round*: beat Yorkshire; *2nd Round*: lost to Nottinghamshire.

1982 *1st Round*: bye; *2nd Round*: lost to Essex.

1983 *1st Round*: beat Cheshire; *2nd Round*: beat Essex; *Q/Final*: beat Warwickshire; *S/Final*: beat Hampshire; *Final*: lost to Somerset by 24 runs.

1984 *1st Round*: beat Yorkshire; *2nd Round*: beat Hampshire; *Q/Final*: beat Somerset; *S/Final*: beat Warwickshire; *Final*: lost to Middlesex by 4 wickets.

1985 *1st Round*: beat Surrey; *2nd Round*: beat Durham; *Q/Final*: lost to Essex.

1986 *1st Round*: beat Scotland; *2nd Round*: lost to Nottinghamshire.

1987 *1st Round*: beat Scotland; *2nd Round*: lost to Derbyshire.

RESULTS IN BENSON & HEDGES CUP

1972 Third in Group South.

1973 First in Group South; *Q/Final*: beat Hampshire; *S/Final*: beat Essex; *Final*: beat Worcestershire by 39 runs.

1974 First in Group South; *Q/Final*: lost to Leicestershire.

1975 Fourth in Group South.

1976 First in Group D; *Q/Final*: beat Nottinghamshire; *S/Final*: beat Surrey; *Final*: beat Worcestershire by 43 runs.

1977 First in Group C; *Q/Final*: beat Sussex; *S/Final*: beat Northamptonshire; *Final*: lost to Gloucestershire by 64 runs.

1978 First in Group D; *Q/Final*: beat Nottinghamshire; *S/Final*: beat Somerset; *Final*: beat Derbyshire by 6 wickets.

1979 Fourth in Group D.

1980 Fourth in Group D.

1981 First in Group C; *Q/Final*: beat Warwickshire; *S/Final*: lost to Somerset.

1982 First in Group C; *Q/Final*: lost to Somerset.

1983 First in Group D; *Q/Final*: beat Hampshire; *S/Final*: lost to Essex.

1984 Third in Group C.

1985 Second in Group D; *Q/Final*: match abandoned; *S/Final*: lost to Leicestershire.

1986 Second in Group D; *Q/Final*: beat Derbyshire; *S/Final*: beat Worcestershire; *Final*: lost to Middlesex by 2 runs.

1987 Second in Group D; *Q/Final*: beat Gloucestershire; *S/Final*: lost to Northamptonshire.

GROUNDS USED BY KENT
1835–1987

Ground	First	Last
Foxgrove, Beckenham	1886	1905
Rectory Field, Blackheath	1887	1971
Phillip's Field, Bromley	1840	
White Hart Field, Bromley	1841	1842
Beverley Ground, Canterbury	1841	1846
St Lawrence Ground, Canterbury	1847	1987
Private Banks, Catford	1875	1921
Hesketh Park, Dartford	1956	
Crabble Ground, Dover	1907	1976
Mont Field, Faversham	1876	
Municipal Ground, Folkestone	1926	1987
Garrison, Gillingham	1862	1968
Bat & Ball, Gravesend	1849	1971
Mote Park, Maidstone	1859	1987

Ground	First	Last
Margate	1864	
Lloyds Bank, New Beckenham	1954	
Midland Bank, New Beckenham	1970	
Preston Hall	1846	1847
Sandgate	1862	1863
Southborough	1867	
Angel, Tonbridge	1869	1939
County Ground, Town Malling	1836	1890
Tunbridge Wells Common	1856	1884
Nevill Ground, Tunbridge Wells	1901	1987

TEAM RECORDS

(1) HIGHEST AND LOWEST SCORE FOR KENT AGAINST EACH COUNTY

Opponents	Highest	Year	Lowest	Year
Derbyshire	615 *at* Derby	1908	25 *at* Wirksworth	1874
Essex	803-4 *at* Brentwood	1934	43 *at* Southend	1925
Glamorgan	490 *at* Gravesend	1934	49 *at* Swansea	1949
Gloucestershire	607-6 *at* Cheltenham	1910	28 *at* Moreton-in-Marsh	1888
Hampshire	610 *at* Bournemouth	1906	32 *at* Southampton	1952
Lancashire	479 *at* Canterbury	1906	38 *at* Maidstone	1881
Leicestershire	551-9 *at* Maidstone	1962	56 *at* Oakham	1935
Middlesex	539-9 *at* Lord's	1928	43 *at* Lord's / 43 *at* Dover	1953 / 1957
Northamptonshire	561 *at* Gravesend	1908	67 *at* Gravesend	1924
Nottinghamshire	507-6 *at* Trent Bridge	1953	36 *at* Town Malling	1878
Somerset	601-8 *at* Taunton	1908	55 *at* Tonbridge	1926
Surrey	579-8 *at* The Oval	1935	20 *at* The Oval	1870
Sussex	580-9 *at* Tonbridge	1939	18 *at* Gravesend	1867
Warwickshire	571 *at* Tonbridge	1898	42 *at* Edgbaston	1925
Worcestershire	602-7 *at* Dudley	1938	50 *at* Dover	1955
Yorkshire	493 *at* Tonbridge	1914	39 *at* Bramall Lane / 39 *at* Bramall Lane	1882 / 1936

(2) HIGHEST AND LOWEST SCORE AGAINST KENT BY EACH COUNTY

Opponents	Highest	Year	Lowest	Year
Derbyshire	437 *at* Tonbridge	1938	36 *at* Wirksworth	1874
Essex	551 *at* Leyton	1900	34 *at* Brentwood	1969
Glamorgan	492 *at* Tonbridge	1939	46 *at* Cardiff	1979
Gloucestershire	563 *at* Tunbridge Wells	1934	31 *at* Tonbridge	1903

Opponents	Highest	Year	Lowest	Year
Hampshire	599 at Southampton	1912	31 at Maidstone	1967
Lancashire	531 at Old Trafford	1906	61 at Old Trafford	1884
Leicestershire	432 at Tonbridge	1928	25 at Leicester	1912
Middlesex	488 at Tonbridge	1925	44 at Lord's	1891
Northamptonshire	445-9 at Northampton	1948	39 at Northampton	1907
Nottinghamshire	602 at Trent Bridge	1904	35 at Beckenham	1889
Somerset	503 at Taunton	1898	50 at Tunbridge Wells	1910
Surrey	617 at The Oval	1897	44 at Maidstone	1884
Sussex	560-9 at Hastings	1930	22 at Sevenoaks	1828
Warwickshire	513 at Edgbaston	1928	16 at Tonbridge	1913
Worcestershire	627-9 at Worcester	1905	25 at Tunbridge Wells	1960
Yorkshire	559 at Canterbury	1887	30 at Bramall Lane	1865

(3) HIGHEST AND LOWEST SCORES IN LIMITED-OVERS MATCHES

	Competition	Score	Opponents and Venue	Year
Highest	Sunday League			
	(John Player/Refuge Assurance)	281-5	Warwicks at Folkestone	1983
	Benson & Hedges Cup	293-6	Somerset at Taunton	1985
	NatWest/Gillette	297-3	Worcestershire at Canterbury	1970
Lowest	Sunday League			
	(John Player/Refuge Assurance)	83	Middlesex at Lord's	1984
	Benson & Hedges Cup	73	Middlesex at Canterbury	1979
	NatWest/Gillette	69	Somerset at Taunton	1979

INDIVIDUAL BATTING RECORDS

(1) DOUBLE-CENTURIES IN FIRST-CLASS MATCHES

Batsman	Score	Opponents	Venue	Year
L. E. G. Ames (8)	295	Gloucestershire	Folkestone	1933
	212★	Nottinghamshire	Gravesend	1947
	212	Gloucestershire	Dover	1948
	210	Warwickshire	Tonbridge	1933
	202	Essex	Brentwood	1934
	201★	Worcestershire	Gillingham	1937
	201	Worcestershire	Worcester	1939
	200	Surrey	Blackheath	1928
W. H. Ashdown (2)	332	Essex	Brentwood	1934
	305★	Derby	Dover	1935
D. G. Aslett (1)	221★	Sri Lankans	Canterbury	1984
J. L. Bryan (1)	236	Hampshire	Canterbury	1923
C. J. Burnup (1)	200	Lancashire	Old Trafford	1900
A. P. F. Chapman (1)	260	Lancashire	Maidstone	1927

Batsman	Score	Opponents	Venue	Year
M. C. Cowdrey (2)	250	Essex	Blackheath	1959
	204★	Cambridge University	Fenner's	1956
A. E. Fagg (6)	269★	Nottinghamshire	Trent Bridge	1953
	257	Hampshire	Southampton	1936
	244	Essex	Colchester	1938
	221	Nottinghamshire	Trent Bridge	1951
	203	Middlesex	Dover	1948
	202★	Essex	Colchester	1938
H. T. W. Hardinge (4)	263★	Gloucestershire	Gloucester	1928
	249★	Leicestershire	Leicester	1922
	207	Surrey	Blackheath	1921
	205	Warwickshire	Tunbridge Wells	1928
E. Humphreys (2)	208	Gloucestershire	Catford	1909
	200★	Lancashire	Tunbridge Wells	1910
B. W. Luckhurst (2)	215	Derbyshire	Derby	1973
	203★	Cambridge University	Fenner's	1970
D. Nicholls (1)	211	Derbyshire	Folkestone	1963
Jas Seymour (3)	218★	Essex	Leyton	1911
	214	Essex	Tunbridge Wells	1914
	204	Hampshire	Tonbridge	1907
B. H. Valentine (2)	242	Leicestershire	Oakham	1938
	201	Nottinghamshire	Trent Bridge	1939
F. E. Woolley (6)	270	Middlesex	Canterbury	1923
	229	Surrey	The Oval	1935
	224★	Oxford University	The Parks	1913
	224	New Zealanders	Canterbury	1931
	217	Northamptonshire	Northampton	1926
	215	Somerset	Gravesend	1925
R. A. Woolmer (1)	203	Sussex	Tunbridge Wells	1982

Note: A. E. Fagg scored 244 and 202★, shown above, in the same match, a unique feat in first-class cricket.

(2) CENTURIES IN LIMITED-OVERS MATCHES
(a) Sunday League (John Player/Refuge Assurance)

Batsman	Score	Opponents	Venue	Year
Asif Iqbal (3)	106	Gloucestershire	Maidstone	1976
	103★	Surrey	The Oval	1976
	100★	Middlesex	Maidstone	1976
D. G. Aslett (1)	100	Somerset	Taunton	1983
M. H. Denness (3)	119★	Yorkshire	Scarborough	1976
	116	Somerset	Canterbury	1975
	108★	Northamptonshire	Canterbury	1976
B. W. Luckhurst (3)	142	Somerset	Weston-super-Mare	1970

Batsman	Score	Opponents	Venue	Year
	124	Essex	Chelmsford	1973
	104	Somerset	Canterbury	1973
C. J. Tavaré (5)	136*	Gloucestershire	Canterbury	1978
	122*	Warwickshire	Folkestone	1983
	110	Glamorgan	Canterbury	1980
	103*	Glamorgan	Canterbury	1982
	101	Hampshire	Canterbury	1985
R. A. Woolmer (1)	112*	Nottinghamshire	Trent Bridge	1980

(b) Benson & Hedges Cup

Batsman	Score	Opponents	Venue	Year
C. S. Cowdrey (1)	114	Sussex	Canterbury	1977
M. C. Cowdrey (1)	107*	Middlesex	Lord's	1972
M. H. Denness (2)	112*	Surrey	The Oval	1973
	104	Surrey	The Oval	1976
B. W. Luckhurst (1)	111	Leicestershire	Canterbury	1974
C. J. Tavaré (1)	143	Somerset	Taunton	1985
N. R. Taylor (3)	121	Sussex	Hove	1982
	121	Somerset	Canterbury	1982
	100	Comb Univ	Cambridge	1983

(c) NatWest Trophy/Gillette Cup

Batsman	Score	Opponents	Venue	Year
M. R. Benson (1)	113*	Warwickshire	Edgbaston	1984
C. S. Cowdrey (1)	122*	Essex	Chelmsford	1983
M. C. Cowdrey (2)	116	Suffolk	Ipswich	1966
	115	Durham	Canterbury	1974
G. W. Johnson (1)	120*	Buckinghamshire	Canterbury	1974
B. W. Luckhurst (3)	129*	Durham	Canterbury	1974
	125	Leicestershire	Canterbury	1974
	114*	Hampshire	Canterbury	1973
P. E. Richardson (1)	127	Sussex	Tunbridge Wells	1963
J. N. Shepherd (1)	101	Middlesex	Canterbury	1977
C. J. Tavaré (2)	118*	Yorkshire	Canterbury	1981
	103	Somerset	Taunton	1984

(3) CARRYING BAT THROUGH A COMPLETED FIRST-CLASS INNINGS

The following opening batsmen have batted throughout a competed innings in which all ten of their partners have been dismissed.

Batsman	Score Total	Opponents	Venue	Year
W. H. Ashdown (4)	150 (303)	Surrey	The Oval	1926
	100 (236)	Sussex	Tunbridge Wells	1928
	83 (223)	Gloucestershire	Maidstone	1930
	305 (560)	Derbyshire	Derby	1935

Batsman	Score	Total	Opponents	Venue	Year
J. L. Bryan (2)	82	(157)	Yorkshire	Tunbridge Wells	1921
	93	(186)	Middlesex	Lord's	1929
C. J. Burnup (1)	103	(209)	Surrey	The Oval	1899
F. G. H. Chalk (1)	115	(215)	Yorkshire	Dover	1939
G. C. Collins (1)	18	(67)	Northamptonshire	Gravesend	1924
M. C. Cowdrey (1)	65	(169)	Gloucestershire	Cheltenham	1956
M. H. Denness (1)	69	(136)	Northamptonshire	Wellingborough	1971
E. W. Dillon (1)	38	(86)	Nottinghamshire	Gravesend	1902
A. E. Fagg (3)	37	(127)	Gloucestershire	Gillingham	1938
	117	(230)	Essex	Maidstone	1948
	71	(134)	Surrey	The Oval	1950
E. W. J. Fillary (1)	28	(146)	Yorkshire	Dover	1964
L. A. Hamilton (1)	117	(205)	Australians	Canterbury	1890
H. T. W. Hardinge (10)	123	(203)	Essex	Tonbridge	1911
	79	(169)	Yorkshire	Headingley	1919
	172	(339)	Essex	Colchester	1919
	62	(163)	Hampshire	Canterbury	1920
	118	(196)	MCC	Lord's	1921
	249	(440)	Leicestershire	Leicester	1922
	71	(161)	Gloucestershire	Tunbridge Wells	1923
	54	(96)	Oxford University	The Parks	1924
	30	(55)	Somerset	Tonbridge	1926
	49	(122)	Essex	Southend	1930
Lord Harris (1)	80	(148)	Yorkshire	Gravesend	1883
A. Hearne (6)	116	(256)	Gloucestershire	Canterbury	1892
	43	(189)	Somerset	Catford	1892
	22	(76)	Gloucestershire	Gravesend	1895
	55	(114)	Sussex	Tonbridge	1899
	79	(172)	Worcestershire	Canterbury	1903
	90	(294)	Gloucestershire	Tonbridge	1904
P. Hearn (1)	12	(32)	Hampshire	Southampton	1952
E. Henty (1)	32	(81)	Yorkshire	Dewsbury	1870
B. W. Luckhurst (2)	126	(253)	Sussex	Tunbridge Wells	1967
	46	(96)	Hampshire	Bournemouth	1969
F. A. Mackinnon (1)	33	(64)	Yorkshire	Bradford	1881
C. Payne (1)	135	(367)	Surrey	Gravesend	1866
A. H. Phebey (4)	54	(126)	Middlesex	Lord's	1951
	89	(209)	Worcestershire	Kidderminster	1951
	85	(181)	Australians	Canterbury	1953
	50	(127)	Northamptonshire	Northampton	1954
L. J. Todd (2)	133	(265)	Leicestershire	Tunbridge Wells	1946
	59	(140)	Worcestershire	Worcester	1946

(4) CENTURY IN EACH INNINGS OF A FIRST-CLASS MATCH

Batsman	Scores		Opponents	Venue	Year
J. M. Allan (1)	121	105	Northamptonshire	Northampton	1955
L. E. G. Ames (3)	132	145★	Northamptonshire	Dover	1933
	119	127	Surrey	Blackheath	1937
	112	119	Gloucestershire	Bristol	1950
W. H. Ashdown (1)	121	103	Middlesex	Lord's	1931
D. G. Aslett (1)	168	119	Derbyshire	Chesterfield	1983
M. R. Benson (1)	102	152★	Warwickshire	Edgbaston	1983
M. C. Cowdrey (2)	115	103★	Essex	Gillingham	1955
	149	121	Australians	Canterbury	1961
A. E. Fagg (2)	244	202★	Essex	Colchester	1938
	136	117★	Essex	Maidstone	1948
H. T. W. Hardinge (4)	153	126	Essex	Leyton	1908
	175	109	Hampshire	Southampton	1911
	117	105★	Hampshire	Dover	1913
	207	102★	Surrey	Blackheath	1921
K. L. Hutchings (1)	109	109★	Worcestershire	Worcester	1907
A. P. E. Knott (1)	127★	118★	Surrey	Maidstone	1972
B. W. Luckhurst (1)	113	100★	Rest of World	Canterbury	1968
P. E. Richardson (1)	111	115	Australians	Canterbury	1964
Jas Seymour (2)	108	136★	Worcestershire	Maidstone	1904
	143	105★	Essex	Leyton	1923
F. E. Woolley (1)	104	148★	Somerset	Tunbridge Wells	1911

(5) CENTURY ON FIRST-CLASS DEBUT FOR KENT

Batsman	Score	Opponents	Venue	Year
D. G. Aslett	146★	Hampshire	Bournemouth	1981
G. J. Bryan	124	Nottinghamshire	Trent Bridge	1920
S. H. Day	101★	Gloucestershire	Cheltenham	1897
A. J. Evans	102	Northamptonshire	Northampton	1921
P. Hearn	124	Warwickshire	Gillingham	1947
A. L. Hilder	103★	Essex	Gravesend	1924
N. R. Taylor	110	Sri Lankans	Canterbury	1979

(6) 2,000 FIRST-CLASS RUNS IN A SEASON FOR KENT

Batsman	Total	Year
L. E. G. Ames (4)	2428	1933
	2156	1947
	2125	1949
	2100	1932
W. H. Ashdown (2)	2247	1928
	2030	1934

Batsman	Total	Year
A. E. Fagg (5)	2420	1948
	2322	1938
	2081	1951
	2034	1950
	2025	1947
H. T. W. Hardinge (5)	2446	1928
	2234	1926
	2126	1921
	2068	1922
	2018	1913
P. E. Richardson (2)	2119	1961
	2081	1962
L. J. Todd (1)	2057	1947
R. C. Wilson (1)	2038	1964
F. E. Woolley (6)	2894	1928
	2540	1934
	2339	1935
	2102	1914
	2040	1929
	2011	1931

INDIVIDUAL BOWLING RECORDS

(1) HAT-TRICKS IN FIRST-CLASS MATCHES

Bowler	Opponents	Venue	Year
W. F. Best	Somerset	Taunton	1891
C. Blythe	Surrey	Blackheath	1910
	Derbyshire	Gravesend	1910
W. M. Bradley	Essex	Leyton	1899
W. M. Bradley	Yorkshire	Tonbridge	1899
	Somerset	Blackheath	1900
G. R. Dilley	Surrey	The Oval	1985
G. R. Dilley	Essex	Chelmsford	1986
A. P. Freeman	Middlesex	Canterbury	1920
	Surrey	Blackheath	1934
D. J. Halfyard	Worcestershire	Folkestone	1957
	Leicestershire	Gillingham	1958
A. Hearne	Gloucestershire	Clifton	1900
G. G. Hearne	Lancashire	Old Trafford	1875
W. Hearne	Lancashire	Tonbridge	1894
C. Lewis	Nottinghamshire	Trent Bridge	1939

Bowler	Opponents	Venue	Year
F. Martin	Surrey	The Oval	1890
W. Pearce	Derbyshire	Derby	1878
F. Ridgway	Derbyshire	Folkestone	1951
	Oxford University	The Parks	1958
D. M. Sayer	Glamorgan	Maidstone	1964
D. L. Underwood	Sussex	Hove	1977
J. Wells	Sussex	Hove	1862
F. E. Woolley	Surrey	Blackheath	1919
A. C. Wright	Warwickshire	Edgbaston	1925
D. V. P Wright	Worcestershire	Worcester	1937
	Nottinghamshire	Trent Bridge	1937
	Gloucestershire	Gillingham	1938
	Gloucestershire	Bristol	1939
	Sussex	Hastings	1947
	Hampshire	Canterbury	1949

Note: J. Wells in 1862 and F. Ridgway in 1951 noted above, took four wickets in four balls.

(2) NINE WICKETS IN AN INNINGS FOR KENT

Bowler	Analysis	Opponents	Venue	Year
G. Bennett (1)	9-113	Sussex	Hove	1871
C. Blythe (6)	10-30	Northamptonshire	Northampton	1907
	9-30	Hampshire	Tonbridge	1904
	9-42	Leicestershire	Leicester	1909
	9-44	Northamptonshire	Northampton	1909
	9-67	Essex	Canterbury	1903
	9-97	Surrey	Lord's	1914
W. M. Bradley (1)	9-87	Hampshire	Tonbridge	1901
G. C. Collins (1)	10-65	Nottinghamshire	Dover	1922
A. Fielder (1)	9-108	Lancashire	Canterbury	1907
A. P. Freeman (8)	10-53	Essex	Southend	1930
	10-79	Lancashire	Old Trafford	1931
	10-131	Lancashire	Maidstone	1929
	9-11	Sussex	Hove	1922
	9-61	Warwickshire	Folkestone	1932
	9-87	Sussex	Hastings	1921
	9-104	West Indians	Canterbury	1928
	9-50	Derbyshire	Ilkeston	1930
D. J. Halfyard (2)	9-39	Glamorgan	Neath	1957
	9-61	Worcestershire	Maidstone	1959
E. Hinkly (1)	10-?	England	Lord's	1848
J. Jackson (2)	9-27	England	Lord's	1858
	9-35	England	Canterbury	1858

Bowler	Analysis	Opponents	Venue	Year
R. Lipscomb (1)	9-88	MCC	Lord's	1871
D. L. Underwood (3)	9-28	Sussex	Hastings	1964
	9-32	Surrey	The Oval	1978
	9-37	Essex	Westcliff-on-Sea	1966
D. V. P. Wright (2)	9-51	Leicestershire	Maidstone	1949
	9-47	Gloucestershire	Bristol	1939
W. Wright (1)	9-72	MCC	Lord's	1889

(3) FIFTEEN WICKETS IN A MATCH FOR KENT

Bowler	Analysis	Opponents	Venue	Year
C. Blythe (4)	17-48	Northamptonshire	Northampton	1907
	15-76	Hampshire	Tonbridge	1904
	16-102	Leicestershire	Leicester	1909
	15-45	Leicestershire	Leicester	1912
G. C. Collins (1)	16-83	Nottinghamshire	Dover	1922
A. P. Freeman (9)	17-67	Sussex	Hove	1922
	17-92	Warwickshire	Folkestone	1932
	16-82	Northamptonshire	Tunbridge Wells	1932
	16-94	Essex	Southend	1930
	15-94	Somerset	Canterbury	1931
	15-122	Middlesex	Lord's	1933
	15-142	Essex	Gravesend	1931
	15-144	Leicestershire	Maidstone	1931
	15-224	Leicestershire	Tonbridge	1928
D. J. Halfyard (1)	15-117	Worcestershire	Maidstone	1959
W. Hearne (1)	15-114	Lancashire	Old Trafford	1893
E. Hinkly (1)	16-?	England	Lord's	1848
J. N. Shepherd (1)	15-147	Sussex	Maidstone	1975
D. V. P. Wright (3)	16-80	Somerset	Bath	1939
	15-163	Leicestershire	Maidstone	1949
	15-173	Sussex	Hastings	1947

(4) SIX WICKETS IN A LIMITED-OVERS MATCH
(a) Sunday League (John Player/Refuge Assurance)

Bowler	Analysis	Opponents	Venue	Year
D. L. Underwood	6-12	Sussex	Hastings	1984
R. A. Woolmer	6-9	Derbyshire	Chesterfield	1979

(b) Benson & Hedges Cup
None

(c) NatWest Trophy/Gillette Cup

Bowler	Analysis	Opponents	Venue	Year
A. L. Dixon	7-15	Surrey	The Oval	1967

(5) 125 WICKETS IN A SEASON (100 SINCE 1969)

Bowler	Total	Year	Bowler	Total	Year
C. Blythe (12)	127	1902	A. P. Freeman	146	1925
	142	1903		177	1926
	134	1904		173	1927
	140	1905		246	1928
	157	1907		214	1929
	174	1908		260	1930
	185	1909		257	1931
	163	1910		226	1932
	138	1911		262	1933
	178	1912		195	1934
	160	1913		212	1935
	170	1914	D. J. Halfyard (2)	135	1958
W. M. Bradley (1)	129	1899		125	1959
A. Fielder (2)	172	1906	D. L. Underwood (5)	144	1966
	159	1907		128	1967
F. E. Woolley (3)	132	1910		110	1978
	164	1920		106	1979
	142	1922		106	1983
A. P. Freeman (16)	163	1921	D. V. P. Wright (5)	131	1939
	129	1921		142	1947
	194	1922		128	1949
	157	1923		141	1950
	159	1924		127	1955

RECORD WICKET PARTNERSHIPS

(1) IN FIRST-CLASS MATCHES

FIRST WICKET (Qualification 250)

Score		Opponents	Venue	Year
283	A. E. Fagg *and* P. R. Sunnucks	Essex	Colchester	1938
256	B. W. Luckhurst *and* G. W. Johnson	Derbyshire	Derby	1973
251	L. J. Todd *and* A. E. Fagg	Leicestershire	Maidstone	1949

SECOND WICKET (Qualification 250)

352	W. H. Ashdown *and* F. E. Woolley	Essex	Brentwood	1934
307	H. T. W. Hardinge *and* Jas Seymour	Worcestershire	Kidderminster	1922
275	A. E. Fagg *and* F. G. H. Chalk	Worcestershire	Dudley	1938
273	L. J. Todd *and* L. E. G. Ames	Essex	Maidstone	1947

262	H. T. W. Hardinge and			
	F. E. Woolley	Warwickshire	Tunbridge Wells	1928
261	E. W. Dillon and Jas Seymour	Somerset	Taunton	1905
260	A. E. Fagg and F. E. Woolley	Northamptonshire	Northampton	1934
255	H. T. W. Hardinge and			
	F. E. Woolley	Derbyshire	Chesterfield	1929
250	H. T. W. Hardinge and Jas Seymour	Essex	Leyton	1923

THIRD WICKET (Qualification 250)

321★	A. Hearne and J. R. Mason	Nottinghamshire	Trent Bridge	1899
304	A. H. Phebey and R. C. Wilson	Glamorgan	Blackheath	1960
283	H. T. W. Hardinge and F. E. Woolley	South Africans	Canterbury	1924
283	R. C. Wilson and S. E. Leary	Northamptonshire	Kettering	1963
280	Jas Seymour and F. E. Woolley	Lancashire	Dover	1922
273	H. T. W. Hardinge and F. E. Woolley	Hampshire	Southampton	1922
259	L. E. G. Ames and L. J. Todd	Gloucestershire	Folkestone	1933
253	H. T. W. Hardinge and F. E. Woolley	Lancashire	Dover	1926
250★	H. T. W. Hardinge and Jas Seymour	Worcestershire	Tonbridge	1921

FOURTH WICKET (Qualification 250)

297	H. T. W. Hardinge and A. P. F. Chapman	Hampshire	Southampton	1926
296	K. L. Hutchings and F. E. Woolley	Northamptonshire	Gravesend	1908
251	C. J. Tavaré and A. G. E. Ealham	Worcestershire	Canterbury	1979

FIFTH WICKET (Qualification 225)

277	F. E. Woolley and L. E. G. Ames	New Zealanders	Canterbury	1931
254	E. Humphreys and A. P. Day	Lancashire	Tunbridge Wells	1910
241★	F. E. Woolley and D. W. Jennings	Somerset	Tunbridge Wells	1911
241	M. H. Denness and M. C. Cowdrey	Somerset	Maidstone	1973
230	Jas Seymour and J. R. Mason	Somerset	Taunton	1907
227	R. C. Wilson and M. C. Cowdrey	Northamptonshire	Tunbridge Wells	1955

SIXTH WICKET (Qualification 225)

284	A. P. F. Chapman and G. B. Legge	Lancashire	Maidstone	1927
256★	C. J. Tavaré and A. P. E. Knott	Essex	Chelmsford	1982
233	R. Mayes and W. Murray-Wood	Sussex	Tunbridge Wells	1952

SEVENTH WICKET (Qualification 180)

248	A. P. Day *and* E. Humphreys	Somerset	Taunton	1908
194	L. E. G. Ames *and* T. A. Pearce	Middlesex	Tunbridge Wells	1932
180	F. G. H. Chalk *and* B. H. Valentine	Hampshire	Canterbury	1937

EIGHTH WICKET (Qualification 150)

157	A. C. Wright *and* A. L. Hilder	Essex	Gravesend	1924

NINTH WICKET (Qualification 150)

161	B. R. Edrich *and* F. Ridgway	Sussex	Tunbridge Wells	1949
158	F. Marchant *and* E. B. Shine	Warwickshire	Tonbridge	1897
158	A. G. E. Ealham *and* A. Brown	Glamorgan	Folkestone	1968

TENTH WICKET (Qualification 100)

235	F. E. Woolley *and* A. Fielder	Worcestershire	Stourbridge	1909
141	J. R. Mason *and* C. Blythe	Surrey	The Oval	1909
103	Jas Seymour *and* A. Fielder	Worcestershire	Maidstone	1904
102	Jas Seymour *and* A. Fielder	Essex	Leyton	1911

(2) IN LIMITED-OVERS MATCHES
(a) Sunday League (John Player/Refuge Assurance)

FIRST WICKET (Qualification 150)

Score		Opponents	Venue	Year
182	M. H. Denness *and* B. W. Luckhurst	Somerset	Weston-super-Mare	1970

SECOND WICKET (Qualification 150)

179	B. W. Luckhurst *and* M. H. Denness	Somerset	Canterbury	1973

THIRD WICKET (Qualification 125)

174	B. W. Luckhurst *and* M. H. Denness	Northamptonshire	Canterbury	1976
170	C. J. Tavaré *and* D. G. Aslett	Warwickshire	Folkestone	1983
150	M. H. Denness *and* Asif Iqbal	Gloucestershire	Maidstone	1976

FOURTH WICKET (Qualification 125)

146	C. J. Tavaré *and* A. G. E. Ealham	Glamorgan	Canterbury	1980
125	C. J. Tavaré *and* C. S. Cowdrey	Hampshire	Canterbury	1981
124★	C. J. Tavaré *and* Asif Iqbal	Glamorgan	Canterbury	1982

FIFTH WICKET (Qualification 125)

163	A. G. E. Ealham *and* B. D. Julien	Leicestershire	Leicester	1977
127	A. G. E. Ealham *and* J. N. Shepherd	Middlesex	Canterbury	1971
126	J. N. Shepherd *and* C. S. Cowdrey	Hampshire	Southampton	1978

SIXTH WICKET
90   A. P. E. Knott *and* G. W. Johnson   Somerset   Maidstone   1982

SEVENTH WICKET
84★   C. J. Tavaré *and* G. W. Johnson   Northamptonshire   Maidstone   1985

EIGHTH WICKET
44   C. J. C. Rowe *and* P. R. Downton   Glamorgan   Maidstone   1978

NINTH WICKET
47   S. E. Leary *and* D. L. Underwood   Essex   Blackheath   1970

TENTH WICKET
44★   D. L. Underwood *and*
        J. M. H. Graham-Brown   Somerset   Taunton   1976

(b) Benson & Hedges Cup
FIRST WICKET
162   L. Potter *and* N. R. Taylor   Sussex   Hove   1982

SECOND WICKET
141   G. W. Johnson *and* M. H. Denness   Surrey   The Oval   1976

THIRD WICKET
139   C. J. Tavaré *and* N. R. Taylor   Worcestershire   Worcester   1986

FOURTH WICKET
146   C. S. Cowdrey *and* A. G. E. Ealham   Sussex   Canterbury   1977

FIFTH WICKET
127   C. S. Cowdrey *and* G. R. Cowdrey   Surrey   Canterbury   1986

SIXTH WICKET
88★   G. R. Cowdrey *and* E. A. E. Baptiste   Hampshire   Southampton   1986

SEVENTH WICKET
67   A. P. E. Knott *and* G. W. Johnson   Hampshire   Canterbury   1982

EIGHTH WICKET
65   R. M. Ellison *and* G. R. Dilley   Hampshire   Canterbury   1983

NINTH WICKET
81   J. N. Shepherd *and*
        D. L. Underwood   Middlesex   Lord's   1975

TENTH WICKET
28   D. L. Underwood *and* K. B. S. Jarvis Surrey   Canterbury   1983

(c) NatWest Trophy/Gillette Cup
FIRST WICKET
188   M. R. Benson *and* S. G. Hinks   Surrey   Canterbury   1985

SECOND WICKET
204   B. W. Luckhurst *and*
M. C. Cowdrey   Durham   Canterbury   1974

THIRD WICKET
149   B. W. Luckhurst *and* M. H. Denness Leicestershire   Canterbury   1974

FOURTH WICKET
110   D. G. Aslett *and* C. S. Cowdrey   Hampshire   Southampton   1984

FIFTH WICKET
90★   M. R. Benson *and* R. M. Ellison   Warwickshire   Edgbaston   1984

SIXTH WICKET
89   Asif Iqbal *and* J. N. Shepherd   Middlesex   Canterbury   1977

SEVENTH WICKET
75   A. P. E. Knott *and* R. A. Woolmer   Nottinghamshire   Trent Bridge   1975

EIGHTH WICKET
54   C. S. Cowdrey *and* R. M. Ellison   Essex   Chelmsford   1983

NINTH WICKET
38★   C. S. Cowdrey *and* G. R. Dilley   Essex   Chelmsford   1983

TENTH WICKET
25   D. L. Underwood *and* J. C. J. Dye   Sussex   Tunbridge Wells   1963

WICKET-KEEPING RECORDS

(1) SIX DISMISSALS IN AN INNINGS

Keeper	Total	Ct	St	Opponents	Venue	Year
L. E. G. Ames (1)	6	4	2	Sussex	Folkestone	1930
J. C. Hubble (1)	6	5	1	Gloucestershire	Cheltenham	1923
F. H. Huish (1)	6	1	5	Surrey	The Oval	1911

Keeper	Total	Ct	St	Opponents	Venue	Year
A. P. E. Knott (6)	6	4	2	Middlesex	Gravesend	1966
	6	5	1	Northamptonshire	Maidstone	1966
	6	6	0	Lancashire	Folkestone	1967
	6	6	0	Worcestershire	Dartford	1973
	6	6	0	Hampshire	Southampton	1975
	6	6	0	Hampshire	Maidstone	1982
W. H. V. Levett (2)	6	4	2	Northamptonshire	Northampton	1934
	6	5	1	Glamorgan	Neath	1939
D. Nicholls (1)	6	6	0	Nottinghamshire	Trent Bridge	1974

(2) NINE DISMISSALS IN A MATCH

Keeper	Total	Ct	St	Opponents	Venue	Year
L. E. G. Ames (2)	9	8	1	Oxford U	The Parks	1928
	9	5	4	Sussex	Maidstone	1929
T. G. Evans (1)	9	8	1	New Zealanders	Canterbury	1949
J. C. Hubble (1)	10	9	1	Gloucestershire	Cheltenham	1923
F. H. Huish (1)	10	1	9	Surrey	The Oval	1911
A. P. E. Knott (1)	9	9	0	Leicestershire	Maidstone	1977
W. H. V. Levett (3)	9	5	4	Nottinghamshire	Maidstone	1933
	9	7	2	Northamptonshire	Northampton	1934
	9	5	4	Sussex	Tunbridge Wells	1935

(3) 75 DISMISSALS IN A SEASON

Keeper	Total	Ct	St	Year
L. E. G. Ames (4)	116	71	45	1929
	114	65	49	1928
	91	35	56	1932
	85	44	41	1930
A. W. Catt (1)	78	65	13	1963
J. C. Hubble (1)	78	44	34	1926
F. H. Huish (5)	101	62	39	1911
	99	69	30	1913
	81	54	27	1908
	77	73	4	1899
	77	54	23	1905
A. P. E. Knott (3)	85	78	7	1967
	81	72	9	1965
	80	72	8	1966
D. G. Ufton (1)	90	76	14	1961

(4) 400 DISMISSALS IN A CAREER

Keeper	Total	Ct	St	Years
L. E. G. Ames	842	512	330	1926–1951

Keeper	Total	Ct	St	Years
T. G. Evans	554	451	103	1939–1967
J. C. Hubble	628	411	217	1904–1929
F. H. Huish	1253	901	352	1895–1914
A. P. Knott	915	828	87	1964–1985

Note: These figures include some catches taken in the field.

FIELDING RECORDS

(1) FIVE CATCHES IN AN INNINGS

Fielder	Total	Opponents	Venue	Year
C. S. Cowdrey (2)	5	Sussex	Hove	1982
	5	Warwickshire	Folkestone	1986
A. G. E. Ealham (1)	5	Gloucestershire	Folkestone	1966
A. E. Fagg (1)	5	Hampshire	Southampton	1952
S. E. Leary (1)	6	Cambridge University	Fenner's	1958
J. M. Prodger (2)	5	Gloucestershire	Cheltenham	1961
	5	Lancashire	Blackpool	1964
Jas Seymour (1)	6	South Africans	Canterbury	1904
F. E. Woolley (2)	5	Middlesex	Blackheath	1926
	5	Hampshire	Canterbury	1936
R. A. Woolmer (1)	5	Worcestershire	Worcester	1976

(2) SEVEN CATCHES IN A MATCH

Fielder (1)	Total	Opponents	Venue	Year
A. E. Fagg (1)	7	Hampshire	Southampton	1952
N. Felix	7	England	Canterbury	1847
S. E. Leary (1)	7	Cambridge University	Fenner's	1958
J. R. Mason (1)	7	Surrey	The Oval	1905
J. M. Prodger (1)	8	Gloucestershire	Cheltenham	1961

(3) 40 CATCHES IN A SEASON

Fielder	Total	Year
M. C. Cowdrey (1)	40	1967
B. W. Luckhurst (1)	43	1966
Jas Seymour (6)	45	1913
	43	1906
	42	1907
	42	1912
	42	1914
	40	1904
C. J. Tavaré (1)	48	1978
F. E. Woolley (2)	44	1935
	42	1923

(4) 350 CATCHES IN A CAREER

Fielder	Total	Years
W. H. Ashdown	398	1920–1937
M. C. Cowdrey	406	1950–1976
A. E. Fagg	411	1932–1957
A. Hearne	352	1884–1906
S. E. Leary	362	1951–1971
B. W. Luckhurst	350	1958–1985
J. R. Mason	360	1893–1914
Jas Seymour	659	1902–1926
F. E. Woolley	773	1906–1938

ACKNOWLEDGEMENTS

The author would like to acknowledge the wide range of help he has received in compiling this history, including many Kent players of the past who have been happy to delve back into their careers.

Thanks are due to Kent County Cricket Club for making available The History of Kent Cricket and its appendices and allowing access to their library, and to Chris Taylor, joint curator of the club, for his generous and unstinting help with statistics and photographs.

A personal note of thanks goes also to Brian Croudy for his assistance and to David Lemmon who has written two biographies on former Kent and England cricketers— A. P. F. Chapman and 'Tich' Freeman.

Unless otherwise indicated, all photographs are reproduced by courtesy of Chris Taylor.

INDEX

298